Date Due

Motherteacher
The Feminization of American Education

Motherteacher

The Feminization of American Education

Redding S. Sugg, Jr.

University Press of Virginia
Charlottesville

THE UNIVERSITY PRESS OF VIRGINIA
Copyright © 1978 by the Rector and Visitors
of the University of Virginia

First published 1978

Library of Congress Cataloging in Publication Data
Sugg, Redding Stancill, Jr.
Motherteacher: the feminization of American education.
Includes index.
1. Women teachers—United States—History.
2. Teachers—United States—History. 3. Feminism. I. Title.
LB2837.S76   371.1′00973   78-2675
ISBN 0-8139-0757-8

Printed in the United States of America

Dedicated, with love and respect,
to the memory of

Redding Stancill Sugg, *1893–1958*
Irene Miller Holloman, *1892–1962*
and
Katharine Miller Sugg, *1896–1972*

Thomas Jefferson to John Adams

I hope the necessity will at length be seen of establishing institutions, here as in Europe, where every branch of science, useful at this day, may be taught in it's highest degrees. Have you ever turned your thoughts to the plan of such an institution?

—July 5, 1814

John Adams to Thomas Jefferson

Education! Oh Education! The greatest Grief of my heart, and the greatest Affliction of my Life! To my mortification I must confess, that I have never closely thought, or very deliberately reflected upon the Subject, which never occurs to me now, without producing a deep Sigh, an heavy groan and sometimes Tears.

—July 16, 1814

The first profession opened to women consisted of the sale of sexual love and was called prostitution; the second, an initiative of nineteenth-century Americans, was a traffic in maternal love and was called pedagogy.

Acknowledgments

This book has been produced without subsidy or institutional backing, but I could not have done it without free access to the resources and services of the John Willard Brister Library at Memphis State University, to which I had only the modest claim, as specified on my stack permit, of a Faculty Spouse. I am further indebted to my wife, Professor Helen White of the Department of English at Memphis State University, for her conversation and criticism. She is only the nearest to me of the considerable number of able women I have known who have made it impossible for me ever to imagine that Motherteacher has been incarnated in women necessarily but never in men.

Contents

Part I. *Toward Anarchy with a Schoolmistress*

Three chapters on factors during the first fifty years of the Republic which predisposed a patriarchal society to accept feminization (in the statistical sense) of the teaching corps after 1837.

Chapter 1. *The Rejection of a National University*

How democratic pedilections prevented development of a hierarchical education system which women could not have monopolized and favored a system limited to elementary education which women could and did monopolize.   3

Chapter 2. *The Wonderful Proportions of Maternity*

How theological rehabilitation of the child helped to magnify the mother as moral influence and provided quasi-priestly credentials for woman, defined in terms of maternity, as teacher.   18

Chapter 3. *Ichabod Crane's Profession and the Profession of Woman*

How the low status of teaching as a male profession made it vulnerable to incursion by women and how improved professional standards, especially as proposed by Catharine Beecher in her notions of the "profession of woman," made the incursion seem reasonable.   38

Part II. *The Transference of Education from Male to Female Hands*

Three chapters on Horace Mann's successful substitution of women for men teachers during the common school revival in Massachusetts, the opposition to his program, and the concern about its consequences throughout the country after the Civil War.

Part III. *The Evolution of Motherteacher*

Four chapters on the influence of optimistic/democratic evolutionist ideology and faith in progress in developing the type of the American teacher from Mann's "normalite," who was female by definition, into "Motherteacher," who may be either male or female but is in either case "feminized" in a sense reflecting nineteenth-century sex-typing.

Part I
Toward Anarchy with a Schoolmistress

Chapter 1

The Rejection of a National University

OUR patriarchal forebears in the middle of the nineteenth century consented not only to the rapid feminization of the teaching corps in quantitative terms but also to the redefinition and development of teaching as a female profession. Feminization was identified with professionalization of education and was thus a qualitative and ideological as well as a quantitative phenomenon. It was not, however, and could not have occurred if it had been, an expression of feminism. At the same time teaching was turned over to women, education was made a function of the state quite against the Jacksonian tendency to restrict positive government. A field of public responsibility, gainful employment underwritten by taxation, and professional aspiration was not only opened to but virtually reserved to women. How did it happen? Several factors in the history of the first fifty years of the Republic predisposed Americans to accept the idea of women as teachers in place of men without feeling that it implied a threat to male virtue and dominance or to laissez-faire democracy.

The factor that probably operated most consciously was the long process, running from the Revolution to the presidency of John Quincy Adams, in which elitist educational policy expressive of Federalist and, to an only slightly less extent, of Republican views was rejected and replaced by the educational preferences of the Democracy. Neither as pupils nor as teachers did females figure more than incidentally in the thinking of the men who devoted themselves to educational theorizing, and women took little part in the discussion, unless they did so privately. The most egalitarian Democrat of 1828 was not more concerned than the most aristocratic Federalist of

1800 had been to reform sex roles or advocate the use of women as teachers. The idea of women as teachers was much more thinkable, however, in the context of the Democrat's educational and political views. First, let us examine briefly the features of the Federalist and Republican educational proposals and discover how improbable it is that women would have monopolized the teaching corps in any educational system founded upon them.

The makers of the Constitution and the adherents of the Federalist party that came to power under the aegis of George Washington held a comparatively realistic opinion of human nature which caused grave doubts about popular sovereignty. They felt that, if it was feasible at all, it must be based upon the widest possible diffusion of knowledge so that the people might take a reasonable view of their own limitations, understand the necessity of delegating their power to qualified representatives, and discriminate between qualified and unqualified candidates at the ballot box. That the masses were potentially capable of self-government took the status of an article of faith, but scarcely anyone thought their capacities were already adequately developed for their sovereign role. Even Thomas Jefferson, away in Paris under the heady influence of the latest French perfectionist ideology while his friends at home wrestled with the problems of forming a national government, knew chaff from corn and had proposed for Virginia an educational winnowing of the populace in order to produce a governing elite.

The Federalists, in rejecting the Calvinist doctrine of total human depravity as the basis of political and educational philosophy, did not fly to the other extreme and assert total virtue. They never imagined that men were in any sense equal by nature, whether in goodness or in evil, or placed, as Benjamin Fletcher Wright expressed it, "any faith in the notion that simple majoritarian democracy will result in the preservation of liberty and justice." They instituted government by the humanly elected to replace government by God's elect but were almost as mystified about how the people could be brought to exercise the franchise intelligently as earlier Americans had been about how to justify the ways of God to man. To their mind, according to Wright, "men are not to be trusted with power, because they are selfish, passionate, full of whims, caprices, and prejudices. Men are not fully rational, calm, dispassionate. Moreover, the nature of man is a constant; it has had these characteristics throughout recorded history. To assume that it will alter for the better would be a betrayal of generations unborn."[1] The Federalists refused to flatter themselves or their constituents that Americans were a blessed exception to the general rule of humanity. In the very defense of the newly proposed Republic, Alexander Hamilton did not hesitate to warn against the "fallacy and extravagance of those idle theories which have amused us with promises of an exemption from the imperfections, weaknesses, and evils incident to society in every shape."[2]

Taking men as they thought they were and would continue to be, the Federalists believed the odds were heavily against the survival of the geographically huge "unmixed republic" they were founding. Benjamin Rush thought it would degenerate inevitably into monarchy within a hundred years. The chances for such success as might be expected must be multiplied in every possible way. The central government must be given enough authority to make up for the lack of any element of monarchy, hereditary aristocracy, theocracy, or military dictatorship from which in a crisis of internal division or external assault nations had always received saving direction. The government must itself be as cunningly contrived as the watch that was a favorite metaphor of their cosmogony, with automatically functioning checks and balances of each branch against the others, so that no ambitious man would be tempted to tyrannize. The formation of the national government was the first order of business, but they felt that the physical and cultural unification of the country was no less essential. According to the conventional wisdom of the time, it was not possible to sustain republican government over a territory as large as any one of the new states, except perhaps Rhode Island, to say nothing of the total area of all thirteen. As soon as it could be put into operation, the federal government must be about the immense work of tying the Republic together physically and commercially by developing roads, canals, and navigation.

"Internal improvements" became, therefore, a Federalist shibboleth; and it is no gratuitous pun to say that the most indispensable of them was the improvement of the inner man, the citizen, by education. To unite and centralize the country physically and politically would be pointless if the people could not be united in culture and sentiment and if the electorate could not be improved in its mind, its information, its skills, its morals. No new type or method of education was thought necessary. The traditional classical education conceived as preparation of ruling elites must be made accessible to talents regardless of birth and wealth, and the masses must be sufficiently educated to be able to consent intelligently to government by qualified representatives. The Federalist notion of a proper educational policy called for a hierarchical system culminating in a national university, in which the university set the standards for the lower schools. Common schooling of the young was to insure a maximum of sympathetic understanding among the different classes of society, but classes were expected to remain.

From as early as 1775 George Washington advocated a national university. The idea was in the air at the Constitutional Convention. James Madison proposed that the power to establish a university be vested in Congress; but it was not done, not because sentiment was against it but because some thought the power was sufficiently implied in the general welfare clause. The failure to write it in, however, later made it possible for strict constructionists, such as Jefferson and Monroe, to doubt the constitutionality of a national university and diverted their emphasis to advocacy of an amendment to clarify the issue. But Washington, John Adams, Madison, and John Quincy Adams all called on Congress to found a university in the capital without getting action. The chances seem to have been favorable in 1806, when Samuel Blodgett and Joel Barlow developed proposals, and again after the War of 1812 when national sentiment was intensified. Congress never considered the university an urgent matter, and the idea shared the growing unpopularity of the Federalist party after the presidency of John Adams. Higher education was identified with "aristocracy."

And of course a university-oriented system would have nourished an elite of intellect, talent, and training, whether or not this should be properly thought of as an aristocracy. Any complete educational system, culminating in a university, must be hierarchical in academic terms and increasingly selective and discriminating at the upper levels. Then as now, nobody knew how to control the implication that admission to and successful negotiation of the higher academic grades guaranteed the perpetuation of class distinctions and privileges. When, in 1777, Thomas Jefferson drafted for Virginia his "Bill for the More General Diffusion of Knowledge," he was liberal if not revolutionary in proposing that able sons of the poor should be given secondary and higher education at public expense. Jefferson meant, however, that the public foundationers, as he called them, should be rigorously selected and commented without much solicitude for democratic sentiment that "by this means twenty of the best geniuses will be raked from the rubbish annually."[3]

The function which a national university was expected to perform in the imminent experiment with popular sovereignty in the new Republic was even more selective than that which Jefferson intended the College of William and Mary to perform in Virginia. His idea was that the college should govern the lower schools and prescribe their curricula. A national university was expected not only to play such an academic role within a national system of education but also to quality candidates for office.

In his proposal of 1788 for a national university, Benjamin Rush asserted axiomatically that the predictions of failure for the American experiment would "certainly come to pass, unless the people are prepared for our new form of government by an education adapted to the new and peculiar situation of our country." He thought the new Congress should promptly establish in the District of Columbia "a federal university, into which the youth of the United States shall be received after they have finished their studies, and taken their degrees in the colleges of their respective states."⁴ He thus proposed, in the secular spirit of the Enlightenment, a university in the most liberal sense of the word, one institution bringing the people by common culture to the service of the federal Constitution as common prayer in an established church had tended to secure the national identity in English tradition.

The importance of a national university as Rush imagined it can scarcely be overestimated, for he meant it to be the exclusive route to office. "In thirty years after this university is established," he wrote, "let an act of Congress be passed to prevent any person being chosen or appointed to power or office, who has not taken a degree in the federal university. We require certain qualifications in lawyers, physicians, and clergymen, before we commit our property, our lives or our souls to their care. We even refuse to commit the charge of a ship to a pilot, who cannot produce a certificate of his education and knowledge in his business. Why then should we commit our country . . . to men who cannot produce vouchers of their qualifications for the important trust?"⁵

Washington's emphasis was always on the national university as a means of controlling the centrifugal forces in the Republic. He thought these came to their most dangerous pitch in political parties and factions, the ultimate danger appearing where different geographical sections became aligned with opposing economic interests and ideological biases. A national university located on the neutral ground of the Federal District seemed to him necessary for producing in the leadership of the country an American character that could transcend state and local loyalties as well as factional politics. Congress failed to act, and Washington continued to urge the matter. Corresponding with Hamilton about the content of his Farewell Address, Washington argued for the inclusion of advocacy of federal initiative in "Education *generally* as one of the surest means of enlightening & givg just ways of thinkg to our Citizens, but particularly the establishment of a University."⁶

The frustration of Washington's proposals seemed to many thoughtful men a distressing defect in the new government. Samuel Knox, for example, one of the winners of the prize awarded in 1797 by the American Philosophical Society for essays on "the best system of liberal education and literary instruction, adapted to the genius of the government of the United States," put the question: "Is it to the honor of the freest country on earth—of the vindicators of that national independence which never could have originated, much less existed, but from the enlightened independence of the public mind, that the wisdom, philanthropy, and patriotism of that man, 'Who Unites All Hearts,' has never been treated with even the appearance of disrespect, save in his liberal endeavors to cherish into maturity and perfection the all important object of a uniform national education?"[7]

A recent authority has characterized the Federalist concept of liberty as "freedom to follow a 'higher' pattern of behavior" and pointed out that this "has its analogues in Puritan thought, and is comparable to the elitist definition of the social order which many Americans, perhaps the majority, held in the half-century following 1770."[8] Unrestricted freedom was not, in the Federalist view, true freedom, and democracy was feared as a threat to popular sovereignty. Could anyone think otherwise who had observed the wild career of the French from the Terror to Napoleon? Self-government must be nonetheless government, and only through education, with emphasis on higher education as tending to guarantee at least a saving remnant of disinterested talent and competence, was it conceivable that every individual could be brought to the degree of virtue at which the consent to be governed, on the one hand, and the ability to govern, on the other, could be rationally secured. The religious prescriptions of higher behavior no longer held. The national university must be instituted as a source of prescriptions and standards, a foundation of reason.

But the tendency of the country was already firmly set in favor of the Republican interpretation of liberty, which implied political antinomianism based on faith in the goodness of human nature and the equitable distribution of it among the people. Every man's opinion being assumed to be as respectable as the next man's, the need for moral prescriptions, objective standards of performance, and powerful government seemed

minimal. Education might be desirable but not, as the
Federalists thought, as a strict discipline designed to control evil
tendencies, supply weaknesses, and keep people up to any pattern of behavior higher than they were casually inclined to
follow. Education was seen increasingly as something an individual had a right to insofar as it seemed to him personally desirable. It was an ornament, an advantage that might be added
to one's already sufficiently admirable self, not a desparate
measure to bring one up to minimal virtue by developing
reason and intelligence as substitutes for the sanctions of religion. The idea of a national university with power to set standards for the lower levels of education and to discriminate
among individuals had never been popular, and with the
triumph of Republicanism in 1800 and the rise of the
Democracy after 1820 it was taken less and less seriously.

By the time John Quincy Adams was narrowly elected to the
presidency over Andrew Jackson in 1824, the idea of a national
university was part and parcel of the American System of
internal improvements advocated by the new president and
Henry Clay. The alignment of parties with sections of the
country so much dreaded by George Washington had occurred. In the division between North and South over in-
dustrialization on the one hand and the protection of agricul-
ture on the other, the national university fell to the northern
side. It was identified with proposals for expanded federal authority and taxation to develop roads and canals, manufacturing, and banking and acquired an ideological coloring such that
it could be made to seem an instrument of class privilege and an
impediment to the realization of the romantic Jeffersonian vi-
sions of inbred agrarian virtue.

As the inheritor of the essential Federalist attitudes, John
Quincy Adams believed in positive government based on law
and principle and held party politics or "electioneering" in contempt. Notwithstanding the closeness of his election and the
frustration of Andrew Jackson's partisans, Adams acted with
plenary decision as if he had received his mandate from an unquestionable majority vote. He knew better than the people did
what was in the interest of the country and did not propose to

concede anything to misguided views or cajole anybody into supporting his policies. The result was a stalemated administration in which the proposal for a national university was sacrificed along with the rest of the American System to obdurate rectitude.

In his first annual message to Congress on December 6, 1825, Adams superbly overrode the realities of what were already Jacksonian politics and in a piece of Roman eloquence delivered the swan song of the Federalist-Republican type of statesman. To men on the lookout for the main chance in all sorts of personal, party, sectional, and economic deals, he took the highest line of presidential decorum, casting himself as "a man of my whole country," and seemed to expect an equally decorous response from the national legislature. He suggested to the parvenu Democracy that presumed itself in no need of criticism that intellectual and moral improvement was as urgently needed as improvement of roads and canals. Adams said:

Roads and canals, by multiplying and facilitating the communications and intercourse between distant regions and multitudes of men, are among the most important means of improvement. But moral, political, intellectual improvements are duties assigned by the Author of our existence to social no less than to individual man. For the fulfillment of those duties governments are invested with power, and to the attainment of the end—the progressive improvement of the condition of the governed—the exercise of delegated powers is a duty as sacred and indispensable as the usurpation of powers not granted is criminal and odious. Among the first, perhaps the very first, instrument for the improvement of the condition of men is knowledge, and to the acquisition of much of the knowledge adapted to the wants, the comforts, and enjoyments of human life public institutions and seminaries of learning are essential.[9]

He recalled Washington's recommendations that a national university and military academy be established and noted that although West Point had been founded, Washington, if he had lived to that day, "would have seen the spot of earth which he had destined and bequeathed to the use and benefit of his country as the site for an university still bare and barren."[10]

Congress did not care to hear Adams's argument that it was constitutionally authorized and therefore morally and legally bound to legislate the university and the advancement of science. "While foreign nations, less blessed with that freedom which is power, than ourselves, are advancing with gigantic strides in the career of public improvement, were we to slumber in indolence, or fold up our arms and proclaim to the world that we are palsied by the will of our constituents, would it not be to cast away the bounties of Providence, and doom ourselves to perpetual inferiority?"[11] So the president came to what he intended as a shaming and inspiring rhetorical question, but the response was hostile laughter.

The fate of the university proposal and the rest of the American System was sealed when Jackson defeated Adams in the election of 1828. The antagonists exemplified the emergent Democratic approach in education among other matters, on the one hand, and the failed academic approach, on the other. Adams, son of Harvard and formerly its professor of rhetoric, opposed the awarding of an honorary degree to Jackson after the latter became president. He could not countenance Harvard's "conferring her highest literary honors upon a barbarian who could not write a sentence of grammar and hardly could spell his own name."[12] For he believed that "democracy of numbers and literature were self-contradictory"[13]—and so did Demos, now in power.

If a national university had been founded and if it had functioned as Rush, Washington, and John Quincy Adams thought it should, one may speculate that teaching would have acquired at all levels professional and social status, an incidental effect of which would have been the prevention of feminization. It is inconceivable that in a patriarchal society the teachers in a university-oriented system designed to produce a governing elite should have been women. Teaching would have taken on the character of an important public function at odds with the private and domestic position which the society took for granted as appropriate for women.

A variety of motives was at work in American society from about 1820, however, which coalesced at the end of the 1830s in what was probably the most important and typical of democratic social inventions, the reformed common school. The result was not so much a policy of nonhierarchical education as a natural development limited to elementary education in which questions of control from above did not arise. Insofar as they were ready at all for public education, early nineteenth-century Americans were tolerant only of piecemeal development without necessary connection between lower and higher education.

Mutually contradictory interests were accommodated in the working consensus in favor of common elementary schools as the heart of democratic educational practice. The establishment and the nascent proletariat of the Jacksonian era joined in support of public education on these terms for their quite different reasons. As Sidney L. Jackson has shown, the intellectual leadership in the East increasingly thought of common schools as a means of social control. They were typically in strong personal and often neurotic reaction against Calvinism and also tended to regard the common school as an instrument of humanitarian optimism and moral progress. At the same time, workingmen in the cities, representing the elements that the intellectual leadership was most concerned to keep in order, could see the common school as a means of multiplying opportunities for rising in society. They demanded state support for common schools while opposing state support for higher education on the grounds that the latter was an instrument of upperclass privilege.[14]

From the point of view of the established middle and upper classes of the East and, no doubt, from that of any thoughtful person regardless of class or location, the need for social control seemed increasingly urgent during the fifteen years prior to the common school revival. In Europe, one nation after another erupted in revolution, and the revolutionary ideas were imported with the arrival of every boatload of immigrants, who brought also the problems of diverse languages, religions, and traditions. The threat to order from across the Atlantic was matched from the West, where the turbulence of the expanding frontier required containment. To the intellectual leadership, popular education seemed necessary as prevention of social disorder which, once allowed to develop, would prove unmanageable.

Lyman Beecher, an instance of the Eastern-bred intellectual worrying about the West on the basis of personal experience there, warned that "the danger is, that our intelligence and virtue will falter and fall back into the dark-minded, vicious populace—a poor, uneducated reckless mass of infuriated animalism, to rush on resistless as a tornado, or to burn as if set on fire of hell."[15] All the while, the note of dissidence sounded from the South. From the near paralysis of government during John Quincy Adams's presidency to the riotous scenes at the first inauguration of Andrew Jackson to riots in many cities over slavery, unionization, Catholicism, and the national bank, and on to the Panic of 1837, the United States gave plentiful evidence of instability.

The intellectual leadership, which might be expected to have preferred a university-oriented system with emphasis on intellectual training, had its reasons for turning to common schools, regarded as terminal educational institutions for the masses, in which moral training should take precedence over intellectual. It seemed only too likely that the burgeoning Democracy would turn into a tyranny of the majority—"a popular despotism under the names and forms of liberty," as Lyman Beecher put it[16]—or sheer mobbishness if moral and religious conditioning of the will were not made the basic tenet of education. The doctrine of depravity was replaced at first with the idea that the will was malleable, especially in early youth, and though not inevitably evil in tendency required strenuous discipline in order to secure a tendency to good. The upper classes were generally convinced that "intellectual" education, meaning little more than literacy, without prior "moral" conditioning of the will was a sure recipe for social upheaval and atheism. Not only was emphasis to shift from intellectual to moral training: the way opened to a subtle perversion whereby the so-called intellectual subjects—just the three Rs—were to be taught less as the means of learning than as the means of moral discipline.

But how was it that Demos, the subject of so much fearful solicitude, came to support the same common school movement
that his betters conceived of as a means of keeping him in line?
Throughout the 1830s workingmen's groups opposed the in-
corporation of banks, the building of turnpikes and canals, and
other internal improvements as machinations of the privileged
classes. They hewed to the Jacksonian line in their opposition to
expansion of government at all levels and were particularly
negative toward the multiplication of the functions and services
and the consequent centralization of power in the federal
government. Yet they demanded publicly supported common
schools.

The basic reason was that they felt that free universal elementary education would enable the poorer classes to govern
themselves and tend to decrease "the authority of established
leaders in the society." Although the system of public education
would depend on legislation, require a major increase in taxation, and represent an anomalous expansion of state function,
they thought that schools once legislated would "make un-
necessary other forms of legislative activity."[17] The workingmen did repudiate "hierarchically oriented education,"
which they regarded as a guarantee of class distinctions.[18] They
felt, however, that common schooling for all classes would
guarantee them or their children an opportunity to compete
for the goods of the society. Common schooling had been instituted as propaedeutic to common prayer of the Calvinist variety, but the sense of the adjective was changing to connote
egalitarian schooling.

On the crucial question of authority, both the upper and the
lower classes were ambivalent for their different reasons and,
while advocating public education, wished to impose restric-
tions upon it. From the point of view of the middle and upper
classes, education as social control meant education that did not
open the Pandora's box of intellectualism and free thinking.
Their emphasis on the primacy of moral training tended to
limit the academic authority of the schools and to replace it with
community sanctions with respect to conduct. This emphasis
also helped to define the scope of public education at the ele-

mentary level and thus limit costs and taxation. As for the workingmen, they were suspicious of authority in the rawer forms of class and state repressiveness and did not want schools that imposed even academic control to any great extent. They, too, were content to limit public education to the elementary level, which, in that simpler era, seemed sufficient for the exercise of citizenship and for getting on in life.

Furthermore, upper and lower classes alike wished to curtail the authority that was associated with the traditional schoolmaster. This was ultimately theological, specifically Calvinist, in character, an extension of clerical authority justified on the basis of the desperate need to curb and correct sinful human nature. Its symbol was the birch rod suspended on the wall behind the master's desk. But Jacksonian Americans no longer tolerated the Calvinist view of human nature, and they were ready for a radically different approach in both the methods and the personnel of education.

The changing estimate of human nature and its rights and capacities, the ambivalence toward authority whether institutional or intellectual, the emphasis on moral rather than intellectual training as the primary function of education, and the tendency to limit public education to the elementary level were all factors which incidentally predisposed Americans to accept the idea of woman as teacher. If the child was not by nature a viper to be scotched at all costs for its own and society's good— and what Jacksonian thought of himself as having been such a child?—but was rather, as people increasingly believed, a seed, of virtue all compact, requiring only sympathetic cultivation, might not the teacher be expected to represent female nurturance rather than male discipline? If authority, whether political, economic, religious, or intellectual, was not wanted in the classroom, the gentler sex, disfranchised and conformist, could seem preferable in a teacher. If moral training was the chief desideratum, it was reasonable to think this could be accomplished more effectually by example and persuasion than by force majeure. On these principles, the woman, conventionally considered purer than the man, was a better candidate for employment as teacher. And if one thought only of ele-

mentary education, the problem of professional qualification of
woman as teacher seemed manageable; she would need little
more than elementary education herself. Considered as a terminal educational institution unbeholden to the logical and
academic requirements of secondary schools and colleges, the
public common school was a theater in which woman's traditional domestic role might conceivably be played on a stage only
slightly extended.

Rush Welter has characterized the Jacksonian consensus in
favor of common elementary schools which replaced the elitist
educational policy advocated by Federalists and Republicans as
the American democracy's redefinition of the Constitution in
terms of "anarchy with a schoolmaster."[19] He is adapting
Carlyle's witticism to the effect that the British constitution
amounted only to "anarchy with a constable." The implication
is that Americans meant to have an individualistic free-for-all
controlled not by the billy club wielded as necessary among
adults in the world at large but only by the birch rod wielded
betimes among the youth in school, with more emphasis upon
the prevention than upon the repression of disorder in society.
However, the Jacksonian taste for anarchy was stronger even
than Welter's percipient phrase suggests and conditioned the
development of an educational system promoting anarchy, not
with a schoolmaster, but with a schoolmistress.

Chapter 2
The Wonderful Proportions of Maternity

THE democratic predilections that predisposed Americans to accept the feminization of education would have been insufficient for the purpose if feminization had implied feminism. It is necessary to show, in addition, that teaching gradually came to be regarded as womanly in terms of the female role traditionally defined. The country was nowhere near ready for the radical attack on "the woman question" which interpreted women's rights "primarily in terms of political and social equality," denied that women were properly subordinate to men, and protested the segregation of male and female functions into the domestic "sphere" for women and public life for men.[1] A far more effectual movement for the improvement of the lot of women, accepted as distinct from that of men, was under way which stressed women's responsibilities within the domestic sphere and insisted on their receiving their just deserts through domestic reform.[2] The employment of women as teachers was advocated by the domestic reformers, so respectable by contrast to the radical feminists, their argument being that teaching was a maternal function and the school properly an extension of the home rather than the first precinct of civil life.

The readiness of Americans in the first half of the nineteenth century to credit woman with a sex-specific gift as educator must be understood in the light of the change from the theocentric piety of Calvinist Christianity to anthropocentric moralism with a tendency to mere individualism and egocentricity. Human nature was radically revalued, and social, political, and educational attitudes were revised accordingly. A key issue was the plight of the child in the Calvinist scheme, particularly the doctrine of infant damnation, according to which children dying before they could be converted and reborn were lost. Under the various influences of natural religion, romanticism, and evolutionary thought, the infant was identified with the human as the human was more optimistically assessed. Incidentally to this process, new value and enhanced status accrued to the mother just as the chosen defender of innocence; and it was woman thus magnified in the maternal role that the nineteenth century saw as divinely ordained to teach.

The attack on orthodoxy usually turned more or less conclusively on the theory of conversion, and the key issue here was the spiritual estate of the child. William Ellery Channing declared in 1819 that the Calvinist system

indeed takes various shapes, but in all it casts dishonor on the Creator. According to its old and genuine form, it teaches, that God brings us into life wholly depraved, so that under the innocent features of our childhood is hidden a nature averse to all good and propense to all evil, a nature which exposes us to God's displeasure and wrath, even before we have acquired power to understand our duties, or to reflect upon our actions. According to a more modern exposition, it teaches, that we came from the hands of our Maker with such a constitution, and are placed under such influences and circumstances, as to render certain and infallible the total depravity of every human being, from the first moment of his moral agency; and it also teaches, that the offence of the child, who brings into life this ceaseless tendency to unmingled crime, exposes him to the sentence of everlasting damnation. Now, according to the plainest principles of morality, we maintain, that a natural constitution of the mind, unfailingly disposing it to evil and to evil alone, would absolve it from guilt; and that to give existence under this condition would argue unspeakable cruelty; and that to punish sin of this unhappily constituted child with endless ruin, would be a wrong unparalleled by the most merciless despotism.[3]

The implications for educational theory were plain: if the child was not born totally depraved and propense to evil, it did not require education on repressive and corrective principles alone and to educate it so would tend to corrupt it in fact.

Nevertheless, the orthodox journal, *Spirit of the Pilgrims,* declared that the aim of religious education—and education in general was still conceived of as religiously oriented—was "obviously, to promote, as early in life as possible, a radical, saving change in the temper" of children's hearts. "What they need is, not so much to be amended and improved, as to be *renewed*—not so much to be kept from falling into sin, as to be delivered from its reigning power. And the great object to be promoted, in every part of their education, is their renewal—their sanctification—and consequent salvation." The *Spirit of the Pilgrims* held that "children possess the same mental faculties as adults—they are, in fact, men and women in miniature—and consequently, the same means are to be used to promote their conversion as are used for the spiritual benefit of those in riper years."[4]

Channing alluded to the "old and genuine" form and to "the more modern exposition" of Calvinism and rejected both, but the latter continued to develop under the influence of such divines as Nathaniel Taylor and Horace Bushnell, coming ever closer to the liberal view. Bushnell, with orthodox credentials, advanced a radical criticism of the doctrine of conversion without becoming schismatic as Channing was. Bushnell's advocacy of the doctrine of Christian nurture should be recalled together with contemporary movements, not particularly theological in character and involving figures both orthodox and heterodox, espousing domestic reform and "fireside education" because they all specified teaching as a distinct function of the mother. They magnified the role of the mother by emphasizing the importance of training and conditioning infants and young children at home according to a program which, though less formal than a school curriculum, was nevertheless an organized attempt to develop the American home as a consciously educational institution.

The fireside education movement rested on a belief that the child is naturally wholesome and that its environment is a decisive factor in determining whether it reaches wholesome maturity. Both father and mother were charged with teaching functions, but the main responsibility was assigned to the mother, thus confirming the tendency to think of women as specially qualified by maternal instinct to teach. Although there was implicit in this tendency a presumption of priestly function in women, bringing in its train grave issues of belief and doctrine, the advocates of fireside education mostly considered themselves devout. As Anne L. Kuhn has observed, "Those who were writing and teaching, and especially those who were encouraging female authorship and the promotion of educational causes, were exposed to a stream of innovation which, whether or not they realized it, was modifying their orthodoxy."[5] Anybody who felt twinges of conscience could salve them by appealing to Bushnell if Channing seemed heretical.

Emphasizing the responsibilities of woman in her domestic and maternal role, the domestic reformers believed that

rights were attained through increased capacity to mold the minds of men [the word being used to refer specifically to the male sex] and of the rising generation. The doctrine of the "middle way" of gradual progress was preached as eloquently by this group as that of immediate action was demonstrated by the other [i.e., the feminists]. . . . The real conflict lay, not between views which dictated female submission on the one hand and female freedom on the other, but in a definition of woman's primary function in a democratic society. The militant feminists felt it necessary to decry the domestic function in their zeal to make a clean break with the old order. The other group felt that the only "emancipation" which was worth while was that which gave first emphasis to the vocation of the wife and mother.[6]

To this analysis should be added the observation that the differences between the domestic reformers and the feminists involved not only a disagreement about the function of woman in a democratic society but also a division of opinion as to the nature of woman. In advancing maternity as the definitive characteristic of woman, the domestic reformers were in tune with other attitudes of the time which tended to reinforce their influence. The feminist view of woman as characterized by something more than the biological function of maternity and the qualities thought to be inherent in the very potential for it, as man was considered more than the function of paternity, hardly resonated at all. But the view of woman-as-mother and the promotion of woman's interests on the basis of maternal instinct and function had profound effect throughout society, and nowhere was it more decisive than in the schools through the redefinition of the teacher.

A third approach, sometimes confused with that of the domestic reformers, should be distinguished both as a matter of interest in itself and as an influence upon the emerging concept of woman as teacher. This approach emphasized the privileges of woman's subordinate status, which even so earnest a reformer as Catharine Beecher could cite on occasion as a value not to be bartered for mere political equality with men. Less responsible ladies, however, included among female privileges that of avoiding even the burdens of traditional wife- and motherhood. For example, Lydia Maria Child, in her *Brief History of the Condition of Woman* (1845), described the lot of American women as comparatively happy and scoffed at agitation for equality of the sexes. What was to be gained from equality while "that true and perfect companionship, which gives both man and woman complete freedom *in* their places, without a restless desire to go out of them, is as yet imperfectly understood?"[7]

In their place, American women—at least middle- and upper-class ones—received such social deference, exercised such private power through what Catharine Beecher and Harriet Beecher Stowe called approvingly the "pink and white tyranny," enjoyed such license to leave the grubby details of housekeeping and child rearing to servants, and claimed such exemptions from the trials of business and the duties of citizenship that many thought there was little to gain and much to lose from acquisition of the franchise, insistence on property rights, or participation in affairs. This frankly selfish line was popular. A classic expression of it was an editorial by Sarah J. Hale in the *Ladies' Magazine* of January 1830 with the complacent title "Privileges of American Ladies."

The divergent emphases on the rights of women (as citizens regardless of sex), the responsibilities of women (in the domestic sphere), and the privileges of women (as compensation for their subordinate status) all continue to echo through public discussion today; but in the formation of the image of woman as teacher the first was left out of account while the second, subtly contaminated by the third, was dominant. The program of the domestic reformers called for the strenuous education of women to fit them for the duties of their sphere, thus implying that those duties had not been performed as well as might be and that the domestic sphere could not be expanded to include the school as well as the home without effort. But people of both sexes who prized the privileges and exemptions of woman in her secondary role rationalized her avoidance of responsibility by claiming that women used their freedom from responsibility in the cultivation of higher things.

Irresponsibility was veneered with genteelism. In the functional segregation by sex, the crude husband got the living midst the barbaric conditions of a competitive business world while his lady wife guarded at home the values of leisure above all and then of art, literature, and religion, thus associating these fields with her secondary status—which is to say, with femaleness as a secondary status. Whatever uncivilized aspects there might be of the husband's getting, his wife might redeem in the spending on home decoration, patronage of the arts and charities, and maintenance of her person.

To the female domestic sphere, soon to be expanded to include the school, affection, refinement, manners, aesthetic values, moralism, and culture were assigned, while in the male sphere of public affairs that really mattered one expected hostility, roughness, crude egoism, money values, venality, and an eye for the main chance. This situation became a theme of fiction, notably that of Henry James after the Civil War, in which he contrasted what he called the two worlds as "uptown"—the location of the genteel, woman-run home—and "downtown," where the men went to pursue "the serious male interest" of commerce. Plainly, the implication was that culture was a nonessential female pastime, pursued less for its own sake than as a more or less cynically recognized mask for the laziness and frivolity at home and the barbarism of business. The point in dwelling here on this situation, still the basic situation of

American life, is that it conditioned the emergence of woman as teacher: it will be a theme of later chapters that implicit in the feminization of American education was subversion of the curriculum and academic standards and license for every true American boy to rebel against them and for American girls to honor them genteelly in the breach. They were only culture. The ultimate allegiance was to life, priced in dollars and cents.

Secularization, however, was never a conscious motive in the common school revival and the feminization of the teaching corps which was inextricably associated with it. Feminization was in part a necessary guarantee that in removing education from the control of the church and placing it in the hands of the state, Christian and Protestant motives would be preserved; and passably orthodox theological credentials had to be provided for woman as teacher before feminization of teaching could be comfortably accepted. Implicit in those credentials, I shall argue, had to be an orthodox sanctioning of the romantic, optimistic view of human nature. If, in providing credentials for woman as educator and approving the liberalization of the doctrine of conversion, the Congregationalist establishment contributed to the shift from piety to moralism, this perception of the case was not that of the nineteenth century but rather an instance of hindsight in the twentieth. At the time, only what was regarded as a more rational and effectual scheme of salvation was proposed, which, incidentally, tended to reorient education.

The apparently heretical doctrine of Christian nurture, according to which the child was born with the capacity to grow all unconsciously into grace without the trauma of conversion, could be made to square with certain elements of orthodox tradition. As the leading proponent of Christian nurture, Bushnell echoed, with the new romantic emphasis, the old Puritan uneasiness about the plight of the child under the strict Calvinist dispensation. Bushnell derived his position from prestigious and sufficiently orthodox predecessors, chiefly Jonathan Edwards himself, Samuel Taylor Coleridge, and Coleridge's American interpreter and Bushnell's teacher, Nathaniel Taylor. These writers had developed intuitionist and idealist lines that encouraged divergence from the rationalist, empiricist rigor of earlier Calvinists and, ironically, tended to subvert the main position of Edwardsean theology.

Bushnell appealed to Edwards's "doctrine of the heart," an essential part of the "New Light" claim of validity for transforming illumination on every man's road to Damascus. This claim involved a contention that there are two distinct kinds of knowledge, the mediate and the immediate. Mediate knowledge was thought to operate concretely and was sometimes also called "notional" or "speculative" knowledge stemming from sense data. An early Puritan formulation described mediate knowledge as "knowledge with a taste," very different from and inferior to the immediate knowledge or nonsensuous experience of God. Bushnell, following Taylor, buttressed this element of the changing New England theology with ideas from Coleridge's *Aids to Reflection* and with his Kantian distinction between Reason and Understanding. He eventually came, in his 1872 sermon "The Immediate Knowledge of God," to such assertions as: "The roads of the natural understanding are in a lower plane, you must rise, you must go up in truth and *know God—God himself*—by the inward discovery of his infinite spirit and person." Knowledge of God was "knowing God within, even as we know ourselves"; and "there is no language in it, no thought, no act of judgment or opinion, you simply have a self-feeling that is intuitive and direct."[8]

Although knowing God is different from experiencing conversion, the two are easily confused and in any case have elements in common. Bushnell's conception of the knowledge of God as an incommunicable "self-feeling" placed an interesting interpretation upon the complementary notion of God as a parent. It implied that Christians were like Christ by reason of a sibling relationship rather than like Adam by reason of genetic descent. For if knowledge of God is a self-feeling, the self must participate in the divine, as Ralph Waldo Emerson was also asserting. An incommunicable self-feeling could be credited by others only on the basis of a man's assertion that he had it, persuasive expressions of his joy in having it, and impressive reflections of it in his conduct; but traditionally the New En-

gland churches had eyed claims of conversion very narrowly
just in order to discount the subjective aspect.

The traditional mode of conversion was formal, technical,
comprising observable behavior consisting of distinct phases in
a climactic order not liable to much individualized variation. It
most decidedly had language in it, a highly conventionalized
testimonial rhetoric; and it involved public delivery. Thought
the most harrowed and analytical was indispensable: every sinner, and all the fellowship, must observe his life with daily attention and derive from the data an impeccably logical conclusion as to his spiritual state. Given the orthodox dogmas, the
most scrupulous evidentiary reasoning was employed.

For skill in this nobody was more respected than the minister.
He was the model of the intellectual, and it was his duty to hold
his people to the standard and to insist upon promulgation of
the conclusion, no matter how painful it might be in any given
case—such as the death of an infant—as to whether or not a
person had received the Spirit. And no matter how gratifying
the conclusion might be in some cases, it was forever in doubt
and there was a lifetime, after sanctification, of proving it.
Opinion and judgment were as inseparable from conversion, as
Edwards had defined it, as from language and thought. A
man's mere self-feeling that all was well with him was likely to
be regarded as a trap of the Adversary and to elicit the most
skeptical and realistic examination.

The orthodox theory and practice of conversion stood behind pedagogy, which, given the dogma of depravity, must approach the young in a judgmental and corrective way from
which intellectuality, evidentiary reasoning, logic, and empirical proof were indivisible. These qualities were associated also
with masculinity and this with deity in the form of a judgmental
God. In order for women to displace men as teachers, the
entire constellation of qualities associated with the old male,
church-dominated pedagogy had to give way before another
constellation associated with femaleness but equally sanctioned
by religion, though religion radically changed.

This constellation, in which compassion and nurture replaced correction and judgment according to external stan-

dards, featured feeling rather than form. Persuasion replaced authority, example replaced force, personal relationship replaced principled requirements. The emerging constellation reflected the concept of maternity, taken as the epitome of womanliness, rather than female personality defined as we do today apart from, or at least as including but not epitomized by, maternity. It calls to mind the elements that went into Mariolatry in the medieval period. Calvinism was reformed medievalism, and part of the reform had been the reinstatement of Jesus Christ in his rigorous role of Judge; now at the decline of Calvinism another reaction against (masculine) harshness took the character, not unexpectedly, of the magnification of (female) mildness. As behind the male teacher had stood the power of male physique and the authority of the male Congregationalist minister, so behind the new female teacher was to stand the example, rather than the authority, of the mother, of whom the nineteenth century came to think as "the minister of the home," as Catharine Beecher liked to call her.

In religion, and then in due course in education, the improving status of woman-as-mother or mother-teacher was a function of the new focus on the child, regarded more and more explicitly as incarnating the divine. When Horace Bushnell asserted in opposition to what he regarded as overemphasis on revivalistic converson "that the child is to grow up a Christian, and never know himself as being otherwise,"[9] he implied revolution in the relationship between child and adult. Bushnell criticized revivalistic conversion as "mechanical"[10] and substituted in theological discourse the metaphors of organicism for those of mechanism, thus implying, probably unawares, a species of predestination very different from the Calvinist doctrine.

To organicism Bushnell added a variety of environmentalism. According to Luther A. Weigle, "He defended this thesis [of unconscious growth in Christianity] with a wealth of argument which rests ultimately upon two propositions: that the nature of the family as a social group is such that the spirit and character of the parents inevitably influence the life and character of the children; and that the life of the family may thus be a means of grace, in that it affords an instrument which God may use for the fulfillment of His promises and constitutes a natural channel for the power of the Holy Spirit." Bushnell matched this attribution of a divine value to the natural family with a similar attribution to the natural body. In Weigle's words, "Physical nurture, he held, may be a means of grace; one cannot be a Christian in his mind, and not be a Christian in his body."[11] Child care in all its aspects took on, in Bushnell's perspective, honorific connotations that it had never had; and mothering gained status thereby.

And so Bushnell declared that "the house, having a domestic Spirit of grace dwelling in it, should become the church of childhood, the table and hearth a holy rite, and life an element of saving power. Something is wanted that is better than teaching, something that transcends mere effort and will-work—the loveliness of a good life, the repose of faith, the confidence of righteous expectation, the sacred and cheerful liberty of the Spirit—all glowing about the young soul, as a warm and genial nurture, and forming in it, by methods that are silent and imperceptible, a spirit of duty and religious obedience to God. This only is Christian nurture, the nurture of the Lord." The celebrant of these rites of the church of childhood and the vessel of this "domestic Spirit of grace" was the mother. Thought of as the church of childhood, *home* took on that special unctuous tone the word still carries; and it was the home so imagined that the educational reformers meant to enlarge by annexing the school, where the female teacher might officiate as the mother did at home. The child was expected to model himself on the Christian behavior of his parents long before he was able to analyze it or understand religion as "a renovated experience."[12] Furthermore, the child was to be dealt with as a child, that is, as a person specially valuable because of his youth.

Bushnell was at pains, however, as he had to be if he was to avoid heresy even by the relaxed standard of mid-nineteenth-century orthodoxy, to deny that to treat the child according to the romantic conception of childhood was equivalent to Arianism or Pelagianism. He insisted that he did not agree with the "many who assume the radical goodness of human nature" and in whose view "the work of Christian education" was "only to educate or educe the good that is in us." Grace was still indispensable, but he nevertheless quoted Baxter to the effect that "education is as properly a means of grace as preaching."[13] In stressing the educative function of mothers, the nineteenth century was able to think of education as an exercise in inducing piety more effectually than the pressures that had been directed toward precocious conversion.

Of the child, Bushnell remarked, "The supposition that he becomes, at some certain moment, a complete moral agent, which a moment before he was not, is clumsy and has not agreement with observation."[14] Implicit here once again is his criticism of the mechanical aspect of the revivalistic approach, which involved putting the fear of God into children by fits and starts and talking in terms unintelligible to them about the necessity of conversion. Instead, parents "should begin with a kind of teaching suited to the age of the child. First of all, they should rather seek to teach a feeling than a doctrine; to bathe the child in their own feeling of love of God and dependence on him, and contrition of wrong before him, bearing up their child's heart in their own, not fearing to encourage every good motion they can call into exercise; to make what is good, happy and attractive; what is wrong, odious and hateful; then as the understanding advances, to give it food suited to its capacity, opening upon it gradually the more difficult views of Christian doctrine and experience."[15] These lines applied to Christian education in particular the advanced general pedagogical theory of the day; and as the minister could recommend the teaching of feeling rather than doctrine, so might the school reformer advocate the teaching of feeling rather than subject matter.

Bushnell asserted "there is a nurture of grace, as well as a grace of conversion; that for childhood, as this for the age of maturity, and one as sure and genuine as the other."[16] He might say the two varieties of grace were equally sure and genuine, but obviously nurtured grace must be preferable. It was of earlier date in the experience of the individual, of painless acquisition and deeper root. In the slow and gradual dynamic of nurtured grace, it was difficult to say when, exactly, a particular child became a complete moral agent not only because childhood was now accounted a condition distinct from adulthood but also because it began to be argued that children differed in rate of growth. The tendency was just to take it for granted that the child of a decent family must, at some point prior to its majority, have been confirmed in a sanctified state. If no specific proof was demanded at any particular time in such an important matter, was it likely that the new feminized education would be any more demanding with respect to proficiency in the "intellectual" subjects?

Although he thought it impracticable to make sharp distinctions between one stage of growth and another, Bushnell ventured for the sake of discussion the possibility that a distinction could be made "between the age of *impressions* and the age of *tuitional influences;* or between the age of *existence in the will of the parent,* and the age of *will and personal choice in the child.*"[17] The two stages in question could also be thought of, he said, as roughly paralleling the periods before and after language. In Bushnell's view, the mother's influence was paramount in the stage of impressions, which was the more important since the child was then supposed most susceptible to example and most pliant. One implication was that in education, taken in the most general sense, nothing definite was to be expected at any particular time in the way of learning. The way was being opened for a large tolerance of variation, not in the stated goals of education any more than in the goals of religious training, but in actual accomplishment in any given component of the regimen. At the same time, given the emphasis on self-feeling and the inability to say of any given child at any given time whether or not he had made satisfactory progress toward moral agency, it seems that the innovation of Christian nurture stood at the source of all that is nowadays meant by "permissiveness."

Not that Bushnell himself or his contemporaries formulated any such doctrine. At every step, Bushnell worriedly reached back to the dogma he was modifying or subverting, to reaffirm it. The principal instance is his denial of radical goodness and reassertion of depravity. He was also very conscious that in magnifying the mother he might be thought to undercut paternal authority in the American family. So he said, "I would not undervalue a strong and decided government in families." He felt, nevertheless, that "there is a kind of virtue, my brethren, which is not in the rod—the virtue, I mean, of a truly good and sanctified life. And a reign of brute force is much more easily maintained than a reign whose power is righteousness and love. There are, too, I must warn you, many who talk much of the rod as the orthodox symbol of parental duty, but who might really as well be heathens as Christians; who only storm about their house with heathenish ferocity, who lecture, and threaten, and castigate, and bruise, and call this family government. They even dare to speak of this as the nurture of the Lord."[18] These are the tones, in some instances the very words, which, as we shall see, Horace Mann used in attacking the male teacher and his rod.

The tone of this passage and of the *Christian Nurture* at large leaves little doubt that Bushnell's heart was with the mother and the reign of love, not with the father and brute force. This distribution of presumptively definitive qualities to the sexes was general in the religious and educational literature of the nineteenth century. Bushnell's bias was explicit. He wrote, for example, that where the husband and father is irresponsible and unbelieving, God helps the wife and mother: "He pledges himself in formal promise to one party, in all such conditions, declaring that the believing wife sanctifies, takes away the defect of the unbelieving husband."[19] This is as much as to rewrite the family covenant, electing the wife and mother as the primary party in the contract with God, and to supply the female sex with a revolutionary theological status.

For the full commitment to the doctrine of Christian nurture, the following passage, in which Bushnell hymned the mother's intermediary relationship to God and to her child, may stand as sufficient witness:

Her love, as she herself feels, looks through the body into the inborn personality of her child,—the man or woman to be. Nay, more than that, if she could sound her consciousness deeply enough, she would find a certain religiousness in it, measurable by no scale of mere earthly and temporal love. Here springs the secret of her maternity, and its semi-divine proportions. It is the call and equipment of God, for a work on the impressional and plastic age of the soul. Christianized as it should be, and wrought in by the grace of the Spirit, the minuteness of its care, its gentleness, its patience, its almost divine faithfulness, are prepared for the shaping of a soul's immortality. And, to make the work a sure one, the intrusted soul is allowed to have no will as yet of its own, that this motherhood may more certainly plant the angel in the man, uniting him to all heavenly goodness by predispositions from itself, before he is united, as he will be, by choices of his own. Nothing but this explains and measures the wonderful proportions of maternity.[20]

Having entered the extraordinary claims that maternity is "the call and equipment of God" and that this call and equipment were given for "a work" with the age of the soul when it is most susceptible of being saved, Bushnell appended a caveat, as he felt impelled to do at other critical points of his argument. Well he might. He had equated maternal with priestly calling and dignity and actually exalted the mother's work above the minister's. If the mother succeeded in her work "on the plastic and impressional age of the soul," the minister was left the lesser work of maintenance or rehabilitation, or of rescue missions in instances where the mother's prior work had failed. By implication scarcely less plain, he had promoted femaleness in general above maleness, if we may read his connotations as well as his conscious denotations. He had said that the virtue of a truly good and sanctified life was not in the rod; now he attributed to motherhood the capacity to "plant" the angel in the man, a much more considerable feat than the father's having planted the seed of the man in the woman. The word *seed* is Bushnell's, as in the title of his 1844 essay, "The Kingdom of Heaven as a Grain of Mustard Seed," which became the heart of his great book. These superb claims for maternity not only undercut the dignity of paterfamilias, ordained minister, and the male sex in general but began to offend against that realism about human nature in which orthodoxy and Bushnell himself were by no means lacking.

So he struck again the chastening note, but as usual it was a second thought. As an intelligent man seeking to liberalize without subverting the orthodox doctrines and as a minister of extensive experience, he knew well the facts of viciousness in parents, including mothers who ruined their children by petty, temperamental, changeable, and un-Christian nurture. He knew that it could and must be admitted that depravity persisted in human nature, male and female alike, that maternity did not necessarily regenerate every woman; he was no uncritical instance of the romantic and democratic optimism of his era. The persistence of depravity "could" be acknowledged. "For the honor of human nature," he went on, "I wish it could not; and that what we call maternal affection, the softest, dearest, most self-sacrificing of all earthly forms of tenderness and fidelity, were, at least, sufficient to save the dishonor, which, alas! it is not; for these wrongs [that mothers commit against their children] are, in fact, the cruelties of motherhood, and as often, I may add, of an over-fond motherhood, as any— wrongs of which the doers are unconscious, and which never get articulated, save by the sobbings of the little bosom, where the sting of injury is felt."[21]

Despite such occasional caveats, the optimism, easily modulated into overpowering sentimentality in the minds of Bushnell's public if not in his own, was first and last dominant in Bushnell's work. He first clearly enunciated it in his essay criticizing the "Spiritual Economy of Revivals of Religion," published in 1838 just as Horace Mann was getting under way with his revival of the common schools of Massachusetts. The outlines of the theory of nurture as an alternative to conversion were developed in his essay already mentioned, "The Kingdom of Heaven as a Grain of Mustard Seed," which appeared in the *New Englander* the year before Mann exulted in the achievement of a statistical trend insuring the displacement of male by female teachers. This essay was incorporated as the chapter "Growth, Not Conquest, the True Method of Christian Progress" in the first edition of his *Views of Christian Nurture* (1847). He revised and enlarged the book repeatedly. The second half, added to the last version published in 1861, went into so many particulars of the rearing of children that it could be regarded as a prototype of Doctor Spock's manual.

Having declared physical nurture a means of grace, Bushnell had a basis on which to approve and encourage, rather than to discourage as the more strictly orthodox did, the playfulness of children, thus supplying clerical backing for this as a chief value of the avant-garde pedagogy of Mann. He expanded his interest in hygiene and psychology, as Catharine Beecher and Mann did with reference to the home and the schoolhouse. This development of the doctrine of Christian nurture in the direction of practical child rearing had its tendency to secularism, which was available for emphasis while still carrying a religious tone, in the new growth of nonsectarian public schools. It was no less available in dignifying the functions of the mother in the home and in rationalizing the extension of those functions to the schools, where women, whether actually mothers or not, might be regarded as divinely called to teach.

Although a careful student can hardly overlook the orthodox qualifications which Bushnell attached to the doctrine of Christian nurture, a people already imbued with the ideology of democratic optimism might not only overlook them but find other themes in Bushnell's work so suited to their predilections as to overshadow the inconvenient elements. Bushnell was, on balance, no sentimentalist; but his ideas, above all about motherhood, were available to sentimentalizing. He was himself evidently a product of the nurturant approach, and his devotion to his own mother is expressed in the tone of his writing. He said of the Bushnell children's relation to their mother: "There was no atmosphere of artificially pious consciousness in the house. And yet she was preaching all the time by her maternal sacrifices for us, scarcely to be noted without tears."[22]

This notion of the mother tacitly preaching through self-sacrifice to her husband and children was extensible to the woman teaching, especially after, as we shall see in the next chapter, teaching was promoted as the best preparation for marriage and motherhood. In the domestic education movement, the mother began to acquire a quasi-public if not professional identity as a teacher. Sanctioned by such theological arguments and sentimental applications as have been instanced, mothers were encouraged to teach formally and to consult with other women in the Motherhood Associations which sprang up in many towns. Although the basic impulse of the domestic education movement was religious, secular motives emerged that in time proved transferable to public education without sectarian character. Compatible though it was with democratic sentiment, the doctrine of nurture could be supported (with suitable shift of emphasis) also by political conservatives who feared the excesses of Jacksonian enthusiasm.

"Most eloquent of the reactionaries," Anne L. Kuhn has noted, "were those who placed their hopes for the salvation of the country in the proper 'nurture and admonition' of the rising generation. Laxness in family government and emphasis on intellectual culture at the expense of religious and moral culture were, they declared, responsible for the deplorable 'atheism, licentiousness and intemperance' which had caused the downfall of the French government, but America might avert this catastrophe by stemming the tide of unbelief by 'seizing upon the infant mind, and training it up under moral and religious influence.' " In the 1830s and 1840s, strict Calvinists were a minority overshadowed by people of transcendentalist and unitarian tendencies; but they were vocal and their strictures carried yet the sting of conscience. Their participation in the cult of the mother and in the fireside education movement guaranteed the respectability of these. They joined in the conclusion that "the mother . . . was of supreme importance to the nation as guardian and guide of the days of infancy, and many definitions of her unique function were forthcoming. While some reformers were to stress the father's responsibility in family education, popular sentiment granted to the mother the chief influence over the emotions, the affections of the soul, through which channels the moral character of childhood was to be guided."[23] The *Parent's Magazine* for March 1841 expressed a commonplace when, in an article entitled "The Responsibility of the Mother," it stated, "Companions, brothers and sisters, the father . . . all perform their part, but the mother does the most."[24]

The compatibility of more or less orthodox religious interests and increasingly secular educational motives in promoting domestic education under the aegis of the mother is apparent in Samuel G. Goodrich's *Fireside Education,* published in New York in 1838. Known as "Peter Parley," Goodrich saw the home as a seminary, the parent as teacher; and he endorsed education for the masses, regarding the common school as "the auxiliary of the fireside." He was preparing a transition from the view of the mother as domestic, nonprofessional educator to woman, whether mother or not, as public, professional schoolteacher. "Infancy, childhood, youth, all advancing to maturity by the process of education, place the design of the Creator before every parent and every member of society," Goodrich said. "Let parents, then, take up and follow out this design; let the community at large engage with providence in carrying to completion its benignant intentions toward mankind. Let our legislators, those who have almost a creative power over the society for whom they act—let these cooperate in the great work of human improvement."[25]

Another aspect of the domestic education movement should be stressed here once again as preparing the way for feminizing the teaching profession, namely, the tendency to prefer the moral to the intellectual or academic values of education. This consorted with the conception of the child as embodying a providential design that parents and teachers had only to follow, and that mothers were specially inclined to follow. It also helped overcome concern about women's academic credentials as teachers. Few nineteenth-century American women were prepared to teach school. It was, therefore, conducive to a change of opinion on the issue that a large segment of opinion was inclined to discount the "intellectual" training women were not as yet qualified to conduct.

The primary concern, as it had always been, was with the training of the will. Under the orthodox dispensation, the child's will must be broken, by force if necessary; the new emphasis was upon bending the will at an early age when it was still pliant. This being seen as preeminently the mother's work, it "helped to break up the patriarchal family pattern in which the father was responsible for the intellectual culture of children."[26] The patriarchal educational pattern, in which memorization of the catechism was the typical enterprise, began to be criticized as damaging to young children, whose hearts must be cultivated before their heads. Intellectual as well as moral instruction was gradually transferred to the mother, and the methods thought advisable in training heart and will were extended to training the mind. In this further sense, education had been feminized through the domestic education movement prior to the common school revival. Jacob Abbott, in the preface to his *The Little Philosopher, or The Infant School at Home,* published in Boston in 1830, provided an instance. "The mother's function in presenting this material [instruction in weights, weather, motion, etc.] is that of questioner and demonstrator," he wrote. "Instead of pouring information into the child's mind, she draws it out of him by appealing, not to memory alone, but to the familiar testimony of the senses and to dawning powers of reason and association."[27]

By the time Horace Mann actively propagandized the feminization of the teaching corps and teaching method in common schools, American society had been accustomed for at least a quarter century to the identification of the idea of the mother with that of teacher. The domestic education movement had popularized the idea of the school as the "auxiliary of the fireside," so it was easy to think of teaching in a public school as merely an extension of the properly private maternal sphere without feeling any great threat to the traditional statuses of the sexes. More fundamentally, "the wonderful proportions of maternity" had been powerfully asserted in a sufficiently orthodox theological sense and could be interpreted as the primary credentials of a feminized pedagogy which did not seem in conflict with the attitudes of a patriarchal society.

Chapter 3

Ichabod Crane's Profession and the Profession of Woman

A THIRD major factor predisposing mid-nineteenth-century opinion to accept the feminization of education was the actual parlous condition of teaching as a male occupation, which meant that jealousy of male prerogative was comparatively weak and that arguments for expanding and improving education by using women as teachers could seem reasonable. Teaching was subprofessional and brought neither status nor remuneration sufficient to attract and hold ambitious men, who could do better in business, law, medicine, or the ministry, or in exploiting the land.[1] Formal schooling was still considered a minor element in education as American society moved out of medieval patterns of family and community into modern industrialized life, in which more education was delegated to the school, the necessity for conscious educational theory and pedagogical method was more generally recognized, and teaching advanced claims to professionalism. In taking over teaching, women won largely by default a field that men neglected. At the same time, their claim to it was given a positive tone by ever more explicit proposals for carrying out the necessary professionalization of teaching redefined as womanly in a traditional, nonfeminist sense.

The best schoolmasters were likely to be transients, young men destined for the professions or business who kept school as a temporary expedient to support themselves and meet college expenses. Teaching was used as a stepping stone to preferable careers requiring formal professional preparation, as teaching did not. The teacher needed only common school education, and even girls increasingly had that and turned readily to keeping summer school or dame school for pupils who were too young for productive labor. Older pupils could be spared from farm or shop chiefly in winter; if the winter school was the domain of the male teacher it was still a secondary affair in the scheme of community values, something that went on when more important things did not. It was his domain more because he was male than because he was specifically qualified to teach. A male teacher was thought necessary for the winter school in order to insure control of the big boys through corporal punishment, which a woman was not physically able to inflict on them.

About the schoolmaster as a type gathered an ambience of transience shading into vagrancy, incompetence, eccentricity, and effeminacy crossed with alienation and sadism. Caricature though it is, Washington Irving's characterization of Ichabod Crane as the butt of the community's ridicule and hostility seems to have reflected reality. That the situation remained much the same a half century after Irving wrote is suggested by Edward Eggleston's portrait of the Hoosier schoolmaster. Through the sentimentality of Eggleston's tale we can sense the frustration of men gentler, more bookish and idealistic than Ichabod Crane who gravitated to teaching only to find themselves in circumstances that tended either to brutalize them or to break their spirit, depending on personality. The male teachers of the late colonial and early national periods were marginal in a social order still more or less intact which did not yet perceive teaching as a distinct function requiring particular training or professional autonomy.

In thinking about the situation of the male teacher during the period preceding the feminization of education, however, one should guard against distortion resulting from long familiarity with feminized public schooling as this developed after the 1840s. Education did not exist as a profession in the sense now used, but this is not to say that for want of public schools and professional educators American education had never been effectual. It appears that, at the time of the Revolution, Americans in general were better educated than they have been since. But by the 1820s changes in American institutions had created a conscious need for public, formal schooling in the hands of professionally qualified teachers which school-masters shaped by the old order could not meet. The reason was not necessarily that they were inferior on their own terms, but that their terms were growing anachronistic.

If men lacked motives either for entering teaching or for inventing a male teaching profession that might suit the times, women, their status subtly enhanced by changes in the family, religion, commerce, and government, were part and parcel of the new situation in which democratic society felt the need for common schooling. The more inclined people were to think every child should be schooled, the more obvious it became that the demand for teachers would increase vastly and that women must be recruited. Teaching, even at a rate of pay from one-fourth to one-half what a male teacher received and found inadequate to support a family, was attractive to women, who had no other opportunities for gainful employment except domestic service, practical nursing, or labor in the new factories at Lowell and elsewhere. It required little preparation, and it was more genteel than the alternatives.

The need to support a family was not expected to arise in the case of a woman. It was the single woman who might take gain-ful employment outside the home but still in occupations that could be interpreted as extensions of domestic functions, cook-ing, nursing, weaving—and now teaching. The unmarried sister, the widow, the girl too young to marry might, without contravening the proprieties, bring in something to help sup-port the household of the father or brother on whom she was dependent. But a woman was supposed to marry! With the opening to the West, however, New England and the Middle Atlantic states found themselves with a surplus of women, for the young men were emigrating to the frontier.

What was she to do, the single woman, especially of the mid-dle class, for whom no husband was to be found? The question was poignant in Boston, New York, and Philadelphia among women who had been educated to the point of asking it with some degree of analytical power and sense of grievance. Society defined them in terms of marriage and maternity, but society failed to provide the necessary men. If a female person came to proper maturity only in subordination to a man and there was no man, was it just—she herself subscribing to the doctrine— that she was relegated to the limbo of spinsterhood? Well-read women found it hard to believe that they were doomed to a supernumerary status and truncated personal development be- cause, despite the best will in the world, they were unable to do their womanly duty as wives and mothers. They felt wronged, not in being denied equality with men, but in being judged less than womanly and denied any role other than wife and mother in which they might prove womanliness: a woman was a woman for a' that!

The perfect instance of this attitude was Catharine Esther Beecher, whose qualities, though appreciated from one angle or another in her lifetime and since, have only recently been placed in proper perspective and analyzed with full respect by Kathryn Kish Sklar. Catharine Beecher embodied all of the ele- ments and conflicts implicit in early nineteenth-century dissatis- faction with the Calvinist dispensation and in the movement for domestic reform of woman's condition within the traditional sphere. She was preeminently what Anne L. Kuhn designated the "active conservative" in the cause of woman and exemplified a powerful irony which is suggested by the para- doxical tone of Kuhn's phrase: a conservative sufficiently irri- tated by the established modes is likely to work from within for change more effectually than the radical who attacks frontally.

Catharine Beecher was earnestly conservative in religion, social attitude, and sexual politics, but the more she acted to put matters right according to the received scheme the more radical her results became. She reduced the ideas of the domestic reform movement to a coherent ideology of domes- ticity but with political bearings, argued for the recognition of woman's domestic functions as a profession, advocated higher education for women to prepare them for it—for "the profession of woman" as she called it—and sought to co-opt the common school movement as the vehicle of her purpose. To her more than to any other figure can be traced the redefinition of the gender of the American teacher,[2] in terms of the traditional sex role of women. However, she did not succeed entirely as she wished. The actual feminization of the teaching corps, when it came, was directed by men such as Horace Mann toward a result different from what Catharine Beecher had in mind.

Catharine Beecher stated that "inasmuch ... as popular education was the topic which was every day rising in interest and importance, it seemed to me, that, to fall into this current, and organize our sex, as women, to secure the proper education of the destitute children of our land, was the better form of presenting the object, rather than to start it as an effort for the elevation of woman. By this method, many embarrassments would be escaped, and many advantages secured."[3] Sklar erred in saying that Catharine Beecher intended to make teaching "the special 'profession of woman,' "[4] for in fact teaching was only an aspect of her conception of the profession of woman which she thought expedient to stress at the beginning. She visualized universities designed for women but equal in academic quality to Harvard, in which teacher education would be only one department, but felt that opinion could be marshaled in favor of higher education for women more easily if it were first presented as necessary to prepare them for teaching rather than for the inclusive profession of woman. Teachers trained in the sort of woman's university Miss Beecher visualized would have been very different from Horace Mann's "normalite," the product of normal schools as these developed on the model of his foundation at Lexington; they would have been comparable rather to the graduates of Bryn Mawr or Radcliffe.

Catharine Beecher's personal development, as well as her ideological formulations and organizational work in behalf of woman and, incidentally, of common schools with women as teachers, illuminates the origins of the type of the American female or—in the case of men—feminized teacher.[5] Catharine Beecher's (female) experience of the classic early nineteenth-century withdrawal from Calvinism—the whole masculine and medieval theology and ethos—resulted in a revaluation of woman which, while overtly orthodox, actually challenged and subverted the primacy of man and asserted the autonomy of woman. As "a daughter of Levi," as she liked to call herself, Catharine Beecher, eldest of a large family, remained Miss Beecher with as much ideological emphasis as many women today place upon the title "Ms." That self-assertion stood against the authority of a formidable orthodox ministerial father, seven ministerial brothers, and a ministerial brother-in-law.

Recoloring everything by the seachanges of gender, Miss Beecher proved herself quite as competent a theologian as they, quite as efficient an organizer of missionary work, quite as able to head a household or an institution. As a young woman, she gave evidence of her mettle by mounting a revival. In fact, on her father's and brothers' own orthodox terms, she made a case for woman, if not exactly as priest, then as more effectual than priests in saving souls. It was not for nothing that her father Lyman, in despair after prolonged efforts to induce a proper conversion experience in his daughter, wrote to her in pre-Freudian innocence, speaking to her as he felt God might: "My rod has been stretched out and my staff offered in vain."[6] It was not for nothing that at the end of her life Catharine stated with satisfaction that "my father never in his life praised me, although he used to say that I was the best boy he had."[7]

Miss Beecher also stood up intellectually against another orthodox minister, even more formidable than her father, the Reverend Nathanael Emmons of Franklin, Massachusetts. A leading exponent of the "New Light" Calvinism, Emmons is of special interest here because of his negative influence not only upon Catharine Beecher but also upon two other key education reformers, Horace Mann and Edward A. Sheldon. She had as personal a motive in this instance as she did in her protracted dialogue about conversion with her father. At the end of 1821 she became engaged to marry Alexander Fisher, the young professor of natural philosophy at Yale, only to lose him in a shipwreck a few months later. It turned out that Fisher, though devout like Catharine, had also never been able to bring himself to experience conversion. A native of Franklin like Horace Mann, Fisher was a member of Emmons's congregation and studied theology with him; and there was no evidence satisfactory to Emmons that the young man, for all his brilliance, died in a state of grace.

For reasons of her own as well as out of revulsion at the interpretation that could account an Alexander Fisher damned, Catharine spent the winter of 1822 with the Fisher family in Franklin, searching her dead fiancé's papers for evidence against Emmons of spiritual well-being. He had kept, in the best Puritan tradition, a diary of his frustrated struggle for conversion. Besides, there was the legacy of his scientific study and writing and his reputation as an exemplary teacher. Catharine pondered all and announced her own interpretation in a letter to her father: "When I think of Mr. Fisher, and remember his blameless and useful life, his unexampled and persevering efforts to do his duty both to God and man, I believe . . . that God . . . does make the needful distinction between virtue and vice; and that there was more reason to hope for one whose whole life had been an example of excellence, than for one who had spent all his days in guilt and sin. Year after year with persevering and unexampled effort, he sought to yield that homage of the heart to his Maker which was required, but he could not: like the friend [and she meant herself] who followed his steps, he had no strength, and there was none given him from above."[8]

The loss of Alexander Fisher, in opening to her his "example of moral rectitude coexisting with an unredeemed heart," helped Catharine finally to believe "there was another path to salvation besides the one her father advocated" and that "she too could lead a virtuous life, remain unconverted, and yet be saved."[9] The loss seems to have helped in another way, too, if it can be put into words connoting due understanding and sympathy. The evidence seems to indicate that the engaged couple was not passionately attached and that Catharine was not psychologically well suited for marriage, whatever the case may have been with him. As the bereaved fiancée, she had a conventionally acceptable explanation to offer for remaining single. Believing that she must lead a virtuous, i.e., an effectual, life though unmarried, she embodied the recipe for the female "active conservative." She survived her oedipal and spiritual crises definitively as Miss Beecher, bolstered by the new bearings on science that carried the sanction of the dead fiancé. In death, Fisher was a more durable ally against paternal pressure than he might have proved had he lived.

She gained identity at a price, however, of severe neurosis, which had public significance because it was reflected in the emergent type of the feminized American teacher. In their relentless efforts to convert her, her father and brothers, especially her brother Edward, "seem to have heightened rather than resolved the contradictory elements of her identity" while "she refused to pretend that the contradictions were resolved when they were not." The species of victory that she won did not amount to the experience of new birth that "had classically enabled men and women to establish psychic contact with their interior self, or at least to resolve contradictions within their sense of self." She could not honestly condemn her life as sinful, jettison it, and start anew; for "this condemnation was not, as in the case of her brothers, a prelude to some new life outside the home, but a prelude to the resumption of those same feminine domestic responsibilities."[10] Yes, but she did not merely resume, she added the dimension of public school teaching to feminine domestic responsibilities.

She pitched upon the received qualities of womanliness— purity, domesticity, and, above all, self-sacrifice—ascribed to them a new theological status, and derived from that a case for the home and the school, with woman supreme, as competitors in spiritual authority and cultural leadership with the church and the male minister. She could do this without feeling herself in conflict with orthodoxy because of the long decline (or, from the point of view of 1830, the long climb) of orthodoxy from Edwardsean piety to democratic moralism. Even Lyman Beecher preached a doctrine of works that would have been heretical a hundred years earlier. In her book *The Elements of Mental and Moral Philosophy, Founded upon Experience, Reason, and the Bible* (1831), Miss Beecher turned the central positions of the common-sense moral philosophy and psychology to her purpose as an apologist for woman. As a conservative, she feared the excesses, without wishing to deny the advantages, of democracy. The common-sense school proposed conscience, which must be conditioned and educated in every individual if it was to function dependably, as the needful control: Miss Beecher proposed woman as the model and educator, as mother and/or teacher.

Sklar has observed that Miss Beecher "turned self-sacrifice and submission—traditional values associated with women—into signs of moral superiority and leadership." In elevating woman's sex-specific quality of self-sacrifice as the "rule of rectitude," she gave "new meaning to inherited Calvinist concepts." Self-centeredness had been the devil's work, the contrary of benevolence, defined by Edwards as "holy love of Being in general"; but now there was orthodox sanction and popular preference for equating social conscience, good works, and civic-mindedness with benevolence. On these terms, self-denial rather than the glorification of God and the enjoyment of him forever was the proof of sanctification. It was compatible with democratic sentiment in that it substituted an internal for an external authority. The persons best qualified to invent the institutions and exercise the cultural leadership needed to control the brawling democracy and shape it into a civilized commonwealth must be virtuosi of self-sacrifice. How were such persons to be recognized? Miss Beecher answered, they were to be known by their positive "longing for purity" and by self-sacrificial behavior in the home, an equivalent of prayer in one's closet far from the plaudits of the crowd. These tests favored women over men and "subtly shifted moral centrality away from the male clergy and placed it on women laity."[11]

Miss Beecher's notion of the profession of woman received detailed development in the book that established her reputation, the *Treatise on Domestic Economy* published in 1841, reprinted frequently, and supplemented by other works to the end of her life. The domestic state was conceived as an *imperium in imperio,* "an oasis of innocence amid the commercial acquisitiveness of American society" where, though "overtly acknowledging male dominance," the *Treatise* "exaggerated and heightened gender differences and thereby altered and romanticized the emphasis given to women's domestic role."[12]

In order properly to understand, much less to perform adequately, their magnified role, women must be highly educated as hygienists, nutritionists, psychologists, teachers, and, yes, as ministers in both ecclesiastical and political senses. Miss Beecher habitually referred to woman as the "minister of the home" when thinking about Christian nurture of the young, and also as the "prime minister of the domestic state" when thinking about the relationship between the sexes and between the domestic state and the inclusive civil state. These relationships were usually thought of in diplomatic terms, but Miss Beecher was capable of thinking war. She advocated an imperialist policy of territorial expansion for the domestic state, meaning to annex the school, and in time the settlement house and hospital.

As a very active conservative, she not only theorized and wrote but set about establishing institutions of higher learning to educate women for their manifest destiny as the regulators of American democratic society. In 1823, at the age of twenty-three, she founded the Hartford Female Seminary as "the means whereby she could define a new relationship with the culture" and "assert social, religious, and intellectual leadership."[13] The school was a success, and on the basis of her experience with it she formulated ideas on the nature of woman, the curriculum appropriate for this, and the social impact that professionally educated woman might be expected to have. Her Hartford program is of special relevance here in that it provided an early outline of her conception of woman as teacher and of the reforms in education she intended the professionally formed woman-teacher to bring about. This conception had a formative influence still operative in American schools, though no doubt much changed by interplay with other influences in the meantime.

The fateful emphasis was upon woman as primarily gifted with moral rather than intellectual talent, which carried as a corollary the belief that the school, once in female hands, should give precedence to moral over intellectual growth of pupils. After five years, Miss Beecher felt that her seminary had made satisfactory progress but needed a new dimension. "The improvements made have hitherto related chiefly to *intellectual acquisitions,*" she wrote, "but this is not the most important object of education. The formation of personal habits and manners, the correction of the disposition, the regulation of the social feelings, the formation of the conscience, and the direction of the moral character and habits, are united, objects of much greater consequence than the mere communication of knowledge and the discipline of the intellectual powers."[14] As a general statement applicable to the education of both sexes, this was available as a basic argument for the feminization of teaching since women were, by virtue of femaleness, thought to be more self-sacrificing and moral than men.

Miss Beecher hoped to add to her seminary a department of moral instruction under Zilpah Grant where the daughters of well-to-do families who enrolled might be influenced to direct their energies and their families' wealth to evangelical uses. All her life Miss Beecher believed it was specifically the genteel women, either born to middle-class manners or capable or rising to them through education for the profession of woman, who could best serve as ministers of the home and as teachers. She observed to Miss Grant, "A woman of piety and active benevolence, with wealth which enables her to take the lead in society, can do more good than another of equally exalted character without it."[15] Miss Grant proving invulnerable to this argument, Lyman came to Catharine's aid. He instructed Miss Grant on the values of "taste and refinement" as embellishments of religion.[16] In founding a moral department, Catharine Beecher meant to provide a boarding home for pupils and teachers on the principle that the hours spent outside the classroom "are the hours of access to the heart, the hours in which character is developed, and in which opportunities for exerting beneficial influence are continually occurring."[17] Thus the emphasis on "character development" in preference to "mere communication of knowledge and the discipline of the intellectual powers" was already, so early in the history of American education, reinforced with a tendency to value the extracurricular above curricular activities.

The proposal to bring female students out of the homes of

their parents into a boarding home operated as part of the school was extraordinary, and Sklar has made the striking comment that this "change in socialization patterns was simultaneous with the shift in women's career options to include teaching as well as homemaking."[18] It implied, in a girl's school staffed by women, the replacement of the paterfamilias by a woman as head of household. It also reminds one of the arrangements in the convent of a Roman Catholic order of teaching sisters, a parallel not lost on Catharine Beecher. In various passages of her writings, especially from the 1830s and 1840s when Lyman Beecher was trying to persuade evangelical Protestant ministers to proselyte the West and forestall Roman Catholic expansion there, his daughter proposed the woman teacher as the more effectual missionary. She thought of the female teacher as the Protestant equivalent of the Catholic teaching sister. Although she asserted belief in male dominance and therefore in marriage and motherhood as woman's definitive state, she seems to have had the idea of the female teacher as celibate. This represented autonomous femaleness.

Her conception of the profession of woman remained constant and consistent, changing with observation and experience in educating women over half a century only in the direction of deeper conviction. Throughout her life, Catharine Beecher proposed it not only apart from but in opposition to agitation for woman suffrage and the feminist view of women implicit therein. She wrote near the end of her career, "This *woman movement* is one which is uniting by co-operating influences, all the antagonisms that are warring on the family state." And in her view it was the family state, with woman supreme within it, that must be defended at all costs. The appeal of the woman suffrage movement was to upper-class women especially, just the ones needed to fill the profession of woman. It enticed them, Miss Beecher said, into spiritualism, free love, divorce, and contraception; the result was to make "the ignorant masses the chief supply of the future ruling majorities" and thus to insure the degradation of the democratic dogma.[19]

First and last, she argued "that woman's usefulness and hap-

piness are equal in value to man's, and consequently that she
has a right to equal advantages for gaining them, that she is un-
justly deprived of such equal advantages, and that organization
and agitation to gain them is her privilege and duty." But she as
steadfastly maintained that the sexes had different natures,
functions, duties, and privileges, those of women being
properly limited to "the family state" enlarged by the school:
"Woman, as mother and as teacher is to form and guide the immortal mind." It was "a fundamental principle" that "the school
should be an appendage of the family state, and modeled on its
primary principle, which is, *to train the ignorant and the weak by
self-sacrificing labor and love; and to bestow the most on the weakest,
the most undeveloped, and the most sinful.*"[20]

This is one of the most illuminating texts from the formative
period of feminized American education. It harmonized with
the humanitarian motives of the common school revival—Miss
Beecher was speaking in 1870, by which date the feminization
of education was an accomplished fact—although these were
not woman- but child-centered and "the child" was tacitly male.
Miss Beecher's emphasis on the woman teacher's self-sacrificial
devotion primarily to the weakest and most sinful children
reflected a religious dogma, namely, that mother-love was the
truest parallel in humankind of Jesus' love of sinners. The
teacher thus conceived sought no easy victories in the battle for
"immortal minds" but rejoiced rather in testing herself against
the heaviest odds. Teachers must resist the temptation to focus
their attention upon "the bright, the good, the industrious," for
it was wrong to assume "that the interests of the more intelligent and docile are to override those of the stupid and
disobedient."[21] We get here a revealing perspective on the
nonintellectualism that was conveniently convertible to anti-
intellectualism in American public education. Democratic complacency could easily discard the Christian rigor behind Miss
Beecher's observation and turn it to the rationalization of
academic permissiveness. She did not mean that the interests of
the stupid and disobedient were to override those of the intelligent and docile any more than the reverse, but her conception of the feminized teacher lent itself to the justification of

"democratic" education taking its cues from what we today euphemize as "the disadvantaged."

If her opposition to feminism strikes anyone as evidence of pusillanimity, it should be recalled how literal she was in speaking for the "sacred interests of woman and the family state" and how stoutly she meant to defend them against encroachments by man and the "civil state."[22] She conveyed the doctrine that woman was to be trained to rule by love but to rule nonetheless, by right of nonapostolic succession from Jesus Christ, whom, in her capacity for self-sacrifice, she so patently resembled. Asking why Jesus Christ had come among men and suffered, she answered, "It was to teach us not only that an immortal existence stretches before us after death, but that the happiness of that immortality depends on *the character which is formed by education here*."[23]

Miss Beecher spoke for woman power, her idea of which grew more positive with the years. Radicals of the period frequently compared the lot of woman to that of the black slave, but she rejected the comparison. Her idea of the minister of the home had more to do with the power to enslave than with inability to resist enslavement. She scoffed at the suggestion that American women were slaves and added: "Moreover, we of the other side are believers in slavery, and we mean to establish it all over the world. We mean to force men to resign their gold, and even to forge chains for themselves with it; and when we have trained their fair and rosy daughters, we will enforce a 'Pink and White Tyranny' more stringent than any other earthly thraldom. And we will make our slave work, and work from early dawn to dark night, under the Great Taskmaster, the Lord of love and happiness, until everyone on earth shall fear him, as 'the beginning of wisdom'; and then 'do justly, love mercy, and walk humbly with God,' as the whole end and perfection of man."[24] One may reasonably read "man" here not generically for the race but particularly for its male component, whose "end" was to be no less certain than his "perfection" at the hands of woman. The prophetess did not speak idly. She and her sister Harriet, now the famous Mrs. Stowe, had resumed the Hartford Female Seminary in 1870 and, as the allusion to Harriet's novel *Pink and White Tyranny* suggested, were jointly about the Lord's work.

Miss Beecher's original connection with the Hartford school ended after eight years in disappointment, which led, however, to her accompanying her father when he moved to Cincinnati in 1832. In the West, she sought to co-opt her father's evangelical missionary work and to adapt missionary organization in behalf of schools taught by women. She saw in the shortage of schools and teachers throughout the developing West a vacuum that women—educated according to her prescription in women's colleges to be founded simultaneously with common schools—were needed to fill. Like priests in parish churches, female teachers in schools would represent to the remotest corners of ignorance and barbarism the cause of civilization. She understood that "ORGANIZATION" was indispensable if women, as women, were to reach the goals of status and higher education for themselves through teaching. In the "foreign mission cause" she saw how secretaries, agents, missionaries, and all their home base of clergy and pious congregations had not only their disinterested devotion to sustain enthusiasm but a complex of mutual professional and personal interests as well.[25]

Pending the realization of her constant object of establishing female institutions of higher education, she decided to create favorable conditions for it by organizing the emigration of surplus women teachers from New England and the Middle Atlantic states—surplus rather in the sense of outnumbering men than in the sense of being unemployed. Her plan called for locating teaching jobs in the western states, recruiting female teachers in the East, escorting them to their places of employment, and providing assistance for them after they arrived. Her views as to the proprieties and expediencies of female behavior precluded her taking a public leadership role, so she had to spend what must have been a prodigious proportion even of her superabundant energy in persuading various men to act for her. It was a nice exercise in pink and white tyranny. Men sufficiently masterful to carry out her ambitions were unlikely to be as manipulatable as she required, but she had within her own family several who served. A Central Committee for Promoting National Education comprised of leading Cincinnati men was established under the chairmanship of Calvin E. Stowe, Harriet's husband; her brother Thomas served, apparently without protest, as mouthpiece; her brother Henry Ward lent a hand. Like a church missionary board, the Central Committee needed an executive staff and the crucial task of finding the right man to be secretary and general agent fell to Catharine.

In 1844 and 1845, the period at which Horace Mann was meeting and surmounting the most telling opposition that was brought against his common school program in Massachusetts, Catharine Beecher collected her ideas in an address later published under the title *The Evils Suffered by American Women and American Children: The Causes and the Remedy*. Her brother Thomas delivered this in her stead, as its subtitle put it, "to Meetings of Ladies in Cincinnati, Washington, Baltimore, Philadelphia, New York, and Other Cities." Catharine was there to follow up on the organizing and the financial appeals. She was the most famous member of her remarkable family at this time, and her presence in the wings must have been as unmistakable as that of the puppeteer at a puppet show.

The subject was an evangelizing account of "an enterprise now in progress, the design of which is *to educate destitute American children, by the agency of American women.*" She meant that the children were destitute not of material things but of schools and moral culture. The treatment was a model of propaganda. She began with an all but Dickensian evocation of the plight of the children, "these despised little ones of our country, whose whole career for eternity depends upon their training in this life, living among civilized and even Christian people, so neglected, so utterly contemned, that anything on earth secures more attention than the work of rearing them to virtue and heaven!" Then came a calculated tweak of the conscience of those "Meetings of Ladies." While the children suffered, "Christian women are sitting in reach of their young voices, twining silk, working worsted, conning poetry and novels, enjoying life and its pleasures, and not lifting a hand or spending a thought to save them."[26]

For any conscience unduly sore, there followed the balm of explanation. The very frivolity just stigmatized was among the evils suffered by American women. She launched into her analysis of the causes of those evils, as already quoted, causes so impressive that she left a vague impression that they more than mitigated the evil consequences, and fetched up in an apostrophe to the Mother. "Oh, sacred and beautiful name! . . . She is to train young minds, whose plastic texture will receive and retain each impress for eternal ages, who will imitate her tastes, habits, feelings, and opinions; who will transmit what they receive to their children, to pass again to the next generation, and then to the next, until a *whole nation* will have received its character and destiny from her hands!"[27] She prophesied remarkably true, although one may today acknowledge the results in tones less joyous than she used in predicting them.

In the emotion generated by her paean to the Mother, it was expedient to remark in passing that American women, whatever evils they suffered, occupied a position superior to that of women in other countries. They had influence, which Miss Beecher pointed out in order to solicit them to use it in the cause of the profession of woman as the true remedy for the wrongs of woman, which the feminists, those "mistaken champions," were "seeking to cure by drawing her into professions and pursuits which belong to the other sex." Then came the pitch for contributions in support of the Central Committee and its efforts to send "missionary teachers" to the West.[28] She thought a hundred dollars per head would do it.

All the while, she was encouraging women's groups in eastern cities to sponsor missionary teachers and searching for a man who would execute the program of the Central Committee. She approached six men without success, but the seventh, the retiring governor of Vermont, William Slade, accepted. Calvin E. Stowe hailed Governor Slade as the prospective Horace Mann of the West, destined to be as much greater as his field of operations would exceed Massachusetts. On November

14, 1845, Catharine Beecher, hoping to shape Slade into the *"competent leader"* she had in mind, conveyed to him the articles of faith: "Our Creator," she informed him, "designed woman to be the chief educator of our race and the prime minister of the family state, and our aim is to train her for this holy calling and give her every possible advantage for the performance of its many and difficult duties." She explained that strategy required that their "first measure presented to the public" must be "the promotion of popular education as the only mode of saving our nation from ruin." The appeal must be adjusted to the predilections of different publics. To the religious-minded, they should present their enterprise "as a missionary effort"; to enthusiasts for the rights of women, "as the shortest, surest, and safest method." But for his ear, she insisted upon the primacy of founding institutions for the higher education of women; everything was to be directed to that end.[29]

From the first, however, the competent leader was mannishly contrary. He never showed the least interest in Miss Beecher's main purpose. It is not clear from her accounts of him whether he actually opposed higher education for women, dismissed it as a distraction from what he regarded as the main job—the transfer of teachers from East to West—or simply bucked against pink and white tyranny. In addition to obstructing her on this matter of policy, Slade obstinately insisted on setting up merely volunteer committees in western towns to receive and look after the missionary teachers instead of employing paid agents as Miss Beecher wished. The ill-matched pair repeated the tour on which "The Evils Suffered by American Women and American Children" had been delivered, reaping the harvest from the seed that Thomas had sowed for her; but their relations became increasingly strained.

Thereafter, Slade made a speaking tour on his own and formed a number of volunteer committees. Then he parted from the Central Committee and started in its place the Board of National Popular Education with a constitution that said nothing about founding female institutions of higher education, employing agents to assist missionary teachers, or providing funds to rescue any who might find themselves in distress.

In this scheme, Miss Beecher was nothing more than a recruiter of teachers. Slade requisitioned one hundred; and she, distrusting his arrangements, recruited thirty-five with the aid of such groups as the Boston Ladies' Society for Promoting Education at the West, put them through training at Albany, and sent them out with misgivings. Although she continued to cooperate, she had Slade announce in the first annual report of the Board of National Popular Education, issued in 1848, that she had severed official connection with the organization.

Slade's recalcitrance was extremely trying, especially since her conscience drove her to make up for his deficiencies. The gritty work of recruitment, involving fund-raising, travel, and masses of correspondence, as well as the training of the teachers, was left to her. When, after formidable efforts, she had secured free board and lodging in Albany for the thirty-five women who comprised the first lot of missionary teachers, provided them a month's training for their western adventure, and got them ready to travel, Slade had not done his part in providing escorts and travel expenses. Miss Beecher found timely aid in the Reverend William James of Albany, and Slade appeared there only the day after the teachers left. Just as Miss Beecher had predicted, the volunteer committees Slade had formed proved undependable, and once arrived in this or that wild western place, many of the teachers were in difficulty with nobody to help them. The next year, the several committees asked for twenty and she risked sending out five more teachers, whom she assembled and trained at Hartford, but the results were discouraging. The organization she had all along advocated simply had not been accomplished. From her frustrations with Slade, she drew the conclusion "that practical housekeepers, mothers, and school-teachers are better qualified to devise and conduct methods of education than men of business and professional men."[30]

But Miss Beecher persisted. She succeeded in founding several female institutions of higher education in the West, one of which survived until recently as Milwaukee-Downer College. Despite periodic collapses into nervous exhaustion, she kept faith with the missionary teachers, rushing out to care for them when they lost their schools or were not paid.

In Catharine Beecher's relationship to William Slade may be observed a foreshadowing of the American profession of education as we know it today with its long-established division of the sexes—women teachers under male administrators. Slade and Beecher did not pull together harmoniously in the traces, but their advocacy of women teachers outside of New England and particularly of the New England female teacher as the serviceable model to meet the educational needs of the West is an important part of the background of Horace Mann's work in Massachusetts. Although Massachusetts had been from the beginning the leader in education among the American colonies and states, the other states might not have been so ready to imitate the state administration of schools that Mann created, depending upon the woman teacher trained at normal school, if this stereotype had not been widely projected.

Although frustrated by Slade's indifference to higher education for women, Catharine Beecher—not alone, be it said, but most prominently—produced effectual propaganda for the simultaneous creation of institutions for the higher education of women to fit them for teaching and of public schools. In Cincinnati, Cleveland, Indianapolis, and Milwaukee, and many smaller towns such as Burlington, Iowa, and Jacksonville, Illinois, the gospel of new-minted woman teacher for new-minted school was preached before, during, and after Horace Mann's work in Massachusetts. The resistance that the male-dominated society would certainly have mounted against a female takeover of any of the established professions was not aroused against the development of a new profession of women perceived merely as woman's work safely under male administration. Nothing so grand as Catharine Beecher's idea of the profession of woman eventuated; the normal schools that Horace Mann started were vastly inferior to the Harvard for women that Miss Beecher visualized. Nevertheless, the "normalite" proved more adaptable to the purposes of democratic education than the traditional male teacher.

Part II

*The Transference of Education from
Male to Female Hands*

Chapter 4

The Pedagogy of Love

DOUBTLESS, there was a common school revival in the sense of a reform of the schools. But according to the motives of Horace Mann and his humanitarian, phrenological, and unitarian supporters, this common school revival was fundamentally a revival of evangelical religion or, if one prefers, the substitution of moralism for religion, by means of common schools. Woman's claim to the holy mission of teaching was advanced and honored in an ambience of religiosity, not of academic, intellectual, or scientific purpose. Her "work" (in the religious sense) was to be character development primarily rather than the diffusion of knowledge or intelligence which had once been regarded as the indispensable function of an educational system in a republic.

Horace Mann and his contemporaries were the heirs of an ambivalent tradition, one element of which they rejected while establishing the other and so, in a new but vaguer orthodoxy, enabled themselves to act single-mindedly. It should be understood how flatly contradictory the elements were. From the point of view of Edwardsean piety, the religious liberals and educational reformers of the nineteenth century were blasphemers and heresiarchs. The disagreement was on the ways of God to man, which, by the time unitarianism became respectable, were understood as determined by the ways of man to man and incidentally to God. In place of the self-regarding Almighty God of Calvinism, whose purpose in creating the world was the furtherance of his own glory and toward whom man's duty was comprised in self-effacing worship on pain of eternal damnation, a conception of God as an indulgent father had emerged. This Americanized God had committed himself to a government of the universe according to the terms of a constitution that recognized that man had rights, rendered inalienable at the ratification of the instrument. It appeared that the government of laws, not of men, which the Constitution of the United States guaranteed was an analogue of a divinely contracted government of natural laws, not of God.

In his *Tenth Annual Report* as secretary of the Massachusetts Board of Education, Horace Mann laid it out as dogma that the fatherhood of God meant that men are brothers sharing a divine origin. God operated scrupulously through natural law, which implants "a powerful, all-mastering instinct of love . . . in the parental, and especially in the maternal breast, to anticipate the idea of duty, and to make duty delightful."[1] From this he derived claims for education, for woman, and for woman-as-educator as means of grace. Governed by natural law, the human heart could not conceivably be naturally corrupt. If a man sinned—he would not say, with Edwards, when a man necessarily sinned—the sin was not evidence of a nature damned from the start and salvable only by the nonnegotiable grace of God. It was merely the result of faulty education or some deprivation, some deficiency of environment, which by taking thought one might have prevented and might yet correct. The glory, to say nothing of the personal honor and mere legal obligation, of God was just in the feasibility of prevention and correction and in the assurance of human progress.

Rousas J. Rushdoony has maintained in commenting on the "messianic" pretensions of American education that Mann argued "that the schools are the means, instruments, vehicles, and true church by which salvation is given to society." Mann also held, as part of his reaction against Calvinism, that education aims at "the fulfillment of Christianity." He did not oppose schools to churches as secular substitutions but as direct competitors in religious function. "In the controversies with the churches," Rushdoony says, "Mann's stand was . . . that true religion would best be served by the schools, and that the churches were in error in their interpretation of their faith and its realm."[2]

Declaring that "no understanding of the American school situation is possible without a recognition of the devout and ostensibly Christian intent in its origins," Rushdoony explains his qualification of the Christian motivation by adding that for Mann "religion was essentially moralism rather than piety." He then usefully characterizes as anti-Calvinism, thus stressing the reactive quality, the moralism which Mann espoused and expressed in educational theory. Rushdoony summarizes the latter as follows: "As against the Calvinist conception of man as sinner, man is good; as against the doctrine of man's responsibility and accountability to God, of life as a stewardship, the non-biblical conception of natural rights is introduced into education. *The pupil is therefore a person with rights rather than responsibilities. Instead of being accountable to God, parents, teachers, and society, the pupil can assert that God, parents, teachers and society are responsible to him.* In this conception, nurtured by normal school principles and germinating in the 19th century, lie the essentials of Dewey's educational philosophy and progressive education."[3]

This establishment of the rights of the pupil (always tacitly the boy, and visibly beyond him Demos full grown) was guaranteed by that other leading dogma of the new moralism, the self-sacrificial responsibilities of woman. While woman remained faithful to the old dispensation, the educational theorists who found it intolerable used her continuing bondage to liberate themselves and the male pupil with whom they identified. The academic antinomianism thus licensed was not endurable by teachers loyal primarily to academic standards, and a new type of teacher with other commitments was needed. The nurturant woman-teacher, nonjudgmental by academic to say nothing of Christian or Calvinist standards, waited in the wings, as "ostensibly" a teacher as the moralism that provided the rationale for her was ostensibly Christian.

Nevertheless, Mann's moralism would have been ineffectual denatured religion just on its own terms without the personal animus he felt against Calvinism. He reacted against it primarily in Nathanael Emmons, the orthodox minister at Franklin, site of the Mann family farm. Mann wrote:

More than by toil, or by the privation of any natural taste, was the inward joy of my youth blighted by theological inculcations. The pastor of the church in Franklin was the somewhat celebrated Dr. Emmons, who not only preached to his people, but ruled them, for more than fifty years. He was an extra or hyper-Calvinist,—a man of pure intellect, whose logic was never softened in its severity by the infusion of any kindliness of sentiment. He expounded all the doctrines of total depravity, election, and reprobation, and not only the eternity, but the extremity, of hell-torments, unflinchingly and in their most terrible significance; while he rarely if ever descanted upon the joys of heaven, and never, to my recollection, upon the essential and necessary happiness of a virtuous life.

Mann went on to explain, "What we phrenologists call causality,—the faculty of mind by which we see effects in causes, and causes in effects, and invest the future with a present reality,—this faculty was always intensely active in my mind." He had been, therefore, particularly affected by Dr. Emmons's hateful logic: "the doom of judgment-day was antedated" for him so intolerably that he had to find premises other than Dr. Emmons's upon which to argue. He could not pursue the essential and necessary happiness of a virtuous life (that is, practice the religion of Heaven) so long as he was paralyzed by the belief that "there, beyond effort, beyond virtue, beyond hope, was the irreversible decree of Jehovah."[4]

Horace Mann was embittered when Emmons preached a sermon at the funeral of Mann's young brother in which, as he had done at the funeral of Catharine Beecher's fiancé, and indeed as he felt he had to do at that of his own son, he held that for want of evidence of regeneration no assurances of the boy's salvation could be given. Mann's brother had played hooky from church one Sunday, gone swimming, and drowned. The minister drew the grim Calvinistic conclusions as an object lesson for the surviving young people in the congregation, in spite of the added grief this meant for the bereaved family. Horace interpreted Emmons's action as gratuitous cruelty, and it is particularly significant that it was the effect on his mother that he most hotly resented.

Mary Peabody Mann remarked of her husband, "He could have said with another remarkable man who emerged from the gloom of Orthodoxy into the light of life and religious liberty, 'My heart is Unitarian; but my nerves are still Calvinistic.' "[5] His affinities were with apostate Calvinists turned unitarian, humanitarian, scientific, phrenological; his mainstay during his crusade for schools was the phrenologist George Combe. But his nerves remaining stubbornly Calvinistic, he was always susceptible to motherly compassion as antidote to pure intellect, heartless logic, all wrapped up with male authority and condemned as hyper-Calvinism.

The year 1837, when Mann accepted the secretaryship, was replete with economic, political, and social disorder, and many people of his class feared that the liberties of Jacksonian Democracy were turning to anarchy, as had often been predicted. The immediate scene in Boston, which was having difficulty absorbing a rising tide of Roman Catholic immigrants, was anything but reassuring. In his journal that spring, Mann recorded rioting and incendiarism. The building in which he kept his law office, where he slept as well, had been fired. Mixed with reflections on the advisability of accepting the secretaryship is a note, dated May 30, "A gang of incendiaries infest the city. What a state of morals it reveals!" He was concerned about the prevalence of drunkenness and full of forebodings of the outcome of the increasing intransigence of the southern states on the slavery issue. He was active in desperate humanitarian causes, notably those of prisoners and the insane. And he asked himself in tones of despair, "When will society, like a mother, take care of *all* her children?"[6]

He overcame his doubts and answered the question by accepting the appointment as secretary to the Board of Education, intending to see to it that through a state system of public schools society should at last perform its maternal duty. Looking back, we see that he was a synthesizer of forces long gathering, but the job looked formidable to him, as indeed it was. "How many men I shall meet," he cried in his journal for June 29, "who are accessible only through a single motive, or who are incased in prejudice and jealousy, and need, not to be subdued, but to be remodelled! how many who will vociferate their devotion to the public, but whose thought will be intent upon themselves! . . . I must not irritate, I must not humble, I must not degrade any one in his own eyes. I must not present myself as a solid body to oppose an iron barrier to any. I must be a fluid sort of man, adapting myself to tastes, opinions, habits, manners, so far as this can be done without hypocrisy or insincerity, or a compromise of principle."[7]

Suspecting, and relishing the idea more than a little, that he might be martyred for his pains, he nevertheless took infinite pains to be a fluid sort of man and gain his end. This he never defined as the feminization of education; the end was the moralization of the democracy, and the question of a female teaching corps was incidental. He found, however, on every important issue the female professional teacher was either most convenient or positively indispensable to his purposes. Neither Mann nor his opponents made a major issue of the female teacher. They argued, rather, the religious question of creedal teaching in public schools; the political question of state versus local control of schools; the economic questions of taxation to support public schools and of standardization of textbooks (the latter bearing heavily on publishers' profits); and the professional questions of teacher training, curriculum making, teaching methods, and school discipline. By 1837 Mann had clear ideas of what he meant to do about every one of these matters, set about settling them on his own terms with dispatch, and rather by the by advocated the female teacher.

The legislative act of April 20, 1837, which created the Massachusetts Board of Education required an "annual abstract of the school returns" and a report on "the condition and efficiency of our system of popular education, and most practicable means of improving and expanding it." The Board was made dependent, however, on the "voluntary cooperation of the people" both in collecting school data and in diffusing information about methods "of arranging studies and conducting the education of the young." Horace Mann needed, therefore, all the persuasiveness and tact he could muster in executing these functions of the new Board, especially since he knew in advance that the data he expected to gather would be anything but flattering to the local prudential committees (which controlled school budgets), school committees (which administered the schools), and teachers throughout Massachusetts. "In pointing out errors in our system, that they may be rectified," he said diplomatically in his *First Annual Report,* "I wish at the same time, to aver my belief in the vast preponderance of its excellencies over its defects."[8] So he attributed such deficiencies as he found not to delinquent individuals but to faults in the system. Nevertheless, he drew up a severe indictment that did not spare individuals. "It is obvious," he declared, "that neglectful school committees, incompetent teachers, and an indifferent public may go on, degrading each other, until the noble system of free schools shall be abandoned by a people, so self-debased as to be unconscious of their abasement."[9]

Having to invent that new genre, the school survey, he drafted a questionnaire, called conventions in almost all the counties (with the significant exception of Suffolk, in which Boston is located), and between August and Christmas rode horseback five or six hundred miles to attend all but one of the conventions. He addressed groups large and small, buttonholed local leaders, kept voluminous notes. In riding his vast circuit, he personally examined or obtained detailed data on the condition of 800 schoolhouses and more general information about 1,000 more. Back in Boston, he had no help in tabulating and analyzing the school returns or in producing, right on time in January 1838, his first abstract and report. Such was his thoroughness that he received returns from 294 of the 305 towns of Massachusetts. Thereafter, when Horace Mann pronounced on education, the mouths of opponents were stopped by the mass of his data even though the purport of these made tact impossible.

The school committees, he found, were failing dismally in their statutory and moral responsibilities. They were tolerating wretched conditions in schoolhouses and providing almost no schoolroom equipment. The new secretary, fearing the committees did not appreciate the new environmentalism—if Catharine Beecher saw the indispensability for moral development of a high standard of comfort, hygiene, and decoration in the home, Horace Mann saw it just as clearly with respect to that adjunct of the home, the schoolroom—promised a detailed and hortatory report on school architecture as soon as he could get around to it. When he did get around to it, he announced that of 3,000 schoolhouses, not more than 100 could be classed as superior. He declared that of all classes of public buildings in Massachusetts, "the schoolhouse, which leads directly towards the church, or rather may be considered as its vestibule" and "which leads directly from the jail and from the prison" was the most disgracefully skimped and neglected.[10]

He addressed himself to the failure of the school committees to examine prospective teachers properly and insist on obtaining the best qualified. The committees were allowing teachers to keep school without any certification of their competence, and town prudential committees were often lax in authorizing payment of teachers who lacked a school committee certificate to teach. In the selection of schoolbooks, the school committees were equally feckless if not actually venal. The result was anarchic variety, with publishers competing for the ungoverned market and books of sectarian bias infiltrating the schools despite the law of 1826, which banned religious particularism.

Furthermore, the school committees of only 50 or 60 out of the 305 towns of the commonwealth were complying with the legal requirement of regular visitation and supervision of the schools; and even fewer were enforcing the attendance of the pupils. The laxity in supervision was an index of the low status of membership on school committees, the penuriousness of the towns and districts that refused to pay adequate salaries to teachers or the expenses of school visitors, and the hostility of the people toward the few school committeemen who did attempt to perform their duties scrupulously. As he thus explained without excusing the delinquency of the committees, Mann advanced a more general and touchy reason for their situation: upperclass families tended to send their children to private schools and shirk responsibilities for public ones.

Under the ominous heading "Competency of teachers," Mann was equally devastating. He remembered the need for tact, but the best he could say for the teachers was that nobody should derogate them—they were "as good as public opinion has demanded."[11] He asserted that "in *two thirds* at least of the towns of the Commonwealth" the teachers were incompetent.[12] He estimated that outside of Boston there were only about 100 male teachers and only a slightly larger number of female teachers "who devote themselves to teaching as a regular employment or profession." Few even of these had any special training to teach. Most teachers were young persons from "mechanical and agricultural employments" or college students, sufficiently well intentioned, he thought, but not able to comprehend the first principle of the art of teaching, namely, "that the great secret of ensuring a voluntary obedience to duty consists in a skilful preparation of motives beforehand."[13]

In its part of the report the Board formulated the issue thus: "Whatever tends to degrade the profession of the teacher in his own mind or that of the public of course impairs his usefulness; and this result must follow from regarding instruction as a business which in itself requires no previous training."[14] Therefore, the establishment of normal schools was advocated from the outset; the school committees were lax about standards in employing teachers, but the fact was, as many committees complained, that no qualified teachers were to be had. The average monthly wages being paid teachers in Massachusetts came to $25.44 per month for men and $11.38 per month for women, inclusive of board, which meant that a male teacher might receive ten or twelve dollars in cash and a female teacher virtually no cash at all. The implication of Mann's discussion of the competence of teachers was that they were worth little more than they were paid. The teachers might understandably feel aggrieved at this assessment; the pedagogy of love, founded upon what seemed to some the miraculous and to others the absurdly pretentious art of ensuring voluntary obedience to duty, could hardly be practiced before it was imparted.

All of the foregoing considerations came, for Mann, to a focus in the concern for a system of education dedicated to character training or moral development, the proof of which must be the capacity for voluntary obedience to duty. For the vitiated common prayer regulated by an established church, he meant to substitute the common school to whose beneficent influence it was essential that all of society's children should be subjected. Hence his criticism of the school committees for not compelling attendance and of the well-to-do for preferring private schools, those redoubts of sectarianism. Hence his criticism of shabby, ill-equipped schoolhouses which did not provide the necessary environment for moral growth. Hence his criticism of textbooks proselyting for this or that sect of revealed religion and interfering with the inculcation of "the beautiful and sublime truths of ethics and natural religion," so necessary as a "poising power" between "fanaticism" and "profligacy."[15]

Hence, too, his criticism of teachers incompetent in the art of teaching founded on an understanding of motivation and feeling. "Arithmetic, grammar, and the other rudiments, as they are called, comprise but a small part of the teachings in a school. The rudiments of feeling are taught not less than the rudiments of thinking. The sentiments and passions get more lessons than the intellect. Teaching is the most difficult of all arts, and the profoundest of all sciences. . . . He [the teacher] has a far deeper duty to perform, than to correct the erroneous results of intellectual processes." A further emphasis was to be placed in social and political terms upon the primacy of moral education. In France, where popular education had been taken farthest and most of the people could read and write, was not atheism rampant? "Their morals have been neglected, and the cultivated intellect presents to the uncultivated feelings, not only a larger circle of temptations, but better instruments for their gratification."[16]

Mann's emphasis upon moral cultivation as the primary aim of education required the practice of the new art of teaching, women were supposed to possess a sex-specific talent for it, and the feminization of education was therefore implied in its moralization. His focus might be upon the latter, but in fact the two were virtually equivalent. In the *First Annual Report,* Mann used the masculine pronoun with the generic noun *teacher,* but it is apparent that he was already thinking primarily of women teachers as the chief candidates for the new pedogogy. This tendency became more marked in the *Second Annual Report.* Frankly stating that the first report had showed "that the Common School system of Massachusetts had fallen into a state of general unsoundness and debility,"[17] Mann and the Board announced the founding of normal schools as "the most important means of improving the character of our common schools."[18] The first normal school, at Lexington, was to be exclusively for women; and if others, which materialized at Barre and Bridgewater, were to be open to men, women were expected to predominate and did so. The original policy was to admit females at sixteen and males at seventeen, to encourage them to take all of the three-year course, but to grant teaching certificates after only one year of study. The curriculum comprised review of the common school "rudiments" coupled with instruction in the all-important art of teaching them, reinforced by practice and observation in a model school. The chief difference between the normal school and a typical male academy, apart from the presence and predominance of females in the former, was the substitution of study and practice of teaching methods for study of classical languages. It is important to note that here at the beginning of American public education as we know it today feminization was coupled with a certain antagonism to literacy as the governing concern.

Mann's main topic in the *Second Annual Report,* to which he addressed himself as part of his obligation to "diffuse" as well as collect information about education, was the new (implicitly feminized) method of teaching spelling and reading. His advocacy of "intelligent" in place of "mechanical" reading was based on theories of what today would be called educational psychology which referred ultimately to the optimistic view of human nature. From the point of view of pedagogy, the important article of this faith was that human beings are capable of voluntary obedience to duty, provided they have the proper exposure to the art of teaching understood as directed primarily to the feelings. If there was a strong odor of indoctrination and manipulation in the verbally contradictory notion of training students to will one thing rather than another, or if the introduction of women teachers specially to work on the feelings of pupils had a covert reference to sexuality implying subversion of academic standards, Horace Mann never seems to have suspected such ambiguities. He just believed that "the acquisition of positive knowledge is not effected by a process of involuntary absorption."[19] Students must be motivated to learn autonomously. Teaching according to the traditional principle that learning could be, and given the intransigence of human nature often must be, effected by a process of involuntary absorption depended on two ancient pedagogical devices, equally repugnant to Mann.

One of these was "emulation," or what Mann regarded as unworthy and maleficent bribing of students to perform with prizes and pride of place; the other was corporal punishment. The entire approach, with its rewards, sanctions, and punishments, was associated with the male teacher thought of as lacking training in the art of teaching. It produced in the teaching of letters, words, and reading the "calamity of unintelligent reading."[20] The results were no better in other subjects. In Mann's opinion, the ability to "prepare" the motive to learn "positively" and "autonomously" was the true teacher's professional hallmark. The teacher who knew how to motivate students did not need to resort to either emulation or punishment. She—and the feminine pronoun for *teacher* as a collective term became more frequent—depended on "love" instead, that is, on affectionate, nondirective personal interaction with pupils, regarded as a perfectly decent expression of maternal instinct.

In the Board's part of the *Third Annual Report* appears a definition of the art of teaching which, though not explicitly comparing the sexes on the score of talent to teach, contained a claim for the female and a condemnation of the male. It is an excellent brief statement of the philosophy of normal school training. The Board said "the art of instruction" is that "of communicating knowledge to the youthful mind and aiding and encouraging its own efforts." It then defined "the art of governing a school" as tantamount to "so forming and influencing it, as to supersede the necessity of that mixture of harsh discipline and capricious indulgence which is called government."[21] Here the gauntlet was thrown contemptuously before the old-line schoolmaster, as if he knew no art of teaching whatever and did not deserve the name of teacher; but the challenge was not taken up, or perhaps fully comprehended, until several years later.

Having sounded warning notes in his first three annual reports, carried a number of approaches to the matter in his newly founded *Common School Journal,* and alluded to it often in his indefatigable lecturing and corresponding in the cause, Horace Mann argued the case for female teachers boldly and at length in his *Fourth Annual Report.* "Nothing but an imperative sense of duty could induce me to approach this most difficult subject," he wrote, "because, to speak of the necessity of higher qualifications, in any department of business, may always be construed into an intentional disparagement of those who administer it. This would often be unjust . . . especially so, in regard to education." Nevertheless, his abstracts had already abundantly shown that there was "scarcely a single instance . . . where the school committee speak with universal commendation of the success of the teachers, they have approved." Teachers were described as deficient in one respect or another, schools were reported as progressing in one branch but not in others, and in other instances committees declared that "notwithstanding all the labor and expense bestowed upon the school" the scholars had "been both intellectually and morally injured." A scandalous number of schools were "broken up" every year throughout Massachusetts by unruly boys.[22]

Then he picked out for deceptively modest effect in a footnote the report of a school committee who admitted "we have had better luck with the female teachers than with the male." To which Mann appended the comment—"as though it were a matter left to 'luck,' what intellectual and moral guides, the rising generation should have."[23] He did not mean to leave the matter to luck. He moved on to an eloquent statement of the case for woman as teacher, the first paragraph of which should be considered as the classical summary of the rationale, indeed as the charter, of the feminized teaching profession:

It is gratifying to observe that a change is rapidly taking place, both in public sentiment and action, in regard to the employment of female teachers. The number of male teachers, in all the summer and winter schools, for the last year [1840] was thirty-three less than for the year preceding, while the number of females was one hundred and three more. That females are incomparably better teachers for young children than males, cannot admit of a doubt. Their manners are more mild and gentle, and hence more in consonance with the tenderness of childhood. They are endowed by nature with stronger parental impulses, and this makes the society of children delightful, and turns duty into pleasure. Their minds are less withdrawn from their employment, by the active scenes of life; and they are less intent and scheming for future honors and emoluments. As a class, they never look forward, as young men almost invariably do, to a period of legal emancipation from parental control, when they are to break away from the domestic circle and go abroad into the world, to build up a fortune for themselves; and hence, the sphere of hope and of effort is narrower, and the whole forces of the mind are more readily concentrated upon present duties. They are also of purer morals. In the most common and notorious vices of the age, profanity, intemperance, fraud, &c., there are twenty men to one woman; and although as life advances, the comparison grows more and more unfavorable to the male sex, yet the beginnings of vice are early, even when their developments are late;—on this account, therefore, females are infinitely more fit than males to be the guides and exemplars of young children.[24]

The pleased accounting of the shifting balance of the sexes in the teaching corps continued through the subsequent annual reports. In the sixth, he reported an excess of the number of female over male teachers of 1,782—"A fact unprecedented in any other State in the Union, and one which would be deemed hardly credible in Europe, where the services of females for this purpose seem to be held in low estimation!" He went on to say that school government was adversely affected when administered by men, for the male thinks primarily of the mischief a pupil's offense would work in society and "chastises it with a severity proportioned rather to the nature of the transgression, than to the moral weakness of the transgressor." Woman, however, with "a gentler, a less hasty, a more forebearing nature," knows how "so to remove the evil as not to extirpate the good"—the good which, in the optimistic view of human nature, was certainly there, as preponderant over the evil in the child as affection was over intellect in the woman teacher.[25]

Here, Mann developed the doctrine of pedagogic love further than he had taken it in earlier reports in order to bring it more fully to bear on his advocacy of normal schools. He repeated that it was "matter for congratulation that females are now so much more extensively employed than formerly, as teachers in our Public Schools." But he promptly added that it was "a duty imperative upon them so to improve their minds, by study, by reading, by reflecting, and by attending such a course of instruction on the subject of teaching, as the recent legislative appropriation for the continuance of the Normal Schools, has proffered to all, that they can answer the just expectations of the public, and discharge, with religious fidelity, the momentous duties to which they are called."[26]

This was the line with which Catharine Beecher could heartily concur and which she vainly hoped that the recalcitrant William Slade would follow in carrying out her plan to moralize the West with missionary teachers. She had only to wait for Mann's *Eighth Annual Report* to see her entire argument for the "profession of woman" enunciated, though limited as a male mind might have been expected to limit it and subordinated to pedagogy under male administration. How, Mann asked, except by taking up the holy work of education, could woman "so well vindicate her right to an exalted station in the scale of being; and cause that shameful sentence of degradation by which she has so long been dishonored, to be repealed? Four fifths of all the women who have ever lived, have been the slaves of man—the menials in his household, the drudges in his field, the instruments of his pleasure; or at best, the gilded toys of his leisure days in court or palace." She now had the opportunity to take a "noble revenge," he said, for in teaching her "superiority of moral power" could "triumph over that physical power which has hitherto subjected her to bondage." As Miss Beecher had been saying for years, perhaps echoing her, Mann added that the profession of teaching could in no way interfere with the primary function of women as wives and mothers.[27]

The best index to the steadily increasing success of Mann's school program was his yearly accounting of the declining number of male and the rising number of female teachers. The watershed was reached in 1845, when the relative number of male teachers continued to diminish and for the first time their absolute number decreased, from 2,595 to 2,585. Mann pounced upon that difference of ten, and when, the following year, the number of male teachers fell to 2,437, he triumphantly proclaimed a trend. "The progressive and systematic transference of the education of the young from male to female hands," he remarked with satisfaction, "is a most interesting fact."[28]

His final report, the twelfth, tabulated "the proportion of the male to the female teachers, employed in our schools" for the period since he began his work as secretary, as follows:

Year	No. of Male Teachers	No. of Female Teachers
1837	2370	3591
1838–9	2411	3825
1839–40	2378*	3928*
1840–1	2491	4112
1842–3	2414*	4301*
1843–4	2529	4581
1844–5	2595	4700
1845–6	2585	4997
1846–7	2437	5238
1847–8	2424	5510

*The returns for these years were not quite complete.[29]

To return to the classic statement of the case for woman as teacher in the *Fourth Annual Report*, I wish to point up two further arguments, in addition to the fundamental argument from maternal instinct, which have proved fraught with omen for the democratic American paideia as this has been mediated by our public schools. For convenience, these may be termed the argument from child nature and the argument from cheapness. Both are only aspects of the argument from maternal instinct but are often adduced without conscious reference to the more inclusive position.

The argument from child nature holds that woman's holy mission to teach is limited to young children, and its corollary is that woman's nature is childlike. It will be a concern of later chapters to observe how, after the Civil War, women became acceptable as teachers of adolescents and eventually of college-age students without any refutation of the argument from child nature. Instead, childlikeness (not to say childishness, with its pejorative connotations) was attributed to students of ever more advanced ages. But Horace Mann probably could not have gained a hearing for his school program if he had not consistently stipulated that woman's gift was to be guide and exemplar of prepubertal children only. As matters stood, his great difficulty in feminizing the teaching corps was resistance to women as teachers in the winter schools, which, though only elementary, typically included pupils in their teens and often enough in their early twenties.

Mann noted in the *Fourth Annual Report* that while the employment of females in the winter schools was "highly commended" in some school committee reports, it was "strongly discountenanced" in others. He himself recommended "a sound discretion" and thought particular decisions should be made on the merits of each case. He said it would be imprudent "to employ a young female, for her first term, in a winter school." And no doubt "where the quiet and harmony of the school are endangered by large and turbulent boys, the power of a sterner voice, and of a firmer hand may be necessary to overawe an insurrectionary spirit." There was the crux of the matter, the turbulent big boys. Even so, Mann argued that while they might exhibit "disobedience and open rebellion against the authority of a master," they might, from "a feeling of chivalry towárds a female ... respect a request from a mistress, though they would spurn a command from a master." Nevertheless, in districts rent with dissension, he thought "it can hardly ever be safe to place a female between the contending parties." This observation, however, he turned to his purpose: it was the responsibility of male educational administrators and town officials to provide the harmonious situation in which a female teacher could function. Given an experienced female teacher and a harmonious school district, "then a female will keep quite as good a school as a man, at two-thirds of the expense, and will transfuse into the minds of her pupils, purer elements, both of conduct and character, which will extend their refining and humanizing influences far outward into society, and far onward into futurity."[30]

Puberty was regarded as a primarily male phenomenon and felt, if not explicitly described, as something infused with the quasi-magical, primitively religious, and quintessentially sinful qualities of maturing sexuality. One need not be psychoanalytically devout to be struck by the way many people in the nineteenth century passionately argued that adolescent boys must come under the domination of "the rod," that is, the rod specifically of male teachers physically able to quell the "insurrectionary spirit" of "turbulent big boys." Intellectual development was generally held to begin at puberty as an adjunct of maturing male sexuality and thus to be of subordinate concern to women teachers in elementary schools, either summer or winter, provided that the older boys who might be in the latter—who were increasingly felt to be anomalous as the grading of schools spread—could be governed through properly authoritative male administration and maternal female instruction.

The argument from child nature prompted no opposition to the feminization of teaching so long as no overt argument for women as teachers of postpubertal boys was advanced; but the argument from cheapness required no exceptions. Much the more effectual argument with the school and prudential committees, it contained elements that ultimately made the idea of woman as teacher in secondary schools and beyond easy to accept. Mann knew that the expansion of the school system and the establishment of normal schools would be tolerated by the taxpayers only if costs could be kept down: in Jacksonian America, he was advocating an unprecedented increase in government function through the creation of a state educational bureaucracy, the training and employment of thousands of teachers, and immense capital outlays. He never hesitated frankly, sometimes crassly, to advance the argument from cheapness although at the same time he advocated raises for all teachers and at least some relative improvement in the pay of female as compared with male teachers. He urged upon the school and prudential committees the "expediency" of hiring women teachers and of introducing reforms that allowed for the use of more women under the direction of fewer men. The consolidation of schools was one such device. Where distances were not too great, he persuaded school committees to consolidate several schools, each under a male teacher, into one school conducted by a single male "principal teacher" with several female "assistants." Although he pointed out the expediency of employing females at "two-thirds" the rate paid males, his own figures show that the rate for females was nearer one-third, on the average, and even one-fourth, in some instances, that for males.

His positions on pay for women teachers from one annual report to the next and sometimes within a given report were inconsistent. Perhaps he was truly ambivalent, influenced on the one hand by his knowledge of the penuriousness of school and prudential committees and, on the other, by his desire to create a professionally trained teacher corps, which implied much increased salaries for all teachers. No doubt he was influenced, probably more than he realized for all his appreciation of the argument from cheapness, by the practices of the rising capitalists and manufacturers who were his chief backers. Michael B. Katz has stressed the "parallels between the methods of educational and industrial reorganization in the period." Moved by scarcity and dearness of labor, industry was creating larger units of production, subdividing manufacturing processes, gathering workers engaged in making a given product under one factory roof, training workers for greater efficiency, and increasing the proportion of female labor in the work force. The grading and consolidation of schools, normal school training, and the advocacy of women teachers were comparable aspects of school reform. "Rationalization, the division of labor, training, and feminization all marked both industry and education."[31]

Mann expressed regret at the insufficiency of "the pecuniary encouragement held out to females to enter this truly noble, truly feminine, and truly Christian employment"; but his very notion of teaching as noble, feminine, and Christian translated into the idea of self-sacrifice, true love of the work transcending

money considerations, and the superiority of heavenly reward
over anything that could be expected from a prudential committee. He boldly, not to say wildly, proposed $500 a year as a
proper salary for female teachers, a munificent figure if compared to anything from $32 to $64 a year depending on school
terms that he cited as average actual pay. He knew of one
woman teacher who made $600, another who made $400, and
several female assistants in Boston schools who made $250 a
year, so in recommending an average salary of $500 he was say-
ing that all women teachers should be paid what the few highest
paid ones received. That was nevertheless only a third of the
$1,500 which the highest paid male teachers, almost all of them
in the Boston schools, were paid.[32]

He never considered it practicable or, so far as I know, desirable that women teachers should receive the same pay as
men for the same work. The argument from cheapness was
after all indispensable. It was remarkable enough, as he said,
that he had reversed the proportions of male and female
teachers and established what looked like a trend that would
eventually result in total replacement of men by women in the
elementary schools. He had done so in spite of the fact that he
had to persuade school districts "which are corporate bodies,
and as independent of each other as England is of France. . . .
Yet, in these separate and independent bodies, acting with
entire freedom from each other, and wholly exempt, on this
point, from all legislative control or interference, a change is
going forward, which, in the uniformity and steadiness of its action, resembles a law of nature."[33] What all these sovereign
school districts were mostly concerned about was costs. A law of
nature might seem to be in operation, and Horace Mann, with
his well-developed phrenological "bump of causality," might indulge a godlike sense of responsibility for it; but his law of feminization was operating in consequence of a prior law, namely,
the maternal, self-sacrificial, Christian tendency of womankind,
divinely ordained subordinate to men and happy in their
place—who happened also to be cheap.

Therefore, Mann's ambivalence about the compensation of
female teachers was ultimately resolved in favor of their cheap-

ness. In 1848, at the end of his secretaryship, he plainly announced:

The expediency of employing a larger portion of female teachers was first urged upon the consideration of the towns and districts, in 1837. The suggestion commended itself to their judgment by its reasonableness. Under certain limitations, the experiment proved eminently successful. . . .the remarkable result is, that the present number of female teachers is much more than double that of males.

Let this change be regarded, for a moment, in an economical point of view. If, in 1846-47, the relative proportion of male and female teachers had been the same as it was in 1837, then . . . we should have had 614 more male teachers, and the same number of female teachers less. Now, the average wages of male teachers, last year, inclusive of board, was $32.46, and the average wages of female teachers, also inclusive of board, was $13.60, and the average length of the summer and winter terms varied but a small fraction of four months each.

He proceeded to work out the arithmetic. The savings for a single year came to $11,580.41—"double," he was quick to point out, "the expense of the three State Normal Schools" which were producing cheap women teachers. The geese were laying golden eggs, and he was quite persuaded "that the educational gain,—the gain to the minds and manners of the children,—has been in a far higher ratio than the pecuniary."[34] Was it nothing but rationalization, perhaps conscious and disingenuous? To this crass exercise in arithmetic, he felt impelled to add: "I cannot leave this topic without adverting to the grossly inadequate compensation made to female teachers."[35] No, his regret was sincere. He did believe, in flat reaction from Calvinist tenets, in the "treasure of unpurchased happiness in the youthful breast . . . referable alone to the benevolence of the Creator." He believed in the pliability of child nature, in its susceptibility to perfection if properly nurtured. He believed "the natural sympathy, the sagacity, the maternal instincts of the female preeminently qualify her for this sphere of noble usefulness."[36] It should be remembered in extenuation that this sphere of noble usefulness, cramped though it was if compared with Catharine Beecher's vision of the profession of woman, exploitive though it was in the view of the nineteenth-century feminists to say nothing of twentieth-century ones, was denied women until Mann did his work. He believed that women who worthily prepared themselves at normal school for teaching "should be rewarded with social distinction and generous emoluments." If these were not forthcoming, he was very sorry but felt that fortunately "for the actors themselves, in this beneficent work, the highest rewards must forever remain where God and nature have irrevocably placed them,—in the consciousness of well-doing."[37]

The expediency of considering the use of female teachers "from an economical point of view" led to settling for a proletarian wage with a hope of something a little better if teachers improved their qualifications through normal training. Those improved qualifications also guaranteed a status somewhat superior to that of the female factory operatives at Lowell. Women teachers could supplement their low pay not only with consciousness of well-doing but with lower-middle-class respectability. If the committees would increase their compensation, not to the $500 a year Mann giddily imagined, but enough at least to enable them to pay for normal school training, the common schools would flourish. They would flourish for the plain capitalistic reason that a better quality of labor would be employed at a rate calibrated to the market. As Mann said, the "school committees, when they go abroad in quest of fit endowments and qualifications to cultivate the immortal capacities of the young, would escape the mortification which they now sometimes suffer, of being overbid by a capitalist who wants them for his factory, and who can afford to pay them more for superintending a loom or a spinning-frame, than the people feel willing to give for weaving the infinitely precious tissue of character."[38]

What Mann really had in mind appears from his remark that, under the conditions of teacher employment he was willing to settle for, even effeminate young men, that is, "those young men whom Nature had preadapted to school-keeping," could be lured into teaching. As it was they were apt to be tempted by more liberal pay "to become head servants in gentlemen's families, or to superintend the affairs of the kitchen in expensive hotels."[39]

Agreed though they were on most of the issues, an important difference remained between Catharine Beecher and Horace Mann on the qualitative aspects of feminizing the teaching corps. That difference stemmed from incompatible assessments of the function and motivation of women in monopolizing public school teaching and latent competition for the cultural leadership they were anxious to wrest from the Calvinist clergy. She saw female monopoly of teaching as the handiest means of remedying the wrongs of American women and only incidentally those of children, and she intended that as professional teachers and housewives women should enjoy higher education, honor, and emoluments comparable to those men commanded in their professions. She encouraged normal schools but always with a view to the ultimate development of true women's universities. She would never have been content with the idea that teachers' salaries comparable to the wages of textile mill operatives could be satisfactorily supplemented by consciousness of well-doing, and nothing could have been more offensive to her than Mann's readiness to equate the status of the female teacher to that of a male majordomo or chef.

The greater intellectual quality and the higher professional and social status that Catharine Beecher claimed for women teachers as one branch of an inclusive profession of woman are to be appreciated in the light of the fact that she never went as far as Horace Mann in rejecting orthodoxy. She did not so much want to destroy the work of her father and brothers, evangelical clergymen all, as to do it better than they. She carried over into her ideas of the education of woman an insistence on academic standards as high as any her father and brothers had met. She felt that she, lacking their advantages of formal education, had surpassed them. What might she not have accomplished if the equivalent of Harvard had been available to her?

Harriet Beecher Stowe came to believe that the movement for domestic reform in tandem with the development of public education would succeed inevitably, the only question being whether it would take its tone from evangelism as mediated by the profession of woman or from Horace Mann and the other educational reformers, with their increasingly secular, statist emphasis. Yet the Beecher men never wholeheartedly supported Catharine. Herself brought to full appreciation of Catharine's program only upon reading *The True Remedy for the Wrongs of American Women,* Mrs. Stowe warned the family that "this thing has *got to go,* and it will go either in your hands and under your influence or it will go by the aid of such men as Horace Mann, Horace Greeley and all that modern reform party who all stand waiting for the moment when Catharine will come to their side." She thought the men of the reform party were "noble minded, noble hearted, energetic, and yet I would rather they came into the movement as accessories than as leaders, that thus they might have their sentiments modified by you, for they need it."[40]

A three-way struggle for power was going on, but it was never articulated or perhaps fully understood by the parties in sex terms. As Catharine Beecher's biographer has observed, Catharine and Harriet became increasingly critical of "the male dominance of evangelical protestantism."[41] They were, as Harriet's remarks just quoted suggest, only less suspicious of male dominance of school and other reforms. Meanwhile, the most significant conflict proceeded between the two male parties, Horace Mann and his sort gaining the upper hand of the declining orthodox, evangelical clergy and their followers. The "profession of woman" as Miss Beecher conceived it was of no more interest to Horace Mann, Horace Greeley, Samuel Gridley Howe, William Ellery Channing, or Henry Barnard than to William Slade. It is doubtful that any of them understood it, if they paid any attention at all, any better than the Beecher men; like the Beecher men, they probably disliked it to the extent they did understand it. Was it not an eccentric female fancy, even a little crazy? The third Beecher sister, Isabella, *was* insane, and her insanity seems to have consisted just in acting out the claims for woman that the others left at pious platitudinous utterance. Isabella Beecher Hooker spoke of "my adorable brother Jesus" and like him expected to "grow into the hearts of men women and children by the power of God our common father." She anticipated being "called to the presidency of a matriarchal government, which would spread from the United States across the whole world and under her leadership be merged with the kingdom of Christ in a great millennial period."[42]

The upshot, so far as the teaching profession was concerned, was an expedient use of women in the schoolroom and the establishment of a male priesthood of administrators and bureaucrats in authority above them, yet of limited authority among them. There was never any question in the male reformers' minds of anybody but themselves assuming cultural and moral leadership, but in instituting the pedagogy of love they gave hostages to fortune. Horace Mann's transference of education from male to female hands meant the creation of a docile labor force for the schools, a schoolroom proletariat. Real status and high pay remained male prerogatives within education but, as measured against those of other male groups, particularly business, disturbingly second-rate. The male educational reformers did succeed, if not in replacing altogether, then in joining the clergy as cultural leaders, but a clergy much reduced in authority by the very moralism the reformers represented. The feminization of teaching made it the example par excellence of what Amitai Etzioni has called a "semi-profession," involving a limitation even upon its male administrative class. School *men,* whether teachers or administrators, suffered diminution by association with the female teaching force they directed.

Chapter 5

The Rod Extended in Vain

HORACE MANN and the Massachusetts Board of Education en-
countered serious opposition first in 1840, when a sizable element of the legislature attempted to destroy their program.
Having surmounted this, they were not dangerously
challenged again until 1844, when the male elite of the teaching
profession came to the defense of the old order. In the first
instance, the protesting interests were ecclesiastical and
political-economic. Orthodox churchmen, both Episcopalian
and Congregational, with a nostalgia for established religion attacked Mann's policy of teaching only nonsectarian Christianity
in the schools and were suspicious of the substitution of state
for church control in education. His most vehement orthodox
critic had a large ax to grind, for he had church-influenced
textbooks to sell and Mann was authorizing only books without
creedal bias. The political and economic issues were the
centralization of school administration, the corollary reduction
of local autonomy, and the increase in taxation needed for the
support of an expanding state school system. The doctrine of
woman's self-sacrificial maternalism and sacred mission to
teach, implying and rationalizing her cheapness, which
guaranteed her docility, was part of Mann's effectual rebuttal
of the whole complex of religious, political, and economic argument against his reforms.

In the second instance, the Association of Masters of the
Boston Public Schools engaged Mann on principles of
pedagogy and the fundamental theological bearings of education. The controversy was fierce and protracted through two
years of pamphleteering, ending in the rout of the masters just
as Mann was celebrating the achievement of a majority of

women in the teaching corps of the state. As part of its disparagement of the Board, the hostile legislative committee of 1840, chaired by Allen Dodge, expressed opposition to the founding of normal schools and scouted the idea that teaching was or should be turned into a profession. By 1844 the normal schools at Lexington, Barre, and Bridgewater had been operating several years; and the Boston masters recognized, but still underestimated, the "normalites" as a threat to their status. The masters did not directly attack the new claims for woman as teacher, any more than the Dodge committee had. Instead, they reaffirmed the traditional principles, derived from Calvinism, of New England education against the whole of Mann's pedagogy of love. Furthermore, the masters correctly perceived themselves to be in conflict, not with the nascent army of normalites, but with another male group which proposed to use the normalites to its own ends.

Having survived the worst that religious and political interests could do, Mann and the Board had time to consolidate their position before being confronted by the most powerful, persistent, and cogent criticism ever brought to bear on them. In 1844 thirty-one masters of the Boston public schools, the most prestigious and highest paid schoolteachers in the country, took the publication of Mann's *Seventh Annual Report* as the occasion to launch what they meant to be a lethal attack on the new system. Mann's seventh report, the masters' *Remarks* on it, Mann's outraged *Reply* to that, the masters' further *Rejoinder,* and finally Mann's *Answer* contain within their musty covers the still electric atmosphere in which public education, as we still have it, emerged like another Frankenstein or Jekyll-Hyde problematically instinct with good and evil. Careers were at stake, and neither side pretended to much disinterestedness or charity. The conflict was waged hotly for two years, the ideological intransigence of the combatants was absolute, and the result was the frankly triumphant imposition of the will of the reformers in Boston and Suffolk County. The victory was so complete, expressing changed attitudes long incubated in society, that for more than a century it was usually interpreted, according to its own democratic, progressive, and optimistic

prejudices, as the triumph of righteousness.[1] Only since World
War II, during a period when changes in American attitudes as
fundamental as those that occurred in the Jacksonian era have
created discomfort with the heritage from that era, have the
views of the trounced Boston masters become available for sympathetic analysis.

Not that anyone is likely to advocate a return to the Calvinistic beliefs and presuppositions of the masters, but many
have been sobered by the consequences of what has been
characterized as the "soft line" in American education deriving
from the common school revival when it was first embodied in
the normalite. It is therefore possible to reassess the Boston
masters' argument for a "hard line" in a pragmatic spirit
enlightened by long experience of the soft line.[2] Taken at a
general level apart from the given cosmological, religious, and
political suppositions of any particular era, the two approaches
express opposed views of human nature and therefore of the
educational methods appropriate for it. Is human nature in-
trinsically as it ought to be at conception and birth, or is it
genetically flawed and capable of achieving a desirable
character at maturity only with direction from outside, if at all?
In the terms used by Horace Mann and the masters, the conflict
was between education conceived as "preventive" or "curative"
and education seen as necessarily corrective and punitive. The
question was whether the teacher should "govern" the schoolroom by love or by authority, that is, by feminine, maternal
love, Christian in the sense of self-sacrificial devotion to the
growth of pupils, or by masculine, paternal power, Christian in
the sense of judgmental decisiveness according to external standards.

Mann's *Seventh Annual Report* contained his account of his
observations of European schools during a short tour in 1843
on part of which he was accompanied, significantly, by his
friend the Scottish phrenologist George Combe, in whom he
confided throughout his campaign to reform the Massachusetts
schools. By this time, he felt secure enough to be more frankly
critical of American schools, including the best of them, those
of Massachusetts, and to make invidious comparisons between

them and the Scottish and Prussian schools he visited. He also found all that he wanted to find in the way of an object lesson for Americans in the Prussian normal schools and professionalized, bureaucratized teaching corps. He had forgotten his resolutions to deal tactfully with the old-line Massachusetts teachers, and the combination of foreign comparisions with a derogatory and sometimes contemptuous tone stung the Boston masters into action. Their grievances had accumulated for seven years, and they now discharged them in a thunderclap that badly rattled Horace Mann.

The masters rose to the defense of what they perceived as the "great cardinal principles" of New England education, against the presumptuous theories of Mann and his heterodox supporters.[3] They rapped Mann as a Johnny-come-lately in the cause of education, which, they asserted with some justice, far from being in the parlous condition he said it was in, "was *never more prosperous than at the time the Board of Education was formed.*" The formation of the Board in 1837 was a major piece of evidence of this prosperity, in fact. They meant, not that education was in no need of improvement, but that through the decade preceding the establishment of the Board opinion had come round in favor of improvement. Not Mann but James G. Carter and others, who had been at work in the cause since the 1820s, had prepared this change in public sentiment. Paul H. Mattingly has recently provided background for the masters' point of view in his account of the initiatives in educational reform prior to the common school revival. His discussion of the activities of the Friends of Education, "an easily discernible yet loosely defined group of citizens" who "used their positions of influence to command the attention of large gatherings of citizens to discuss the condition of common schools," is particularly illuminating.[4] But "the desire was for *improvement,* and not for *revolution*" in the schools, according to the masters; Mann had misread the mandate. "A sacrilegious hand," they asserted, "was laid upon every thing mental, literary, and moral, that did not conform to the new light of the day."[5]

The masters placed the new light according to Mann—and the sharpness of the expression should be realized: it alluded to

"New Light" Calvinism and suggested Mann's heresy—among other recent "hot-bed theories" of education. There had been, for instance, the "infant school system" according to which the "fond parent, the philosopher, and the philanthropist were equally captivated by the scintillations of infant genius." In a more direct hit at Mann, the masters said, "Next came Phrenology with all its organs and propensities, rejecting all fear, emulation, and punishments." Then there was a vogue for "the monitorial system," in which older taught younger pupils. The masters imputed faddishness to Mann by adding, "Next, the antipodes to the monitorialist, came the *Normalist,* who thinks there will not be good schools in Massachusetts, till all the teachers shall be trained, for a course of years, in some seminary for teachers."[6]

If the secretary imagined he had handled teachers diplomatically, the masters sought to disillusion him. From his very first report, they felt, "no little injustice has been done to the general character of teachers, by those who have been over-anxious for the reputation and success of the Normal schools." Alluding to the secretary's energetic proselyting throughout the state with the notable exception of Boston and Suffolk County, they stated, "A spirit of distrust in teachers was created through the State, before the establishment of the first Normal school," which "was to be the Propaganda from which this new light was to be irradiated for the advancement of the moral and intellectual welfare of coming generations." They noted that according to the new light pedagogy neither emulation nor corporal punishment was tolerable as a motivation to learn; for phrenology held with what the masters thought was pseudo-scientific certitude that everyone was endowed with a cranial bump of self-esteem which could be relied upon to motivate pupils. All that they required was a nurturant normalite environment. Was it surprising, on such principles, that Horace Mann was modeling the public school for normal children on the "sanative" institutions for the retarded, the criminal, the deaf, the blind, such as his friend Samuel Gridley Howe's asylum for the blind? "It is hard to conceive," the masters declared, "of anything more *radical* and less *conservative,* than such views. . . . Nothing can be more at war with approved principles."[7]

Over against the new light pedagogy, the Boston masters raised the point that "the teacher must take the world as he finds it," and no realist could doubt that the rod, rather than love, must be his ultimate resort. They were unimpressed by a report that "'a large majority of the young ladies' of the Lexington Normal School, under Mr. Pierce, 'were of opinion, that it should not be resorted to in any case.'" Regardless of what the normalites might think, "experience, philanthropy, and wisdom, still dictate the necessity of its use, or of the *right* to use it." They added a snort at the mere idea of "Normalites!!!" having the temerity to oppose the use of the rod.[8] The sex issue was not specifically addressed but it was pervasive. The masters had been driven to attack the new feminized pedagogy by the realization that if they remained silent "it might well be supposed they [the masters] have neither the qualifications of teachers, nor the feelings of *men,* and it seems that the secretary must have supposed them destitute of both, or he would not have so trifled with public credulity."[9] A small but telling index to the situation was the masters' assertion of their rights as teachers, the most fundamental of which was the right to use corporal punishment according to approved principles; the emergent type of female teacher knew only responsibilities.

The false "philanthropists" of Mann's stripe were, in the masters' opinion, sentimentalizing the child and warping education accordingly. They ridiculed the reformers' faith in teaching methods and the improvement of school equipment, ventilation, and so on as the sure means of doing everything for both "the refractory dunce" and "the well-bred child." On the contrary, they asserted that the "material to be wrought upon" must be realistically perceived if the teachers' job was to be properly appreciated. "It is one thing to give form and figure to the wax," they said, "and quite a different affair to bring out the living expression from the flinty marble, and worse than flinty granite." Horace Mann might indulge a fancy that children were wax in warm loving hands, but the masters knew flinty granite when they saw it. The difficulty of dealing with the material was increased by the fact that the children were chips off old blocks, namely, parents who in their Jacksonian complacency were hostile and defensive about teachers' strictures upon the flintiness of their recalcitrant offspring. The masters pointed out, therefore, that the teacher who did his duty might "often find himself a stranger to sympathy and gratitude." For the public school teacher in Jacksonian America worked "for a sovereign, who seldom acts alike at two given times, or in two different places."[10]

Billing themselves repeatedly as *"practical educators"* in contrast to Mann as a mischievous theorist, the masters turned to Mann's claims for the superiority of Prussian methods which he had observed. The key point was the value and function of the textbook. According to Mann, American teachers depended on it too much, requiring pupils to memorize whether or not they understood, presiding over schoolrooms held to sepulchral stillness under the sign of the birch rod hanging on the wall behind the master's desk. Scottish and Prussian teachers were much livelier and altogether more engaging personally than American teachers, he reported. They entered into noisy give-and-take with pupils, gave varied Pestalozzian "object-lessons," Socratically educed knowledge, and used textbooks only incidentally. The American dependence upon textbooks implied, Mann said, that it was the teacher who was really dependent upon them. To the masters, however, the textbook represented focus on delimited matter and the individual responsibility of pupils to learn it. If the teacher were as active as Mann wished, he would become a sort of entertainer and reduce pupils to passivity. Mann might be correct in thinking the Prussian way would for the nonce "interest" pupils, "but it will in no degree induce that habit of patient and constant attention to a subject" that is the true consideration. Instead, "the mind of the pupil . . . would become accustomed to act only through the force of that excitement which is supplied by the teacher."[11]

The masters accused Mann of dwelling only on the abuse of textbooks in horrible examples and ignoring their proper use. At the least, textbooks provided a dependable "method" and "certainty of accurate information," they said. The masters believed "text-books to be necessary, not only as the medium of distinct and accurate information, but also to enable the pupil ... to acquire habits of discrimination and patient investigation." The teacher should take care not to make the pupils' task "too easy," and Mann underestimated the need for "a rigid course of study."[12]

But the heart of the controversy, as both Mann and the masters recognized, was school discipline and in particular the use of corporal punishment; in Joseph Hale, the master who wrote on this theme in behalf of his colleagues, Mann met the ablest, most disinterested, and telling of his critics. Hale got through repeatedly to the Calvinist nerves that underlay Mann's liberalism, but the issue was crucial also in the most obvious practical terms. The rationale for the normalite stood or fell on the question whether she could govern the schoolroom in spite of her physical inability to whip the big boys.

Mann always denied that he wished to ban corporal punishment altogether, but the masters did not believe him. Given the turbulence of democracy, Mann consistently held that corporal punishment should be used as a last resort, but the tone in which he affirmed this position was unconvincing. As his friend George Combe only too revealingly described his view of the matter, Mann believed "the rod should be used seldom and never in passion."[13] He believed that his pedagogy of love in the hands of normalites would gradually reduce social unrest to the point where corporal punishment would become a dead letter, and he rated teachers higher the less they had to punish since he tended to attribute sadistic motives to teachers who used the rod. The masters, however, took the seventh report "to present the practical fruits of this long-cherished notion" that the "total disuse" of both corporal punishment and emulation could be achieved through "the science of teaching" as dispensed in the normal schools.[14]

Joseph Hale believed that the case for "kindness" as the appropriate and almost exclusive "means of influence" in motivating ordinary common school pupils to behave well and learn their lessons was based not only upon false theory and heretical

religion but also upon irrelevant examples. The latter were the
new humanitarian "*sanative* schools" for the disabled, diseased,
or delinquent; the Prussian schools; and the model schools at
the new normals. He denied that methods that might be required to teach or rehabilitate the various sorts of what today
are called "disadvantaged" pupils were applicable to common
schools. With regard to the Prussian schools, he was dubious of
Mann's claims for them but conceded that "the strong arm of a
government beyond the control of the people may enable judicious and accomplished teachers to avoid, in a great measure,
the necessity of an actual appeal to force." The implication was
that "kindness" in the schoolroom was bought at an excessive
price if it depended on prior regimentation of society as a
whole according to the pattern of Prussian autocracy. And Hale
judged the results obtained by the model schools at the normals
"unsatisfactory, being the results of moral experiments, made
under limited and controlled, not to say, selected circumstances."[15]

Hale then proposed to show "that all school order, like that
of the family and of society, must be established upon the basis
of acknowledged authority" and to maintain "not only the
right, but the duty to enforce it, by an appeal to the most appropriate motives, that a true heart and a sound mind may select,
among all those which God has implanted in our nature; preferring, always, the higher to the lower; but rejecting none,
which circumstances may render fitting; not even the fear of
physical pain; for we believe that that, low as it is, will have its
place, its proper sphere of influence, not for a limited period
merely, till teachers become better qualified, and society more
morally refined, but while men and children continue to be
human; that is, so long as schools and schoolmasters and
government and laws are needed."[16] He mistrusted even
Mann's caveat that corporal punishment should be retained as
only the last resort: there were degrees. Above all, he resented
Mann's allegations that the use of corporal punishment was
shameful to the teacher and a sign of incompetence. Speaking
of New England teachers, Hale prayed, "May their firmness of
principle be commensurate, at least, with their sensitiveness to

reproach; so that, however much they may suffer in their feelings, from the contemptuous sarcasm of those who denounce them as brutes and barbarians, they may yet stifle feeling, and, listening rather to the dictates of conscience, and duty, be guided more by fixed principles of a true scriptural philosophy, than by the changeful notions of fluctuating experimentalism."[17]

American children, increasingly obstreperous and backed by their parents in their obstreperousness in an egalitarian democratic era, were not as Horace Mann chose to believe, said Hale. The schoolmaster actually engaged in teaching the American young had "no alternative but to present to their senses, in tangible shape, the actual rod."[18] Mann might argue for the substitution of expulsion for the rod in intractable cases. Hale asserted, to the contrary, "The community have a right to expect that the pupils of the public schools shall be really taught and governed within them" and not weakly expelled from school only to find their way to prison.[19] "We must take human nature as it is," Hale repeated; and taking the case as he believed it to be Hale was sure that Horace Mann underestimated its desperateness. Mann was generalizing from abuses of corporal punishment, but the existence of these did not qualify the truth that "everything is to be used as not abusing it. Nothing is to be despised."[20]

"We object, then," Hale continued, ". . . to the idea, that the relation of a pupil to his teacher is one 'of affection first, and then duty.' We would rather reverse the terms." For the first necessity was that "implicit obedience to rightful authority must be inculcated and enforced upon children, as the very germ of all good order in future society. . . . Yet it is quite offensive now-a-days to ears polite, to talk of authority, and command, and injunction. We must persuade, and invite, and win. . . . The present is an age remarkable for the ascendency of sympathy over the sterner virtues. Kindness . . . has stepped beyond the limits of its legitimate control. . . . Kindness cannot supply the place of authority, nor gratitude that of submission. . . . True obedience is a hearty response to acknowledged authority."[21] The "Utopian theorists" professed "to elevate themselves above the region of physical influences, and to scorn their control"; but Hale pointed out that "it is this very physical organization that they appear most anxious to protect from outrage. They seem willing to forego that sound moral and intellectual training, which they so fully appreciate and so truely prize, rather than to receive it, through the degradation of that lower nature which they affect to despise."[22]

Horace Mann reacted with a neurotic attack of logorrhea to the masters' *Remarks,* especially to Joseph Hale on discipline. It is not clear that the masters were a real threat to Mann although no doubt their approval would have helped to legitimize the new eduational bureaucracy and its new light pedagogy. After more than seven years' labor worthy of the hero and potential martyr he knew himself to be, Mann was succeeding and by his own account knew he was succeeding; but the masters' criticism impinged at a deep level upon the apostate Calvinist. Writing on February 10, 1844, early in the controversy, he informed his physician that he had not slept for three weeks. "I can feel the flame in the centre of my cranium, blazing and flaring round just as you see that of a pile of brush on a distant heath in the wind. What can be done to extinguish it?"[23] Throughout the affair he kept George Combe posted; in a letter dated December 1, 1844, he declared, "The orthodox have hunted me this winter as though they were bloodhounds, and I a poor rabbit. . . . They feel in respect to a free education, that opens the mind, develops the conscience, and cultivates reverence for whatever is good without the infusion of Calvinistic influence, as the old monks felt about printing, when they said, 'If we do not put that down, it will put us down.'"[24] Feeling thus harried so long as the battle raged dubious, he was vindictive in eventual victory.

He was persuaded that their separate attacks on the particular innovations he advocated contained only intimations of "their views of the proper incitements to study and persuasives to good conduct." He characterized those intimations as "only a few clouds rushing, here and there, athwart an angry sky" which scarcely prepared one for the horrors of the complete formulation of the masters' "system" in the fourth section of their *Remarks,* the section on "School Discipline" by Joseph Hale. It was only there, Mann asserted, that the *Remarks* finally "introduce us to a frozen midnight, where the light of love is extinguished, and all moral sentiment and humanity are congealed." He went on to quote what he read quite accurately as the key parts of the masters' "system," confident that the public would react to them as he did.[25] Seldom has an old dispensation confronted a new so intractably and gone down to such definitive defeat.

Mann stigmatized the masters' philosophy of school discipline as a doctrine of "Authority, Force, Fear, Pain!" Without squarely addressing the dogma of original sin from which the masters' position derived, Mann expressed and appealed to the humanitarianism of the time by sentimentalizing childhood. He was appalled by a doctrine in which "the ideas of Childhood and Punishment [were] indissolubly associated together," and he could only throw up his hands on finding Joseph Hale saying that the most that could be expected, even from the most passionate application of authority, force, fear, and pain, was "to develop and bring to light latent evil" in the young. Hale based this view on the ground that God alone has the power of "educing good from ill." Mann's reaction was that "surely if such a philosophy is to prevail, and our practice is to be conformed to it, He, whose prerogative it is to bring good out of evil, will be supplied with a superfluity of the raw material upon which to work."[26]

The nature of the impasse as an absolute conflict of world views and religious commitments is further illustrated by Mann's derogation of authority, force, fear, and pain as motives "taken from the nethermost end of the scale of influences."[27] As he made clear in returning to the theme later in the affair, when the masters had published their *Rejoinder* to his *Reply* and he a further *Answer,* he was setting the masters' philosophy of school discipline in the context of the Scale of Being, that shibboleth of natural religion, natural law, and human rights. To do this was to supply a basis for charging the masters with libeling human nature by attempting to educate it through motives appropriate only to subhuman levels of the Scale of Be-

ing. Mann reasserted the reformers' claim that they worked
through the higher, distinctively human motives of love, self-
esteem, conscience. He condemned the masters in terms echoing the tenets of phrenology: "That powerful class of motives
which consists of affection for parents, love for brothers and
sisters, whether older or younger than themselves, justice and
the social sentiment towards schoolmates, respect for elders,
the pleasures of acquiring knowledge, the duty of doing as we
would be done by, the connection between present conduct,
and success, estimation, eminence, in future life, the presence
of an unseen eye,—not a syllable of all these is set forth with
any earnestness, or insisted upon, as the true source and spring
of human actions."[28]

Mann's arguments begged the question, and Hale shrewdly
observed, "perhaps the 'Remarks' are objectionable to Mr.
Mann, because they settle something, and consequently differ
so widely from his own *argumentative* writings. By contrast they
may seem to mean a great deal inasmuch as they cannot be resolved into absolute nothing."[29] Hale had ridiculed Mann's
ideologically skewed logic as being similar to a complex alge-
braic statement which after many minuses and pluses came to
zero.[30] As logicians, the orthodox had always been exasperat-
ingly superior to optimists and Arminians as now they were to
humanitarians, phrenologists, and "philanthropists" in general.
The controversy simplified itself to the question whether or not
there was any sanction in human nature for corporal punishment in schools, with Mann and his associates veering off the
point to vilify the masters as professionally incompetent and
brutal. Returning to this ad hominem tendency of Mann's,
Hale evenly declared in the *Rejoinder* that "physical coercion"
was "equally honorable, when used in its true relation with any
other agency, to both giver and receiver"—to which Mann
could only cry that "this last remark out-Herods the 'Remarks'
themselves."[31]

The reformers' effectual reply to the Boston masters came
not in the form of conclusions from rational dialogue but in a
species of demagoguery, in a political power play, and finally in
the feminizing of the public schools under the reformers'

administration. Mann was shaken by Hale's observation that
men who, like Mann and his supporters, disbelieve that "there
is in the nature of man an innate element of evil, prompting
him to rebellion," implicitly confess a creed according to which
"the impulses are all that is necessary to secure duty," "temptation is at an end," "virtue is a negation," "vice is a nonentity,"
and "repentance is a work of supererogation." Indignantly rejecting these imputations, Mann declared that nobody in
Massachusetts held any such creed; but he turned the debate to
demagogic effect by accusing the masters of promoting their
"private denominational views." Apart from any merits of the
argument, he could count on appealing to a majority of the
public, especially in Unitarian Boston, when he asserted of the
masters with a good deal less than justice, "Private opinions
have been thrust forward only by that small but persistent and
intolerant party, who are determined to force dogmatic
theology into our Common Schools, or to scatter those schools
to the winds."[32]

The demagoguery took the further form of a muckraking attack on what the reformers presented as the sadistic abuse of
the rod in the schools. There seems to have been a certain
amount, and perhaps a great deal, and the public in Boston and
elsewhere had been for some years displeased about it. Exactly
how serious the situation was in the Boston schools does not
seem to have been well documented. Joseph Hale, with Mann's
touting of Prussian mildness ringing no more strangely in his
ears than in ours, claimed, "Should the Prussian Minister of
Public Instruction see fit to honor the schools of this country
with a visit, we presume he would not be shocked with a single
exhibition of cruelty or anger."[33]

Nevertheless, Mann and his friends mounted a campaign in
the press against the alleged abuses, and Mann produced
examples. Applying his statistical approach, he declared that in
one Boston school there were $65\frac{3}{5}$ floggings per day on the
average; a boy's palm had become infected after it had been
beaten; in some schools masters, he asserted, made "large girls
lie down flat on their backs;—thus, in order to produce shame,
wounding and crushing the tenderest and most delicate sensi-

bilities of modest, maidenly feeling."[34] He readily injected personalities. Joseph Hale had come to Boston from a school in Salem four years before, and Mann asserted that his successor, Edwin Jocelyn, had not struck a blow since taking over. The result was such excellent order in the school that the Salem school committee had rewarded him by electing him principal of its high school for girls. "Now," said Mann, "a fact like this cannot be owing to any differences in human nature, *in general,* but only to a difference in the teacher's nature, *in particular.*"[35] He published this slur without evidence that Hale had struck any blows in Salem, that Salem had been dissatisfied with Hale, or that his move to Boston had not been as much a professional accolade as Jocelyn's promotion.

With sentiment aroused against corporal punishment, the reformers threatened the masters' jobs by campaigning for places on the Boston school committee. Once on the committee, Mann's friends, especially Samuel Gridley Howe, stiffened the evaluation procedures through which the masters were annually reelected to their positions, brought their professional competence into question by staging unprecedented written tests of the masters' pupils and publishing results that seemed to discredit the masters, instituted a requirement that every case of corporal punishment must be recorded and be subject to review, installed a superintendent of schools sympathetic to the reformers, and reorganized the administration of individual schools in order to insure more centralized control. Four of the thirty-one masters who had originally criticized Mann's seventh report were removed, and others were transferred. By September 1845 the balance had shifted in Mann's favor, and he reported with satisfaction to Combe the dismissal of the four. He declared that "the old notion of the perfection of the Boston grammar and writing schools is destroyed . . . and the masters are hereafter to stand upon their good behavior."[36] Writing again to Combe on April 27, 1846, Mann reported that the masters had not attempted to counter his *Answer.* "I think they never will; but I almost wish they would. One of the already ripened and gathered fruits of the controversy is, that it is admitted on all hands, that, since the controversy began, corporal punishment has diminished in the masters' schools at least eighty per cent!"[37]

If any one view of the masters went at once to the quick of Mann's detestation of Calvinistic (male) hardness on the one hand and his preference for optimistic (female) softness on the other, it was Joseph Hale's assertion, "Kindness cannot supply the place of authority, nor gratitude that of submission." Mann thoroughly misinterpreted this statement, in a way that has proved perennial in American educational thought, as meaning preference of submission, that is, compulsion to domineer. It did not occur to him that the masters might be propounding simple truth, not necessarily related to Calvinist doctrine: to substitute kindness for authority in teaching may be a fatal unkindness.[38] Hale had first stated, in the *Remarks,* the axiom, "The governed, on his part, is not, from sympathy, and affection, and harmony of opinion, to obey the individual, but the authority residing in him rather, from a sense of obligation."[39] He tried to reinforce this with irony in the *Rejoinder* by turning the proposition around: "The child, animated with a sense of duty and love, and seeing the reasonableness of the teacher's requisitions, is not to obey them from sympathy, and affection, and harmony of opinion! *Such* a child cannot but obey from sympathy, and affection, and harmony of opinion."[40] Mann did not see that Hale was pointing to a contradiction between the idea of obedience and the function of sympathy, affection, and harmony of opinion. In his perfectionistic optimism, Mann was postulating a very wise child indeed, as it were a preeducated child already possessed of capacities that Hale thought all of the engines of authority might very well never be able to educe from (sinful) humanity.

Whereas Hale's point was that education could not proceed from personal affection between pupil and teacher, with a governing emphasis on the feelings of the pupil, but must be founded on obedience in the pupil and academically qualified authority in the teacher, Mann countered with a parable about a female teacher governing with love. This young lady, harassed in a school which "seemed rapidly resolving into anarchy" under the influence of big rowdy boys, did not punish them because she could not. Her inability to do so was two-fold. She was physically too weak; but, more important, her gentle exemplary female nature, reinforced by normal school principles, recoiled from the idea of authority backed by the threat of punishment. That cure, even if it had been available, was worse than the disease. After vainly appealing to the ring-leaders, she "wept bitterly" and dismissed school. Gathering her strength in the recess, she made one last appeal. Mann declared,

At this juncture of indescribable pain, several of the ring leaders arose from their seats and approached her. They said to her that they appeared on account of the school, and particularly on their own, to ask pardon for what they had done, to express their sorrow at the pain they had caused her, and promise, in behalf of all, that her wishes should thereafter be cordially obeyed. Her genuine sorrow had touched a spot in their hearts which no blows could ever reach; and, from that hour, the school went on with a degree of intellectual improvement never known before; and, like the sweet accord of music, when every instrument has been attuned by a master's hand, no jarring note ever afterwards arose to mar its perfect harmony.[41]

This young lady should be examined as a prophetic figure, not yet, in 1845, fully emergent from the brow of Horace Mann but available as the pattern of the normalite. The fairy tale in which he set her contains only one slightly jarring note. Surely he did not mean that it was a *master's* hand that attuned

> The trembling living wire
> Of those unusual strings

—the heartstrings of the pupils! Otherwise, Mann's parable exactly illustrates the pedagogy of love, the substitution of personal interaction between pupil and teacher for properly professional relations.

It should be specially noticed that in Mann's parable of the normalite the teacher succeeded by appealing as a woman to insurrectionary pupils as men. The argument from the first had been that women were divinely apt to teach young children through an extension of maternal solicitude and compatibility from home to school, but Mann unconsciously shifted the terms in exhibiting his female teacher's success with postpubertal boys. She succeeded through a sexual appeal no longer maternal, or if so, not very healthfully so. That school may, as Mann claimed, have hummed along thereafter "like the sweet accord of music," but one may doubt if it also "went on with a degree of intellectual improvement never known before." Two further aspects of the interplay of the sexes implicit in Mann's parable should be mentioned for development later, in reference to the consequences of the feminization of education. One is the effect of the feminized teaching corps on its male administrators, and the other is the effect of the total situation on female pupils—aspects that defined themselves gradually and that are still generally ignored although surely of profound importance.

The female teacher in the parable should be considered further in the light of Mann's attitude toward feminism, which, like Catharine Beecher's, remained negative. He saw the schoolrooms of the state, each with its female teacher, as so many rooms of the house where he and his kind ruled paternally and not without a species of droit du seigneur. Woman's place was the domestic sphere and the schools only an enlarged domestic sphere. After his death, Mary Peabody Mann memorialized her husband's attitude in the devotional tones of the nineteenth-century widow, and all the more revealingly for that:

He had never been pleased with any desire on woman's part to shine in public, but it was his opinion that the divinely appointed mission of woman is to teach, and it was his wish to introduce her into every department of instruction as soon as it could be done with good effect. He had watched teaching long enough to know that woman's teaching, other things being equal, is more patient, persistent, and thorough than man's; and that to equal intellectual advantages, that of moral culture, which should never be divorced from these, is more surely added thereby; and that this grows out of the domestic traits, which are not marred by this use, but only thus directed to the noblest ends. Nor does it interfere in any degree with the peculiarly appointed sphere of woman. She is better fitted for the duties of wife and mother for having first used her faculties in imparting knowledge

under circumstances that are free from distracting cares. He had no
desire to shut out men from the enjoyment of the same privilege; but
he hoped, by the union of the two in the vocation of teaching, to an-
nihilate as it were, certainly to banish, all brutalities of growth in
young men, and frivolities in young women, and this without check-
ing the hilarity or interfering with the simplicity of youth.[42]

The last sentence should be remembered as an early sounding
of a note that has been repeated from time to time to the
present, but always tentatively—the notion that the union of
the sexes in the vocation of teaching is the ultimately desirable
thing.

It remains to resume one more theme, introduced earlier as a
factor that predisposed American society to accept feminization
of education, which emerged unmistakably in the controversy
between Mann and the masters. This was the educational
preference of egalitarian democracy. Male teachers once
identified with authority, and authority symbolized by the rod,
the attack on corporal punishment was politically effective.
After the reformers gained control of the Boston school committee, one of the annual examining committees opined with
respect to corporal punishment that "if our schools are to be
places where human beings shall be taught and trained, there
must be discipline, restraint, and positive authority. He who
hopes for an escape from this necessity, knows nothing of
human nature." So Joseph Hale had insisted; but the committee continued, in a fashion that has proved constant in
American educational affairs, to subvert the principle so
roundly announced. "We are forced to believe," the committee
added, "that there has been a gross abuse of the power of corporal punishment." They said they had taken steps to curb it although aware that "there are some persons who look upon the
rod as if it had a magic power; as if chaos must come again, if it
were abandoned and forgotten." But such worries were merely
superstitious, and corporal punishment was obviously incompatible with American democracy. "In this country," the committee observed complacently, "when the boy escapes from
school, he never hears the word *Master* again"—they did not
reinforce the point, but I shall, by observing that they had fixed

things so the boy would hear the word less and less frequently even before escaping from school. They commented on the absurdity of the "parent or schoolmaster who seeks to prepare a child to become an American citizen, by no better discipline than that of corporal punishment."[43]

The citadel of the traditional, hard-line, objectively oriented education in the hands of male teachers, the highest paid, best prepared, and most prestigious in America, had been sacked. The examining committee exulted in the humiliation of the Boston masters, in whom the committee now found "a want of a feeling of manly independence and of fearless frankness." Some of the masters turned servile and seemed, the committee said pityingly, "to fear a secret power which may govern them and the committee too." That all concerned might indeed be governed by a power as yet, in 1845, only latent in democratic society will be suggested in the following chapter. The masters had given way not only on corporal punishment but on textbooks too, relating as these did to the traditional line in education as nearly as corporal punishment; the committee professed surprise that the masters had little to recommend regarding the improvement of textbooks and touched the issue "as one would handle the edge of a very sharp instrument." And the committee capped its sarcasms by concluding that if "for blows upon the hand there must be blows upon the soul, then we say, give back the rod to the master."[44] This imagery of sharp-edged instruments and the taking away of the rod from male teachers speaks a plain obbligato to the committee's overt message.

Chapter 6

Sentiment Out of Season

ONCE instituted during the 1840s in Massachusetts, Connecticut, and Rhode Island, the feminization of the teaching corps steadily increased in those states, was imitated in the Middle Atlantic and western states, and was then imposed after the Civil War as a feature of Reconstruction in the southern states. Concern seems to have developed only as people realized that women were monopolizing public secondary schools, when these multiplied after the Civil War, as they had already monopolized the elementary schools. The most commonly expressed worry was the effect on adolescent boys. Formerly, the problem had been taken to be that women teachers were not strong enough to inflict physical discipline on big boys; now the problem was usually said to be the psychological influence of women teachers on adolescent boys, who were thought to need masculine example as well as discipline at school. Few questioned the effects of a predominantly or, in many instances, exclusively female teaching corps on female students or on the character of male teachers and administrators.

In 1875 Charles W. Eliot delivered a controversial address to a county teachers' association in which he asserted there were "too many women teachers" and stigmatized the cause as "false economy" on the part of taxpayers and school committees. Thirty-five years earlier, Horace Mann had made the argument from cheapness respectable by interpreting the willingness of women to teach for low wages as proof of their sex-specific, self-sacrificial motherliness. Eliot bluntly declared, "It is true that sentimental reasons are often given for the almost exclusive employment of women in the common schools; but the effective reason is economy. Sentiment is charming in its season, and true economy is always wholesome; but sentiment and economy make a very suspicious mixture. If women had not been cheaper than men, they would not have replaced nine-tenths of the men in the American public schools." He went on to characterize the disproportionate employment of women in the schools as "an unwise economy, because it inevitably tends, first, to make the body of teachers a changing, fluctuating body, fast thinned and fast recruited; and secondly, to make teaching, not a life-work, as it ought to be, but a temporary resort on the way to another mode of life."[1]

Eliot's criticism discomfited male administrators as much as female teachers. He would not allow that (male) "superintendence" was a compensation for inadequate teaching by young women on a brief detour on their road to the altar. "A school committee hires a superintendent, and then thinks it can safely employ an inferior class of teachers, just as an inferior class of laborers may be safely employed for digging or sweeping if a smart overseer is hired to watch them." He observed that the increased superintendence necessitated by inferior teachers—he did not present the inferiority of women teachers as inherent in femaleness but in the actual condition of women—was acquired by robbing the schools of what few male teachers there were. "Now a gain in superintendence which is procured at the expense of a loss of direct teaching power is too dearly bought," Eliot said.[2] Thus early was it possible to analyze the perniciousness of the practice of promoting male teachers out of teaching, as work suitable for an inferior group, into administration.

Eliot took his stand for the necessity of the teacher being a superior professional person regardless of sex. It is unlikely he imagined that, given the conditions of his time, many women would be found among a superior professional group. Without making invidious remarks about women, however, he focused on the "honor of the profession"; and that, as soon appeared, was inseparable from a species of elitism. Like Horace Mann, he thought "teaching should be as much honored as preaching." He thought the teacher's office should be made "tenable during good behavior and efficiency" and thus protected from the caprices of public opinion or individual grievance, and he did not think that free schooling should extend to secondary school. Free common schooling was feasible only in a homogeneous community and even there only through the elementary grades. It had become a doubtful enterprise as the population became heterogeneous, with cleavages along ethnic, religious, economic, and educational lines.[3]

Eliot was nevertheless willing, though with reservations, to continue free common schooling through the age of twelve "on the ground that so much is necessary for the safety of the State." Secondary education, however, should be for children who could profit by it and whose parents could pay part of the cost, with a Jeffersonian proviso that public scholarships be available to the academically talented children of the poor. He plainly made the honor of the teaching profession depend upon academic standards, frankly admitting the selective effect of these in the face of egalitarian democratic sentiment.[4]

To the cry that he must have known would be raised against his recommendations, Eliot replied with a summary of Jeffersonian principles, startlingly anachronistic though they were by 1875. "The equality upon which modern republican institutions are founded is not social equality, or the equality of possessions, or the equality of powers and capacities," he asserted, "but simply the equality of all men before the law. Republican institutions obliterate hereditary distinctions, level artificial barriers, and make society mobile, so that distinction is more easily won by individual merit and power, and sooner lost through demerit or impotence; but they give free play to the irresistible natural forces which invariably cause the division of every complicated human society into different classes." If society should cease to give "free play to the endless diversities of innate power, inherited capacity, and trained skill which humanity exhibits," Eliot argued, Americans would be frustrated in their characteristic desire to better themselves and held to a dead level incompatible with republican virtues and public liberty.[5]

While proposing, like Jefferson, to rake from the rubbish the bright children of poor parents who could not pay for secondary education, Eliot did not hesitate to express one of the most un-American of sentiments: "The dull children whose parents are unable to pay for them will of course get no further than the compulsory limit [of free elementary schooling], but the community will lose little or nothing thereby."[6] He seems to have been politically naive though a case can be made for his realism from an academic point of view. The public and public school administrators acted on political, not academic, imperatives. One concludes that a truly professional teaching corps based on academic standards that conflicted with democratic sentiment was not possible.

The feminization of teaching was an effectual social solution to American ambivalence about education. Free common schooling to ever later ages and ostensibly higher levels could be safely instituted if only it were in the hands of a class of persons too weak to insist on professional honor and impose academic standards. Women were such a class. The profession of education had been turned over to them on the unstated condition that they forever subvert it by their prior allegiance to matrimony and motherhood and the concept of schooling as extended mothering. As a class physically weaker than men, politically disfranchised, conditioned by normal school training, and occupationally limited, they were in any case too weak to trouble the democracy with authoritative criticism, much less to establish a logical system of education with strict intellectual requirements.

The administrative officials, mostly male, of the state and city systems of public schools held their positions on the same terms. Though they enjoyed a higher status than the female teacher it was still lower than that of men in the true professions, commerce, and government. In the sense that they administered a self-subverting sector of public life, male school administrators were "feminized." Susan B. Anthony predicted this result in 1852 when she appropriated the floor of the convention of the New York Education Association, which had not admitted women teachers to membership though women already outnumbered men in the teaching corps. In suggesting that nineteenth-century schoolmen created for themselves a "classless" profession, Paul H. Mattingly credits them with virtuous democratic intentions;[7] but his study seems to imply that what they came out with could be characterized equally well as a déclassé profession because of their association with the feminized teaching corps.

In the circumstances, it is not surprising that such warnings as were raised about the monopolization of teaching by women were halfhearted. From the 1870s on, concern was expressed in city after city and in one annual report of the U.S. commissioner of education after another. But the matter was increasingly treated just as given, or at the most as one of those perennial "challenges," to use a term still dear to our educationists, never to be decisively met, forever to be faced with a show of martyred virtue.

In his report for 1873, the U.S. commissioner of education, John Eaton, called attention to the fact that there were many more female than male teachers in every northern state except Indiana and Missouri and that the women teachers' success had led to the idea of employing them also as school visitors, members of school committees, and county superintendents. It was this encroachment by women upon administration, regarded as properly a male domain, that seems to have aroused the commissioner's interest in the whole question of sex as a consideration in the conduct of education. He put a number of questions: "Should the fact of sex make any difference in the relation of individuals to education either as trainer or trained? In the education of the young has one sex any work to do which the other sex cannot equally well perform, and are the children in our schools trained actually so different, on account of the difference of sex, as to render modifications in their respective trainings necessary?" He recognized the ideological conflict that made discussion inconclusive. On one side—presumably that of the opponents of feminization—he recognized "gross conservatism"; on that of its advocates, "immoderate theory." The lines were still as clearly drawn as they were in the controversy between Horace Mann and the Boston masters, and the commissioner could only recommend "a philosophical study of accumulated facts and human experience."[8]

Such study as followed, so far as can be judged from subsequent reports of the commissioner, was not philosophical but loosely statistical. Through the 1870s and 1880s one may trace the increasing incidence of women, not merely in elementary education where they were considered appropriate but also in secondary education and administration where their presence was disturbing. The trend was most marked in the large cities; feminization of education was identical with its urbanization, amplifying the mother's influence at home from which urban working conditions tended to abstract the paterfamilias. Figures on the use of women were regularly culled from the annual reports of the state commissioners and the city superintendents of education but were not analyzed. At most general comments were recorded. Feminization of teaching on the Massachusetts model was coincidental with the development of public school systems in western states and territories. For example, the Washington Territory reported 120 male and 100 female teachers in 1875, but the next year the scale shifted as 134 male to 145 female teachers were employed. The Wisconsin superintendent's report for 1877–78 included the observation: "The tendency in the cities to engage a larger proportionate number of women teachers has been growing for several years, the ratio employed in 1878 being nearly six to one. In the country districts, nearly one-third as many men as women were employed."[9]

The enfranchisement and qualifying for office of women occurred in school elections long before women obtained the privileges of general elections. This must have reflected acceptance of the idea of schools as part of woman's affairs. In 1880 the election of women to school boards was singled out as "a noteworthy feature" of the past decade, and the change was traced to the controverted election of four women to the Boston school committee in 1873. The Supreme Court of Massachusetts ruled them ineligible, but the legislature then removed their disability.[10]

Toward the end of the 1880s, the preponderance of women

teachers was so great throughout the country that mere common sense, apart from ideological considerations, was raising questions. The expressions of concern were mild and typically led to the observation that a better balance between the sexes in teaching was desirable without going deeply into reasons. The feeling was general that, however compelling the reasons might be, the country was not willing to pay for male teachers. Male school administrators were so far from being the leaders of the culture that Horace Mann had in mind that they were disinclined to stand against public preference. In 1886 Virginia's superintendent of education reported, "At the same [present] rate of increase our schools in a few years will be pretty largely in the hands of female teachers. No unfavorable comment is to be made on this tendency, yet it ought not to go too far."[11]

The strongest reaction may be exemplified by a Rhode Island superintendent. He regretted the extreme feminization of his schools, observing: "The two types of mind and heart [i.e., male and female] are distinct and were designed to have their combined effect on the youthful character. Any scheme of education and training that leaves out either is defective and cannot secure that symmetrical development which is possible under the other plan."[12] This was, by implication, a much more searching comment than any contained in the most detailed account of the subject that appeared in the U.S. commissioner's reports, an essay on "The Teaching Force of New England from 1866 to 1888" in the commissioner's report for 1888–89. Though it dealt more fully with the feminization of the schools than anything previously published, this essay ended in discreet inconclusiveness.

Alarm was nevertheless widespread and seems to have reached its peak early in the 1890s as dismayed recognition of feminization as an intractable accomplished fact rather than as determination to alter it. The commissioner's report for 1891–92 observed that "the proportion of men in the teaching force has been growing less for a long time" and had further decreased that year from what might have been thought an irreducible 7.20 percent to 7.16 percent. The report cited as typically distressing situations those of Wilmington, Delaware, which now had only 5 male teachers out of a total of 193— those 5 all being in high schools—and of Minneapolis, where of 605 teachers all were women except 4 male high school principals, 6 male special teachers, and 6 male manual training instructors. The change from male to female teachers, "begun at the instance of Horace Mann, Henry Barnard, and their contemporaries," had gone "much further than was ever intended or dreamed of by the original advocates of the employment of women, and further than the general sentiment of school men now approves."[13] Superintendents of the city systems, which had been almost totally feminized, were apparently the most alarmed officials; state commissioners had less sense of being overwhelmed by women because rural districts still had a good many male teachers and because the commissioners dealt with a male bureaucracy.

Consequences of feminization, characterized by the commissioner as "not foreseen" and "difficult to overcome," were described by him as follows:

The business of school teaching is coming to be considered a woman's business, and therefore, offers less attraction to young men than formerly, especially in the subordinate positions, where the low salaries also operate to repel them. The appointment of principals, too, presents new difficulties. The assistants' positions were formerly the training schools of principals, and from them it was always easy to select a man to fill any vacancy; but now it becomes necessary either to employ a new and untried college graduate, to import a rustic schoolmaster, or to transfer a high-school assistant. The first two sources of supply are open to the objection that there is too much uncertainty about the men of whose fitness for the position so little can be known, while the third expedient invariably weakens the faculty of the high school. With the source of supply so curtailed it is not surprising that in many cases women have been promoted from subordinate positions and made principals because no man was available about whom enough was known to justify the belief that he could fill the place better. The tendency thus gains force as it proceeds by constantly making it more and more difficult to secure good material, and there is danger that the increasing femininity of the schools, if such a term is permissible, may be productive of serious results. The already noticeable decrease in the proportion of boys in the higher grades is ascribed by many to this cause, and with some show of plausibility.[14]

Foreign observers, long fascinated by the American common school system as the nursery of democracy, were nonplussed by its feminization. An inquiry into the extent and consequences of feminization in American schools requested by the Joint Education Committees of Wales and Monmouthshire provided the occasion in 1891 for American officials to make the most thorough investigation of the subject to date. The school superintendents of New York, Chicago, Philadelphia, Brooklyn, Boston, Cleveland, Jersey City, and Denver—the cities employing, in that order, the highest numbers of women teachers—answered questions, reproduced in the U.S. commissioner's report for 1891–92:

I. Are women employed as teachers of classes either (a) of boys only, or (b) boys and girls together?

II. If so, (1) in what subjects; (2) to children of what ages; (3) of what classes of life?

III. How far are they successful (a) in giving intellectual training; (b) in maintaining discipline and order?

IV. Does their work under any of the foregoing heads require supplementing by that of men?

V. How does their remuneration compare with that of male teachers of the same social and intellectual standing?

VI. In what proportion do married women act as teachers, and is it found that they are at any disadvantage as compared with those who are unmarried?[15]

In answer to the first question, every city replied that women were employed as teachers of classes both of boys only and of boys and girls together, except Chicago and Cleveland, which had no separate classes for boys. The answers to the second question revealed that women were teaching all subjects and children of every age and social class in elementary schools, where indeed they were practically 100 percent of the teaching force. Although still largely excluded from teaching in secondary school they were steadily gaining access to it, for example in girls' high schools. Almost everywhere they were teaching through the eighth grade; in Philadelphia they were teaching throughout the girls' high school and the normal school; in Chicago, Boston, and Denver they were teaching straight through high school. For the United States as a whole, the census of 1890 revealed that 65.5 percent of all teachers were female, and the U.S. commissioner stated that "in general the salary of women is about 60 per cent. that of men." It appears that there was a sharper discrimination in favor of men in administrative work. The sex bias came out markedly in the circumstance that the whole scale, from principal to least assistant, for girls' high schools was usually much lower than the scale for boys' or coeducational high schools. Married women teachers, though barred by many systems, were described generally as superior to unmarried women teachers.

The responding city superintendents uniformly declared for equality of the sexes with respect to teaching ability. The U.S. commissioner agreed that women "as a rule succeed better than men in getting work out of pupils of all kinds. The intellectual training which they give is therefore better up to a certain point, than that given by men. They also maintain better discipline and order than men, and with less corporal punishment." He added, however: "But there is a drawback to the intellectual training and discipline of women in the fact that their training is more like that of the family and less like that of the State. It is evident that the child needs both of these kinds of training, and therefore he should have instruction from male as well as female teachers."[16] The commissioner's last remark points to a central characteristic of the tradition of feminized schooling and labels it a drawback.

In view of the inspiration Horace Mann took from his quick look at the Prussian educational system in 1843, the reactions of a Prussian educator to the American system fifty years later are instructive. Having attended the Congress of Education that was held at the Chicago World's Fair in 1893, E. Schlee, director of the Real-Gymnasium at Altona, bracketed as "unfavorable peculiarities" of American schools deficient professional preparation of teachers and "the extraordinary preponderance

of female teachers." He made it plain that the one condition implied the other. Schlee was surprised to find such a high incidence of female teachers in a system supposedly modeled on
that of Prussia. He noted that in 1890 only 34.5 percent of
American teachers were men and observed, without fully ap-
preciating its significance, the fact that feminization was the
characteristic of the most developed state systems and not, as he
would have expected, a temporary expedient in the
underdeveloped states of the West and South. Only 20 percent
of the teachers in the North Atlantic states were men, and the
enrollments at the normal schools in Massachusetts, Connecticut, and New Hampshire were more than 90 percent female. It was clear that the preponderance of female teachers,
tending to complete monopoly through the operation of the
normals, was the defining characteristic of American public
education. Thus Schlee remarked that Chicago seemed to be
"about the most American city," with only 219 male teachers
and 3,081 female teachers in 1892.[17] The Massachusetts model
had indeed become all-American if the metropolis of the West
had accepted it.

Schlee gained the correct impression that the country owed
the policy of feminization to Massachusetts primarily but
thought it had started there as an expedient to staff schools
during the Civil War when men were in the army. Being
unaware of its origin in Horace Mann's highly articulated
reform propaganda of the 1830s and 1840s, he was in a position to observe without having the information needed to
analyze its influence in teacher training. Quantitatively, the
United States had an abundance of normal schools—135 public
and 43 private ones with 34,440 students enrolled in 1890,
which might seem, even in comparison with Prussia, more than
sufficient to insure professional quality. For Prussia had fewer
normal schools. "But the difference is reversed," said Schlee,
"by firmness of purpose and fixed order."[18] Prussia had imposed much stricter requirements in professional training
upon its predominantly male teaching corps. But the Prussian
firmness was a matter of rational, external—perceived as
precisely masculine—order; the German educator did not ap-

preciate the perdurability of the heritage from Horace Mann and the common school revival which, rooted in reaches of democratically conditioned psychology, was more unshakable than any external rationale.

Like most Americans who expressed concern about the preponderance of women in teaching, foreign critics, almost always men, singled out its effect on male pupils for comment. Only rarely did anyone worry about prepubertal boys, and never about girls of any age; but everybody thought boys over twelve should have male teachers. According to the Reverend Herbert Branston Grey, warden and headmaster of Bradfield College, Berkshire, the preponderance of women teachers was "an anxious problem to many thinkers in the Eastern, and still more the Middle States" when he visited them in 1903. The British headmaster observed "a certain highly-strung nervous system, a want of power of concentration, and often an effeminate appearance, as being characteristics of the American schoolboy" traceable to female tutelage.[19]

A colleague of the Reverend Mr. Grey, Professor Henry E. Armstrong, who taught chemistry in the City and Guilds of London Central Institute, put the sentiment more crudely. He thought that "the boy in America is not being brought up to punch another boy's head or to stand having his own punched in a healthy and proper manner" and asserted he had found "a tendency towards a common . . . sexless tone of thought" which he attributed to female teachers. He felt it imperative in both the United States and Britain to attract able men to careers as teachers, for he believed that however nearly equal in "creative and imaginative power" the sexes may originally have been, women had suffered such damage—such negative evolutionary effects—through millennia of being "man's slave" that there was no immediate prospect of removing their "mental disabilities" through education.[20]

In the American teaching profession, opposition to the preponderance of women teachers reached a peak in the Male High School Teachers Association of New York City in 1904. One may bracket opposition to women teachers, which lost its theological bearings and gradually redefined itself as masculine protest, by the movement against Horace Mann mounted by the Boston masters in 1844 and 1845 and by the protest of the male high school teachers of New York City sixty years later. Whereas the Boston masters expressed themselves as the elite of a threatened order, the New York male high school teachers had the tone of an aggrieved minority who knew they could not count on public support. The public had been accustomed to think of teaching as a feminine profession whose male members had classified themselves as second-class men by entering it. What had been a serious public issue between strong men in Boston in 1844–45 was seen in New York in 1904 as an intramural squabble between a group of marginal men teachers and the legitimately female majority of teachers.

Since the consolidation of the borough school systems to form the city system in 1898, the women teachers had vociferously demanded equal pay with men for equal work. The men teachers felt impelled to defend the differential rates as the guarantee of such status as they enjoyed, but the public was less interested in their status than in the threat of increased taxes to pay all teachers at the male rate. If the public attitude tended to help the male teachers on the immediate issue, it implied no opposition to the feminization of teaching, for the cheapness of women was the great desideratum. Retaining a tiny minority of male teachers at a rate somewhat higher than the female majority received was only a way of keeping education cheap and so limiting the authority of the schools.

The male high school teachers cited figures showing that feminization had accelerated throughout the country since 1880, when 42 percent of all teachers were men, a proportion which declined to 33 percent in 1890 and to 28 percent in 1900. The trend seemed headed for absolute zero within ten or fifteen years; and Massachusetts, where it began, seemed to provide evidence for the worst fears. In 1880 only 13 percent of Massachusetts teachers were men, and the decline had continued to 9 percent in 1890 and on to 8 percent in 1900. Comparable figures were usual for city systems everywhere. The male percentages for states, including data from rural districts where men were still employed in greater numbers, were

somewhat higher. "In all the schools of the cities of this country
... 93 per cent. of the teachers are female." In elementary
schools, 97 percent of all teachers were female. The minute
proportion of male teachers in elementary schools were almost
entirely in administrative work and carried the title of teacher
by courtesy: actual teaching was totally feminized for all
students to the age of twelve. The trend toward a similar situation was obvious in the high schools also; in New York state
high schools "there are two female teachers to one male
teacher." And once again, the minority of men counted as
teachers were generally performing administrative rather than
teaching functions. Even in colleges, "where 25 years ago all
teachers, were men, over 10 per cent. of their faculties are now
women."[21]

The Male High School Teachers Association then called attention to a parallel between the numerical feminization of
faculties and that of student bodies. This development had
been arbitrarily prevented in elementary schools, but by 1900
the public high schools of the country reported three girls to
every two boys, and the divergence was growing. In New York
City high schools the ratio was four girls to two boys; in
Chicago, two to one; and in Philadelphia four to one. Furthermore, "in many colleges, where a few years ago there were no
women now over 25 per cent. of the students are women," and
in coeducational institutions "women students have increased
from 51 per cent., in 1880, to 71 per cent. in 1900." There was
nothing to regret in the more widespread and longer continued
education of girls and women; yet the growing proportion of
women students in high schools, normals, and colleges was
mostly destined for employment as teachers while the supply of
educated men from whom teachers might be drawn was dwin-
dling.[22]

The favorite argument of the common school revival, that
the school was but an extension of the domestic sphere and
woman was therefore properly in command (under male
supervision), was questioned by the male high school teachers.
They argued that the family was "the fundamental institution
of society," that there were "many reasons for believing that the

ever lessening regard of educated people for the family ideal should be viewed with alarm," and that "perhaps the maintenance and extension of so large a body of unmarried women teachers may be, along with the other public employment of women, one of the agencies which is diminishing the extent, power, and influence of the home."[23]

Nor could they take it so complacently for granted that women should teach just until they could marry. "Teaching has been used as a temporary employment. This is a condition most unhealthful to any vocation. . . . The practice of entering the profession and leaving it after a short period has made teaching the most unstable of all professions in its personnel. Some authorities refuse even to place the calling in the category of professions." They were bent on exploding Horace Mann's argument from cheapness for the use of women as teachers and did so partly on the grounds Charles W. Eliot had advanced in 1875 but, more originally, also on the basis of a claim for men's superiority as teachers. They asserted that "penurious expenditure" on education was no "economy." "Women have been employed in many places for a mere pittance. The average salary of a woman teacher in the United States is $39 per month, or about $350 per year. The people have been taught a wrong standard of expenditure for so great a public work. They have objected to men on the ground of economy, and have persistently asked, 'Why pay men more for the same work?' The answer is very simple. The woman is not doing, or cannot do, the same work. She works as a woman, and after all cannot quite undo her true, womanly self."[24]

Here was a direct denial of the basic tenet of the common school revival that woman's "true, womanly self" was just what fundamentally qualified her to teach. The male high school teachers made several points in support of this extraordinary criticism of the feminization of teaching on qualitative grounds. They observed that women qualitatively "feminized" both the course of study and the methods of teaching. "The curriculum taught by a woman will most naturally receive a feminine interpretation" and be weakened by a "constant tendency to overvalue the softer and more showy arts at the expense of the hard essentials." In regard to methods, the male high school teachers accused women teachers of influencing students "thru a personal motive altogether" instead of appealing to "notions of right and justice." "The sentimental question ever is, 'Now won't you perform this task for me?'"[25] This was mordant criticism of the pedagogy of love, amounting to the accusation that women teachers subverted the profession of teaching by substituting a personal relationship with students.

The male high school teachers' criticism of the qualitative aspects of female teaching showed, however, sex chauvinism. They were thinking throughout of school as properly the place for male teachers and male pupils which had been outrageously invaded by females. Not so long ago, men, not women, were "considered the ideal teachers." The feminization of American schools, "unprecedented in the educational history of the world," had "as yet scarcely the sanction of a generation." When it came to asserting the superior capacity of men to teach, these male teachers spoke too flatly in the accents of male chauvinism: "The man, as a man, is bringing into the boy's life what no woman can bring."[26] One looks vainly for any comment on what the man, as a man, might bring into the girl's life or for any appreciation of what the woman, as a woman, might bring into the life of boys.

The male teachers observed, "The woman influences the boy thru a personal motive altogether." Her approach was sentimental in the sense of coquettish: "The boy's feelings are used as a constant and immediate lever for all action. The man [teacher] never appeals to a boy in this way, but rather thru the notions of right and justice. 'You should do so and so because it is right or more beneficial.'"[27] This criticism certainly implied a preference for impersonal standards as the basis for teaching but was, in the absence of the orthodox theological context, far weaker than the Boston masters' assertion of the teacher's right and authority as an extension of the authority of the father in his several manifestations as paterfamilias, magistrate, minister, and God.

The situation between men and women teachers in New York City reached a crucial stage in the year 1906–7, which, according to Superintendent William H. Maxwell, was "memorable for an agitation carried on by women teachers in elementary schools and high schools to secure legislation making it mandatory upon the Board of Education to pay the same salaries to women that are paid to men." Admitting the validity of the women's cause, Maxwell nevertheless had to dwell on difficulties. "If there is to be 'equal pay for equal work' . . . either men's salaries must be reduced . . . or women's salaries must be raised." In the first instance, the city would lose its "strong men" teachers; in the second, an immediate increase in expenditures variously estimated from about $8 million to about $11 million would result which, in Maxwell's opinion, would induce a taxpayers' revolt.[28]

Maxwell did not blink the fact that the salary issue was "really a question of the relative merits of men and of women as teachers." He did not think it possible to settle the question by examinations but offered a comment on it which he made contingent upon two axiomatic positions, first, "that the prime object of education is not so much the imparting of knowledge as the development of character," and second, that there are indeed sex differentiae in "intellectual and emotional characteristics" that affect teaching. Both axioms faithfully reflected the tradition of the common school revival, but the premises of the argument for sex differences were no longer theological but rather evolutionist and sociological. In lieu of Catharine Beecher's and Horace Mann's case for woman as self-sacrificial and therefore Christian in the expression of maternal instinct, Maxwell cited Herbert Spencer's view that "the maternal instinct delights in yielding benefits apart from deserts." He quoted Spencer further to the effect that women are characterized by a propensity to generosity over justice, the concrete over the abstract; they were said to be more competent in dealing with "the personal, the special, and the immediate" than with "the general and impersonal." Spencer held that women have "the predominant awe of power and authority" which "tends towards the strengthening of governments, political and ecclesiastical." Maxwell, ascribing opposite tendencies to men, concluded that "girls as well as boys, should in their school work, come under the influence of the mind of the man as well as of the mind of the woman." A balance of the sexes in the teaching corps would insure the inculcation of respect for both equity and justice, power and freedom, and so on.[29]

Maxwell believed, like most other people, that the influence of the male teacher was really important only in secondary education. He stated that the majority of teachers was rightly female since younger children were more numerous in the schools than older and women could be had more cheaply than men to teach them. "Some" men should be employed to teach the higher grades; he thought high school pupils should discover, by exposure to male teachers, "that culture and refinement are not the peculiar province of women." Male teachers were also needed to guide older boys in athletics, which was where the male teacher, as distinguished from the administrator, might count on something like full masculine status. The pattern of principal and coach presiding in defensive masculinity over female teachers, among whom might occasionally be found a hapless male teacher with merely academic functions, was already set.[30]

In New York City the movement for the equalization of salaries of men and women teachers came to a dead end, for the time being, in the report of a special commission set up by Mayor George B. McClelland to study the matter. At the end of 1909 this commission hastily put together a report which dwelt upon the great costs of equalizing salaries. It purported to be inconclusive for lack of time, but it consisted at bottom of a sufficiently conclusive syllogism: (1) "In the general market for labor, men command higher wages than women." (2) "Schools . . . depend for their supply of teachers upon the general labor market, and if they pay what that market demands, they are forced to give to men more than they give to women of the same grade of ability and attainments." Matter-of-factly, they restated the second premise: "The very large proportion of women now employed in the public schools is due to the fact that they have been and can be obtained at a smaller compensation than that paid to the male teachers." (3) The report did not draw but clearly implied the conclusion: "Whether it would or would not be equitable to give to women the very large premium above market rates which would result from raising their pay to the level of that of the male teachers is one of the questions submitted to us."[31] As capitalists righteous in their commitment to social Darwinism, the commissioners could be expected to give only one answer, to which feminized school administrators, not less than female teachers, must accede.

The commission's language was again revealing when, in turning from the "unquestionable facts" of the market, it addressed matters "which may be questioned but are sanctioned by a nearly universal opinion." Among these, the commission affirmed, was the following: "A school system officered only by men would be improved by exchanging many of them for women; and one conducted wholly by women would be improved by exchanging some of them for men; since neither sex accomplishes the best results when it works quite alone." But this was only lip service to an unrealistic ideal. The commission obviously thought that the existing proportion of men to women in the New York City system was all right. Opinions, it admitted, differed seriously as to "what the best proportion should be." It was sure an efficient school system "should include men and women in proper proportions; and it is safe to affirm that in all probability school systems will actually do this."[32] The commission lacked data from which it felt it could make an authoritative determination but made a determination anyhow by acting on the data it felt it had in abundance—the arithmetic of anything remotely approaching the costs of equalizing salaries of male and female teachers.

Such inclination as there was at the beginning of the twentieth century to reassess the feminization of American education was never strong enough to challenge its financial expediency. Horace Mann had used the word unblushingly in his propaganda for women teachers but had also, in his quasi-Christian concept of woman nature and his idea of the normal school, anticipated future extenuations. If he used the argument from cheapness to audiences with whom it might do the most good, he also advocated the professionalization of women teachers and appropriate increases in their salaries to what for his day was no mean level. At $350 a year for women and $450 for men teachers, the salaries paid in New York City in 1908 were still much lower than he advocated in the 1840s.

By 1908 it was possible to see male teachers as demeaned by their "hireling occupation," in which they were "at the mercy of boards of education or trustees" so that "even the public patronizes male teachers." The view was abroad that "teaching usually belittles a man" because he deals with "petty things, of interest only to his children and a few women assistants, and under regulations laid down by outside authority." Evidently, the school curriculum no longer expressed the values of the culture and so provided no basis for truly professional pedagogy. The male school administrator was inevitably belittled in his degree; "men principals are often petty tyrants" terrible to the women lorded over in the school but seen as more petty than tyrannical outside. "How often you see a principal and his assistants coming in a body to an association," said the observer of 1908, "the women cluttering about him and he strutting majestically like cock and hens in a barnyard."[33]

The same author, C. W. Bardeen, superintendent of schools at Syracuse, who in 1908 saw the male principal as Chanticleer, four years later attacked "the monopolizing woman teacher" in terms which would seem ludicrously extreme if one did not suspect they expressed sentiments which are still common today. After surveying with alarm the rapid feminization of the schools since the middle of the nineteenth century, he made the usual concessions to woman's ability to teach. His sex attitude showed, however, in his belief that "the masculine women teachers" were effective in the classroom, "but one never thinks of them as women except by accident." The reason female compared favorably with male teachers was that teaching, with its woman-wage, attracted the best women but not the best men. Although he said women teachers were at least adequate as scholars and maybe superior as disciplinarians, Bardeen feared that many boys were "going to the bad" for want of masculine vigor in their teachers. He regretted the passing of corporal punishment. "School discipline, like salaries, has been adjusted to women, and may as well be abandoned to them."[34]

Nevertheless, the beleaguered Bardeen felt impelled to assert an age limit to women's teaching ability, for reasons that briefly illuminate for us the abysses of sex prejudice. Women teachers did well enough until they were twenty-eight, whereas men teachers kept improving until they were forty. His explanation was that a woman ought to be in bed one or two days a month, but not being able to take the time female teachers were apt to become "nervous wrecks." The wreckage of their nervous systems was the more certain *"parce que la femme est l'instrument de plaisir"*—out in the world as she must be, the woman teacher had constantly to rebuff the advances of "coarse men." Past twenty-eight, the superintendent thought, women teachers therefore developed "a pessimism, a contempt for mankind, that is not healthful, and that boards of education shrink from."[35]

"Then," Bardeen glumly continued, "there is the influence of confirmed maidenhood." Bardeen mentioned in passing that he would not engage a man teacher "thirty-five years old without an adequate explanation of his being single"; and added, "but to a woman marriage is far more important; she must be a wife and mother to realize her possibilities."[41] Obviously suspecting the unmarried male teacher of homosexuality (though without saying so even in discreet French) and assuming that the unmarried woman teacher would be either unpleasantly nervous or aggressive, the superintendent was instantly put in mind of "the dilemma of the married woman" as a teacher. This classification did not quite do, either; if only, he exclaimed, all women teachers were widows! Widows, having had "experience," were not subject to the "mummification" that made of unmarried women teachers such poor examples of womanliness. The proof of the value of widows as teachers was, for Bardeen, not that they steadfastly continued in the profession, but that in his experience they were more likely to remarry than old maids were to marry at all.[36]

The superintendent found women, to say nothing of women

as teachers, a maddening conundrum, whether they were young or old, unmarried, married, or widowed. His reflections issued in random and somewhat hysterical exclamations. It occurred to him that women could not even vote or play baseball, from which circumstances he concluded that as teachers they are really most questionable. As a finale, he rounded on one of the key elements of the early propaganda for women as teachers, taking a witheringly negative view of the contention that their maternal instinct led them to a self-sacrificial, "Christian" kind of service to children. The truth of it was, in his opinion, just that "a woman does not grasp what a man means by a sense of honor."[37] If the connection seems unclear, he hastened to explain and in an ambivalent way to excuse it. Woman's obliviousness to honor was, he said, one of the sex characters that differentiated her from man; it was not a deficiency; he interpreted it rather as a function of her prime quality as a woman, the instinctive talent for uncritical sacrificial love—which subverted education.

Superintendent Bardeen's tirade was calmly answered by Harriet R. Pease, who noted the confusion of his argument and denied what was as near a central point as he made, the idea that marriage and childbirth are indispensable to female maturation. While assuming woman's natural superiority to man as a teacher, she acknowledged that students need teachers of both sexes. The most interesting aspect of her statement was the axiomatic tone in which she reasserted the line advanced by Catharine Beecher in the 1820s to the effect that teaching is a legitimate and healthy, indeed a divinely ordained, outlet for the maternal affections of childless women. The great weakness of the superintendent's indictment of the woman teacher was that he "ignores the mother love, that, deprived of personal treasures, expends itself freely on the larger group of other people's children."[38]

Over against the Chanticleer tones of the male school administrator may be placed those of Admiral F. E. Chadwick as an instance of the "tough-minded" man's man. He believed that the capacity for education beyond a simple level was rare and reasserted the conservative dogma that in the United States men were equal before the law but not otherwise. For most pupils, "book work" was a waste of time; "the main effort should be toward the training in character." His emphasis on character training as taking precedence over literary or intellectual training was verbally the same as that of Horace Mann but, amusingly, opposite in content. Feminization had seemed to Mann the necessary condition for securing emphasis on character, but the admiral meant by character "manliness in boys," which women teachers were sure to subvert, although of course they might sufficiently nurture "womanliness in girls."[39]

Admiral Chadwick's warnings against "the woman peril" elicited a response from Florence H. Hewitt, who, while apparently retaining affection for him as a late instance of a disappearing type, thought that he naively underestimated the situation. The feminizers had by no means lost sight of the subconscious, psychical influences; on the contrary, these were what had duly produced the feminized manhood of which the admiral complained. According to Florence Hewitt, "the all but hopelessly feminized men now in charge of our educational system are constitutionally incapacitated for taking Admiral Chadwick's view." The American mother, glorified since the collapse of paternalistic religion, was accomplishing the constitutional incapacitation of boys before they ever reached school, where to be sure the work was confirmed by women teachers. She said the country no longer had any ideal males after "generations of feminine tutelage" from the cradle to adulthood. The feminized (male) taxpayer revealed his condition, she thought, in his refusal to pay for men teachers. Although she saw the need for a balance of male and female influences on the young, she informed the admiral that "the American system has, unconsciously, recognized [maternal influence] as natural, and paralleled it in the schools by employing a large proportion of women teachers."[40] She thought it would be better if all except the youngest children could be well taught partly by men, but in the circumstances felt the only realistic policy was to prefer the able woman teacher over the inadequate man teacher.

Horace Mann would not have been happy with the idea of settling for less than the best teachers. He envisioned a much more splendid result to be accomplished by a feminized teaching corps under the direction of a quasi-priesthood of male administrators. Nothing less than the moral regeneration of the democracy was to be the work of the common schools, in which the maternal nature of woman was to be focused by male intellect and reinforced by male authority and the combined influences of the sexes brought to bear upon the education of the young. He expected that in time schools so staffed and administered would command the highest professional status, at least for the administrators. He found it expedient, however, to make use of, while deploring, the cheapness of female labor, which he could rationalize with respect to teachers by naming it a proof and consequence of the Christian, self-sacrificial nature of woman defined as essentially maternal. In the event, expediency prevailed as the Christian motive weakened in public education. The prestige of the (male) ministry, which the new schoolmen were meant to expropriate, declined; and the schoolmen never equaled it, even as it declined. The cheapness of women teachers tended to depress the market value of their male administrators, who never inherited the moral and intellectual leadership of the society as Mann hoped they would, and continued to discourage men from becoming teachers. The situation suited Demos, who had never been enthusiastic about being subjected to an educational system with real power to winnow the moral and intellectual chaff from the corn; democracy had brought education to terms by feminizing it.

Part III
The Evolution of Motherteacher

Chapter 7

From Normalite to Motherteacher

AMONG the consequences of his educational reforms, none would have startled Horace Mann more than the metamorphosis of the stereotype of the female teacher from the normalite, as he conceived her, to what I am calling Motherteacher by considered analogy to a popular obscenity. The most characteristic elements of his educational theory and the expedients he adopted to put his theory into practice, especially his advocacy of woman as teacher, in which theory and expediency coalesced, were co-opted by the very democratic social forces he wished to control and newly rationalized by adaptations of the process philosophies and the doctrine of evolution in biology that so preoccupied the latter half of the nineteenth century. Phrenology, respectable enough when Mann adopted its tenets, provided a supposedly scientific developmental account of human nature that suited Mann's religious and educational predilections, which Demos shared in his rounder, more vulgar terms. The next generation, however, found more impressive rationalization for these predilections in philosophy of Hegelian inspiration and in Darwinism, which tended to render Christian moralism, the central concern of Mann's pedagogy of love, irrelevant and to alter the idea of the female teacher accordingly.

The qualities, purposes, and functions thought proper for the teacher are derived fundamentally from convictions as to the character, capacities, and needs of the child in relation to socialization and, beyond that, to a cosmology. According to the romantic and democratic views of the nineteenth century, the child was tacitly the male child and, as Wordsworth described him, father to the man: closer to his divine origin, the child was the purer stage of (male) humanity. The idea of the child as father to the man perfectly implied superiority in the child and presumptuousness in the man who dealt with the child authoritatively. The normalite was an American response to this new perception of the child to which had been added, by authority of an orthodox divine, Horace Bushnell, the doctrine that the child had been created to grow "organically" into Christian grace and so required of the teacher chiefly nurture. Convictions about child, i.e., human male, nature continued to change in the new direction. The normalite, therefore, proved to be a temporary definition of the teacher which was modified as a function of the changing idea of the child.

The normalite was still an expression of the responsibilities of woman within the traditional scheme, not a feminist expression of the rights of woman per se. This consorted well with the Bushnellian doctrine of Christian nurture and saved the Christian pretensions of the "new light" pedagogy of love. The goal of education remained Christian; theoretically, only its methods and personnel changed, just in order to make more certain that the goal was reached. The child was still perceived as needing, on peril of his soul, vigorous encouragement and example and constant appeal to every appropriate motive in order to realize the best and overcome the worst that was in him. No doubt the odds had been adjusted in the child's favor as compared with any assessment that Jonathan Edwards or Nathanael Emmons would have been prepared to offer. No doubt the saved Christian person whom the normalite was expected to help on the way was a good deal other than the recipient of God's mysterious grace, escaped from His richly deserved wrath. No doubt he was reduced in practice to a nineteenth-century paragon of unitarian respectability, very like Horace Mann. But that was still a standard external to the child and a demanding one, toward which his conscience, properly nurtured by the normalite, must propel him.

As a responsible moral agent within this scheme, the normalite was forceful, a bender of the twigs. It is only over against the standards of a Joseph Hale that her standards may seem less than demanding or her methods less than powerful. Hers might not be the hand that could wield the rod even if she wished, but her hand was reinforced by the male principals of the renovated teaching profession. We are discussing, after all, the New England school marm. Does anyone remember her as weak or irresponsible toward moral and social requirements? If she had not done so already, she proved her mettle in the Reconstruction of the South. Though she may often have cut a comic or exasperating figure there, she was nonetheless effectual as an agent of the imperial victorious half of the nation and a standard-bearer, as she had been already for twenty years in the West, of the bloodily affirmed manifest destiny of the nation under the hegemony of the North.

In the meantime, however, influences were at work that tended to discredit the external standards, whether generally Christian or specifically academic, to which the teacher might hold the child. The new value attributed to the child was magnified until it actually outweighed the value of adulthood. The child of the romantic poets, the optimistic seers, and the democratic ideologues was held to be nearer perfection than the adult. Insofar as this was felt to be the case, the telic character of teaching was subverted and the way prepared for insistence upon the process of education as valuable just as process, without reference to prescribed results. If the human ideal was relocated prior to the educational process, every pupil was in a position to make as little or as much of it as might suit his antinomian preferences. As for the teacher, she—and the gender change accomplished with the emergence of the normalite of course proved lasting—had committed herself to love as her professional principle in place of authority and power to enforce it.

Gradually, the teacher's method of love, reinforced chiefly by her personal moral example, preempted the end to which it was supposed to lead. She could only love the child as he was rather than as he might become. The goal of responsible (Christian) adulthood no longer organized the educational process. The image of the prelapsarian child now determined the goal, or rather whether there should be a determined goal, of education. Wherever these circumstances appeared, the normalite was turning into Motherteacher, and the analogy weakened between the idea of the common school and the lost common prayer.

The very concept of mothering changed. As perceived in the fireside education movement, the doctrine of Christian nurture, and Catharine Beecher's theory of the profession of woman, mothering was directive. Perhaps it inherited something of the Puritan desire for early conversion and therefore continued to value precocity, so that the child might be hurried through the hazards of innocence into the comparative safety of instructed maturity. Association with children was no doubt often pleasant or amusing, but the mother did not blink the duty, the drudgery, the boredom in it. The appeal of childhood was more apparent to maternal instinct, people felt, than to the unbiased adult mind.

The supposed female propensity for self-sacrifice caused woman to subordinate her own interests as an adult person to the interests of others, especially children. In so doing, she of course further subordinated her interests to those of the men whom her service to the young freed for more personally gratifying activities. The sacrifice expected of her was real sacrifice, the pains and frustrations of which were tolerable only by the grace of maternal instinct and justifiable only on the grounds that, like the sacrifice of Jesus Christ, it ransomed souls. In thinking of the mother as the minister of the home, one should sometimes employ the sense of "rector" of the home to connote a regulative element.

Although there was in it from the beginning a fatal tendency to sentimentality, the idea of the normalite had antecedents in this sterner conception of maternal love. The professional sacrifice the female teacher was expected to make as her part in the cure of souls consisted of acquiescence in low wages and also just in enduring, for their sake, the company of the young and having to cater to their needs. The mother, if she was a good mother, might look forward to weaning and the first day of school as second and third deliveries, good for the child but not less a relief to her. Similarly, the normalite, as a teacher motherly in the sense described above, might properly look forward to graduation day. For the wife, a new pregnancy and, for the normalite, a new class of first-graders meant fresh sacrifices that might frankly and realistically be accounted such.

The element of realism about children in the original idea of the normalite is further attested by the circumstance that she was expected to deal in her maternalistic fashion only with prepubertal children. The extension of mothering beyond the home, the dame school, and the summer school was envisaged, at first, with the provisos that it be limited to young children and used to condition their more rapid and lasting growth to maturity according to a prescribed model. The normalite's emphasis on moral rather than intellectual training was not intended as derogation of the latter but as an improved means of making sure that intellectual development, including socialization, when its season arrived, would be thorough. As the embodiment of a protobehavioristic philosophy of education, the normalite was expected to accomplish better through love, or the positive reinforcement of desirable tendencies in her pupils, what the traditional schoolmaster sought to accomplish through authority backed with force.

The normalite meant to nurture automotive conscience as the guarantee of adult Christian character and preventive of anarchy in an individualistic democracy. The old regime of emulation and punishment was held to be productive of pride and envy, on the one hand, or of rebelliousness, on the other: the very works of the devil. In short, though representing enlarged claims for mothering, the normalite was not child-centered, except insofar as maternal sympathy with the young enabled her to bring them on efficiently in the direction of an ideal of adulthood.

Nevertheless, the extension of mothering from home to school involved softening the adult approach to pupils and delaying the application of adult (external) standards—indeed involved redefinition of adult standards. The recognition and, soon enough, glorification of childhood for which the nineteenth century is famous rested upon a developmental theory of human nature. The ascription of positive value to the successive stages of human growth and development implied reduction in the value ascribed to the ultimate stage of adulthood. This was the case even if value was only democratically parceled out among the several phases, but the nineteenth century tended to ascribe greater value to childhood, considering it the uncorrupted quintessentially human stage, than to maturity.

As parents and teachers were persuaded that their duty was to study the child and adapt their demands to the child's "interests"—its spontaneously expressive movements—the child's duty to study a prescribed curriculum decreased. The normalite's pedagogy of love already priced autonomous, internal motives above external standards and enforcement, and "self-activity" in the pupil was increasingly posited as the necessary condition of learning. Add, as in time the nineteenth century did, reasons for assuming that the child was better qualified to select as well as to motivate his own activities than the adults in authority over him, and the last condition needed to transform the normalite into Motherteacher was in play.

I believe the most telling change was the weakening of the idea of womanly self-sacrifice as the key qualification of woman as teacher. With the ascription of value not only positive but higher than adult values to childhood and youth, the teacher's sacrifice began to be accounted privilege. Instead of being seen as an adult specially graced by her sex to endure tedious association with children, the female teacher was perceived as empathetic with children and happy to be among them. A large part of the normalite's professional self-sacrifice was the abundant patience required to persuade pupils to conform themselves to the curriculum and thus to change themselves from worse to better. If the child was thought to be all right to begin with, possessed of an integrity that must not be violated, and if—as soon happened—he was expected to change in his own good time according to the laws of his own nature, the teacher was less and less authorized to specify the changes or insist on them in any given sequence or at any given rate. She became less the agent of the prescribed adulthood pupils must achieve and more one of them, supportive and compassionate rather than critical and directive.

So long, however, as the female teacher worked only with prepubertal children, this tendency was automatically limited; the definitive transformation into Motherteacher waited upon the further extension of mothering, perceived as supportive and nondirective, to secondary and higher education. The feminization of education is still defined here basically in quantitative terms, with reference to the staffing of public high schools when they multiplied after the Civil War. The majority of women on high school faculties became nearly as absolute as on elementary school faculties and was effectually 100 percent in most of the subjects, most notably in English, with a minority of men concentrated in mathematics and the natural sciences (the male teachers of these subjects often doubling, however, as coaches and administrators with the prospect of being promoted out of teaching altogether). Dealing now with adolescent and older pupils on a basis of specialization in intellectual subjects, the female teacher was well beyond her supposed sex-specific competence as a general moral influence upon young pupils. The element of compassionate, supportive mothering in her approach was described increasingly not as a biological feminine character but as a professional aspect of teaching regardless of the sex of the teacher. Formal education thus came to depend upon professional skill in establishing personal relationships with pupils, with their self-asserted interests or lack thereof paramount, as if the one did not tend to contradict the other.

This development toward pupil-centeredness may be traced in the successive changes in the idea of the child and the correlative idea of the teacher which characterized the most influential normal schools. These included, first, the Massachusetts normals as shaped by Horace Mann; then the Oswego, New York, State Normal and Training School under Edward Austin Sheldon; then the Cook County, Illinois, Normal School under Francis W. Parker; next Clark University during the presidency of G. Stanley Hall; and finally the apotheosis of the normal school, Teachers College of Columbia University, a more complex institution than the others where, if a single figure may be emphasized, William H. Kilpatrick was most significant in a succession of educators who contributed to the evolution of Motherteacher. During the period from about 1840 to 1920 when teacher training and professionalism were being developed under the leadership of these institutions, Americans appropriated and adapted the ideas and methods of a number of European educators, above all Pestalozzi, Froebel, and Herbart.

In addition, Americans were influenced by European thinkers of higher power, Hegel and Darwin, in the rationalization of democratic education. Operating at a much more theoretical and philosophical level than the normal school principals and professors, the most important adapter of Hegelianism to American education was William Torrey Harris, while the most important adapter of evolutionary theory was G. Stanley Hall. These strains were synthesized and transformed in the pragmatism of John Dewey, to whom Kilpatrick stood in a relation like that of Harris to Hegel or Hall to Darwin while simultaneously popularizing the doctrine, now the complete doctrine of Motherteaching, in the huge classes he conducted at Teachers College.

The Oswego Movement in American education occurred during the principalship of Edward Austin Sheldon at the Oswego State Normal and Training School from 1861 to 1886. It echoed and amplified the themes of Horace Mann's common school revival in Massachusetts, modulating them toward new conceptions. A generation younger than Mann, Sheldon resembled him in important respects, altered just by the differences a generation would make. The similarity and the difference are evident in the approaches the two made to the treatment of religion in the schools. Both took the goal of education to be religious and thought the schools must assume the work of the church in promoting common cultural and spiritual values. Mann, however, was part of the final difficult change in New England from piety to moralism and had to fight the churches in order to secure the inculcation of his nonsectarian "religion of heaven" by the agency of the normalite. Not merely Unitarians but people still regarding themselves as orthodox had, by Sheldon's day, come to accept "the state as the truly catholic realm because it was the ethical and moral realm." In helping to emphasize "moralism and patriotism in the state-supported schools," the Oswego Movement sought to make the schools "the 'catholic' church of the people of America and the moral identity of the body politic."[1] Sheldon no more than Mann thought of secularization as desirable in education but helped bring it about, for the schools inevitably reflected and were put to the service of the controlling state.

Again, like Mann, Sheldon was attracted by the ideas of Pestalozzi, which provided an authoritative rationalization for predilections he already shared with most of his countrymen. Pestalozzi was more distinctly the presiding genius at Oswego than he had been in the early days of the Massachusetts normals. Pestalozzianism was the aspect of the Prussian school system that most attracted Mann, but his unitarian and phrenological attitudes were more in play. Sheldon imported English apostles of Pestalozzi to help organize the curriculum and set the tone at Oswego. The chief article of the faith there was "object-teaching," derived from Pestalozzi, which seems to have been a confused and inconsistent method whose devotees were as much opposed to the textbook and the old education it symbolized as they were enamored of any particular or systematic use of objects. The underlying point was the child-centered character of object-teaching, in which the child was supposed to be "led" through the exercise of his "faculties" to general moral and intellectual competence. Once he had achieved this, he might direct his own education. This variety of what nowadays is called permissive education provoked in the town of Oswego a reaction in favor of what nowadays would be called a return to the fundamentals, as later varieties of ever more permissive education provoked ever weaker reactions. Graduates of the Oswego normal were soon widely distributed through the country, and other normal schools followed in its train.[2]

In emphasizing both missionary moralism and Pestalozzian methods, the Oswego Movement tended to make the incompatibility inherent in the two more apparent and to make it likely one would give way to the other in the normalite. She could be permissive only up to a point if her basic job was to develop conformity to a code of conduct. As the metamorphosis of Calvinist piety into moralism might lead one to expect, it was the missionary moralism that weakened in the normalite; but enough of it remained to put a respectable face on pedagogic permissivism. The latter, in fact, itself borrowed a creedal tone and became the self-consistent philosophy of Motherteacher.

Sheldon, like Mann, thought of himself not as an apostate but as an improved model Puritan, supporting Unitarian doctrine "as the best version of the old faith." In its extreme tolerance and its ethical, social emphasis, Unitarianism approved of the transfer of responsibility for education from church to state and "helped materially to make the school the new established church of the realm, the mother-teacher-savior of the flock."[3] The Oswego Movement not only did much to popularize this conception of the school but contributed a great deal to the professional training of Motherteacher as celebrant of its rites—Motherteacher in her several orders, with male administrators in charge and female teachers as their handmaidens, all avowing the same creed. But something, after all, was missing: a focus of worship; and this proved to be the child, implicitly the male child as the teacher was implicitly female or feminized.

The divinization of the child expressed native inclinations of long standing for which new grounds were imported during the last half of the nineteenth century from European, especially from German, philosophers, psychologists, and educators. The holiness imputed to the child was in part a sentimental extension of native democratic and individualistic self-esteem but also had, as has been explained, native theological sanctions in the doctrine of Christian nurture, in the Unitarian doctrine of infant innocence, and in Horace Mann's religion of Heaven comprising elements of Christianity held to be common to all Christian sects. Americans imbued with the secularized Puritan ethic were ready to accept any philosophy that presented the universe as changing for the better, any psychology that presented human nature as fundamentally good and part of universal progress, any educational scheme that purported to provide practical methods of insuring and hastening improvement.

In Herbart, Hegel, Pestalozzi, Froebel, and Wundt—to extend the roll call of leading figures—Americans found much to their purpose and tended to overlook what was not. They liked speculation and assertion about the world as dynamic process and about human growth and development as the epitome of it but shied away from definition of ends or goals, since the latter implied control of process. Open-ended change, change for its own sake was what they wanted to believe in, and they incorporated this as an article of faith in the pedagogic creed.

When Friedrich Froebel died in 1852, he was a prophet without honor in his native Prussia but felt prophetically that his *kindergarten* principles would be vindicated in America, as Hegel had felt America would be the scene where the dialectic of history would produce the next expression of the "concrete universal." American readiness for Froebel is exemplified in Elizabeth Peabody, who is of added interest here because of her association with Horace Mann before and during the common school revival in Massachusetts. She hoped to marry Mann, and her sister Mary did marry him. A devotee or associate at various times of Bronson Alcott, William Ellery Channing, and Ralph Waldo Emerson as well as of Mann, she had before 1840 absorbed and given a turn of her own to every attitude and belief required in the definition of the kindergartener as she eventually learned it from Froebel's work about 1860. The kindergartener and the normalite were sister types. Froebel's work organized with the éclat of German authority the sort of educational claims and methods she had espoused as early as 1834, when she became Bronson Alcott's assistant in the Temple School.

Elizabeth Peabody started a kindergarten and became probably the most effectual of early kindergarten propagandists. To the audiences that attended her lectures, she asserted that she felt *"Divinely authorized* to present him [Froebel] to you as an authority which you can reverently trust." On either God's or Froebel's authority she magnified the child in Wordsworth's phrases as a "seer blest" who came "trailing clouds of glory . . . from God" and was, therefore, not so much to be taught as religiously served by the teacher. For, she said, "kindergartening" was "true education . . . a religion . . . a vocation from on High."[4] The teacher's vocation was not to impose adult categories upon the child; the child garden was an environment favorable for growth of children according to their innate principles.

The horticultural imagery hinted at dimensions beyond the commoner imagery of maternity. A school imaged as womb or as home implicitly looked to a delivery of the child. Imaged as a garden, it carried connotations of Eden, so that *kindergarten* translated easily into *The Paradise of Childhood*, as in the title of a book by Edward Wiebe published in 1869 as a manual for kindergarteners. Departure in this context was no longer desirable. Who would wish to leave Eden? It was also tempting to think of extending the boundaries of the kindergarten through a sort of Edenic imperialism to include higher levels of education, so that nobody really had to leave.

From Froebel came the assurance that the child's growth was literally creative in the sense that it was a divinely ordained process expressing the child's direct participation in the Absolute. Such doctrine harmonized with native attitudes, above all with Emerson's pantheistic paeans to individualism, self-reliant because of the divine element in every American. The "creativity" and "self-expression" so much touted to this day in our schools at all levels testify to the pervasiveness of the kindergarten model. To "teach" a roomful of "creative people," or simply of "people"—the word uttered in an ineffably sentimental tone—whether five or twenty-five years old, remains a hatefully un-American thing. At most, Motherteacher seeks to "communicate."

Froebel struck the keynote in one of his Mother Songs avowing,

> Dear Little children, we will learn from you.

Kindergarteners and soon, by extension, all teachers of the

evolving Motherteacher type were assigned these sentiments in regard to their relation to pupils:

> Gardens we'll make, and you the flowers shall be;
> Our care shall seem no tedious drudgery—
> Only a happy trust that's ever new.[5]

Through the horticultural imagery, Catharine Beecher's and Horace Mann's self-sacrificial female teacher, the normalite, is to be seen transformed. Instead of helping their charges to control their evil and encourage their virtuous tendencies and thus regulate their relationship to a severe God, the kindergartener was to assume all tendencies blest and God's presence within.

The ultimate touch is Froebel's putting into the mouths of adult (female) teachers the grateful acknowledgement that, through privileged association with the divinely planned young, they might themselves retain or retrieve a measure of infantilism themselves. Continued growth, the definitive aspect of youth, was becoming the shibboleth for all ages. The kindergartener was thus much less the model of moral, to say nothing of intellectual, maturity, and less authoritative even than the normalite.

Froebel has been interpreted by a critic of our own day as having defined evil just as "faulty education which interferes with the fundamental nature and direction of the cosmic process," which the child spontaneously "expresses" if not repressed.[6] Given a cosmos characterized as process, not even the following generation of kindergarteners who might themselves have been kindergartened could prescribe and enforce a curriculum, for the rising generation would still express a further and higher stage of the cosmic process. Acknowledging that there might be at least some elements of inherited culture that the young should know, Froebel nevertheless supplied a further reason for being casual about the curriculum: "For the purpose of teaching and instruction is to bring ever more *out* of man rather than to put more and more *into* him; for that which can get *into* man we already know and possess as the property of mankind, and every one, simply because he is a human being, will unfold and develop it out of himself in accordance with the laws of mankind."[7]

A teacher whose forte was compassionate admiration of childhood as it was must have had new and stronger reasons than those with which Horace Mann endowed the normalite for deprecating the importance of inculcating "mere knowledge" in her pupils. She must, in consequence, have had less reason for acquiring a great deal herself. She could have no faith in the logic of whatever subjects she taught as the source of teaching method or the basis for judging the results of her teaching. Instead of increments in knowledge and skill, she was to look primarily for evidences of continuing growth, in both her pupils and herself, toward undefinable and ever receding stages on the way to the millennium.

Froebelianism, as summed up at the end of the nineteenth century, advanced the following as principles:

self-activity, to produce development; all-sided *connectedness* and unbroken *continuity,* to help the right acquisition of knowledge; *creativeness,* or expressive activity, to produce assimilation of knowledge, growth of power, and acquisition of skill; well-ordered physical *activity,* to develop the physical body and its powers; and *happy and harmonious surroundings,* to foster and help all these. If a school, therefore, includes amongst its aims the true acquisition of knowledge—as distinct from the more or less temporary possession of information—and with this the development of power and the production of skill—and most schools at least profess to do so—it follows at once that the school must look to these same principles for guidance and help, unless it denies their efficacy altogether, or holds that the life of a human being is a series of discontinuous separate existences, the natural laws of which differ for each successive existence.[8]

The connotations of this terminology are strikingly of the womb, of what about the time the passage was published Freud described as polymorphous perversity, of masturbation; and the advocacy of this condition, this attitude, and this activity was here explicitly extended beyond kindergarten to the rest of education. Having long since rejected hierarchical education organized from above, Americans felt their prejudices flattered by any impressive philosophy of education that allowed for influence from the bottom up. They did not mean to be shaped by an elite, they meant to prevent the development of an elite at all.

Froebel himself thought the kindergarten ought to shape the school. American devotees assumed that kindergarten principles should be paradigmatic for all education. Nina C. Vandewalker, a figure in the mature Americanized movement after the turn of the century, delivered the following matter-of-fact summary of the Froebelian law and the prophets: "That education is a process of development rather than a process of instruction; that play is the natural means of development during the early years; that the child's creative activity must be the main factor in his education; and that his present interests and needs rather than the demands of the future should determine the material and method employed,—all these principles underlying kindergarten procedure the psychologist approved, not for kindergarten alone, but for all education."[9]

The generic "psychologist" who approved, according to Nina Vandewalker, the extension of kindergarten princples to all education was most closely identifiable with William James and G. Stanley Hall, and it will be essential to consider the influence of experimental and genetic psychology in the development of Motherteacher. First, however, one should consider the influence stemming from an earlier psychologist and another German, Johann Friedrich Herbart, the successor of Kant at Königsberg.

Dead in 1841, Herbart did not become a major influence on American educators until the 1890s. They found congenial his view that education must be directed primarily to moral development, and he provided a welcome change of emphasis by defining this in social rather than religious terms. Morality, according to Herbart, was "a matter of adjustment of the individual to society." Americans also found to their taste Herbart's "fundamental postulate," namely "the plasticity, or educability of the pupil."[10]

By choosing certain elements in Herbart, avoiding certain connections, and failing to draw certain conclusions, majoritarian democrats could rationalize first one and then the other of the contradictory aspects of the "soft line" in education without giving up either or coming to an impasse. The idea that social adjustment might properly be the purpose of education flattered the belief in the correctness of the majority and in the majority as standing for society. But majoritarian democrats also feel that each individual has a right to his own way, so that social adjustment is only adjustment to a changing society without inconveniently fixed principles.

It happened that Herbart provided, in addition to his social emphasis, a complex theory of apperception from which he derived an educational principle, namely, that "interest" is the basic condition for educability. By this he meant that a pupil is able to learn only what his previous experience has equipped him to learn or desire to know; new percepts are attainable if they relate to elements of what nowadays is termed the "apperceptive mass," that is, the accumulated experience and knowledge existing in the learner. The pedagogical implications of this doctrine seemed clear and persuasive to American educators. They descend to us in such a truism as "you have to take the student from where he is" and help in justifying forgiveness of failure to master subjects.

But in Herbart's German the term which is translated into English as *interest* does not seem to carry the same connotations as the English term, and I suspect that American Herbartians tended to be enthusiastic about just the connotations that would have been most surprising to Herbart. He seems to have meant that, in order to learn, the learner must be an interested party, someone already possessed of a share in what is to be learned sufficient both to motivate him and to provide necessary links. Americans, however, tended to equate "interest" with spontaneous inclinations of pupils, their "likes," and were ready to excuse them from meeting academic standards if they lacked inclination and their dislikes seemed sufficiently spontaneous. "Not only must education be adjusted in ends and means to the society in which we live," wrote the leading Herbartian, Charles De Garmo, "but it must also be adjusted to the individual to be educated."[11] This observation was directed to secondary education; the double adjustment of education, to the changing preferences of democratic society on the one hand and to the interests of the individual pupil on the other, was incompatible with the subject-centeredness of the high school.

The Herbartians found in the master two further psychological doctrines that served to rationalize the educational antinomianism of the pupil and the corresponding degradation of the curriculum and diminution of authority in the teacher. Herbart, long before Freud, stressed the dominance of the unconscious; and he cast doubt upon the notion of psychological faculties that might be trained, per se. De Garmo interpreted the pupil's "interest" as "a feeling that accompanies the idea of self-expression."[12] Intellectuality or the mind was conceived as governed by and expressive of the unconscious and the racial heritage rather than as something that could be developed and formed by willed exercise. The Herbartians thought of mind as a force that might work to evil as well as to good and of social pressure as the means of rendering it moral. Social conformity took precedence over academic or intellectual accomplishment in the Herbartian educational program, which thus reflected an ingenuous faith in the rightness and stability of democratic social norms.

One of the most specific effects the Herbartians had on the curriculum and, therefore, on the idea of the pupil and of the teacher was to weaken further the old credit of mental faculties. Mistaken though the faculty psychology may have been, it served to insure, by means of the corollary belief in the transfer of training, respect for "hard" subjects. These were exemplified by Latin and mathematics, which, however impractical they seemed, could be justified on the ground that they "trained the mind." Once past parsing Caesar, Cicero, and Virgil, and once all the answers had been found in the back of the algebra book, a student was assured he would think straighter in all the affairs of life. In exploding this contention, the Herbartians unfortunately overlooked further aspects of the situation.

Latin and algebra had, after all, intrinsic values; they symbolized the value of meeting an external standard by overcoming personal disinclination as necessary; and they were constituents of common education which, once discredited, were not replaced with anything more defensible. Training and experience in Latin and algebra were, if not literally transferable to other subjects, important as touchstones of academic integrity. This can be experienced only in particular subjects, whether Latin, algebra, or some other that is sufficiently "hard" to require the pupil to work disinterestedly. Herbartian criticism of the concept of the transfer of training tended to make stronger the case for the indispensability of the pupil's interest as the criterion whereby the curriculum should be determined or left undetermined. It was easy for teachers to mistake caprice for interest and, conversely, to overestimate a negative attitude as evidence of real incapacity or lack of "readiness."

Herbartianism tended to subvert education according to the impersonal and objective principles and social desirability of whatever was taught, whether the subject was called academic or vocational. The relationship between teacher and pupil was rendered more casual, personal, less professional, and less mediated by the exigencies of the subjects taught and so less accessible to rational assessment. With the waning of religious consensus in society, no customary and unexamined source of authority was available to validate the claims of any particular subject matter or sequence of subjects. Even the claims of literacy were reduced by the decline of biblicism. The difficult business, by no means accomplished today, of conscious, deliberate choice and commitment had begun.

Motherteacher embodied, in part, an adaptation to this cultural situation in which any teacher who sought to act authoritatively in terms of subjects taught lacked a context in which to do so. Subject-centered teaching exposed the teacher to attack by parents and pupils for authoritarianism, since Americans were ever ready to interpret academic authoritativeness as an outrageous personal presumptuousness, and by administrative superiors—with their sensitivity to popular attitudes—for insubordination. Teachers in general, especially the normal-trained ones, were in fact not sufficiently well educated to be authoritative, and their loyalty had never been bespoken by the subjects they taught in the first place.

In the meantime, the outright glorification of the child as the palladium of teacher training was preached in the most unqualified rhetoric and amplified through the land by Francis W. Parker. He, too, received impetus from Germany, *gemütlich* Germany, during a stay from 1872 to 1875, but his were largely native wood-notes wild. On returning from study in Germany, he instituted reforms in the schools of Quincy, Massachusetts. After several years as a school supervisor in Boston, he assumed in 1883 his most influential position, principal of the Cook County Normal School in Chicago. In 1899 he became the first director of the School of Education at the University of Chicago. During the 1890s his impact on John Dewey was considerable. Parker's *Talks on Pedagogics,* based on Chautauqua lectures delivered in 1891 and published in 1894, is one of the authentic books of the bible of Motherteacher.

"The child," Parker declared, "is the climax and culmination of all God's creations, and to answer the question 'What is the child?' is to approach nearer the still greater question, 'What is the Creator and Giver of Life.'"[13] In school, according to Parker, the child must be reverently left free to do his, not the teacher's, will on the principle that "the spontaneous tendencies of the child are the records of inborn divinity."[14] One senses his identification with the child: I can find no passage in which he explained why the teacher, who must have once been a child, was credited with no records of inborn divinity herself that might deserve at least some attention. Parker was at any rate apparently susceptible to a certain confusion about his own identity. He was perfectly certain, however, that "God made the child His highest creation, [that] He put into that child His divinity, and that this divinity manifests itself in the seeking for truth through the visible and tangible."[15]

The truth Parker supposed the child to be seeking by the aid of his divinely implanted compass went undefined; but Parker believed that it was the child, not the teacher, who could recognize the truth whatever it turned out to be. Each child must be an arbiter of truth. Education could not be accomplished by means of a prescribed curriculum designed to inculcate testable knowledge or information. "The working out of the design of a human being into character is education," said Parker, meaning, of course, God's design incarnate in each child.[16]

And so teaching, according to Parker, was "the presentation of external conditions for educative self-effort."[17] This was what he called "quality" teaching, which in one place he would say was professional application of the "science of education" but in another an "art"; on the whole it was the "artist teacher" he seemed most taken with. Quality teaching stood in magnificent contrast to outmoded and wickedly misguided "quantity" teaching, which so overrated "mere knowledge" and set such store by the curriculum, that Procrustean bed to which divine children were cruelly fitted.

Parker regarded the child as the ablest and most perspicuous of students prior to any vagaries of the curriculum-planner or ministrations of the teacher. The child "studies" anthropology, he stated, beginning with his naive family relationships. He should be recognized as a zoologist: is not his pet cat to him "a thing of beauty and a joy forever"? He has standing as a botanist, for the farm boy indisputably "comes in direct contact with worm-wood, sorrel, rag-weed." And so on for history, physics, meteorology, geology, mineralogy ("especially upon a rocky farm"), geography.[18] By means of the divine afflatus, the child spontaneously begins "the whole round of knowledge" just "because it breathes, it lives." The teacher, therefore, "should recognize the great dignity of the child, the child's divine power and divine possibilities"—specifically as a student, among all his other capacities—and then "present the conditions for their complete outworking." "If the child loves science and history, and studies or attends to them instinctively, then he should go on, and we must know the conditions or subjects and means which should be presented to him for each new demand or need."[19]

The American common school, as soon as it should be properly staffed by quality teachers, from Cook County if possible, was in Parker's propaganda the institution which could be relied on to bring about the realization of democratic

America's manifest destiny. Already this destiny extended to global moral imperialism, as a sort of monstrous metamorphosis from the Edenic imperialism of the kindergarteners. Parker asserted that the American citizen "should say in his heart: 'I await the regeneration of the world from the teaching of the common schools of America.' " All that stood in the way of this regeneration was "tradition and its methods," which he anathematized as aristocratic and still to be rooted out.[20]

And what did this man, in whom so much of the popular ideology came to application in the profession of teaching, think the fully developed common school would be like once the people were "ready to move, to demand that the methods of quantity shall go, and the methods of quality shall come"? He visualized it thus:

> A school should be a model home, a complete community and embryonic democracy. How? you ask. Again I answer, by putting into every schoolroom an educated, cultured, trained, devoted, child-loving teacher, a teacher imbued with a knowledge of the science of education, and a zealous, enthusiastic application of its principles. Where shall we find such teachers? They will spring from the earth and drop from the clouds when they *hear the demand*. We have asked for quantity teachers, and they have come by the tens of thousands. Now, let us demand the *artist teacher*, the teacher trained and skilled in the science of education—a genuine leader of little feet.[21]

Parker was the prophet destined for vindication with the passage of time. It remained only to work out a somewhat more convincing rationalization than he was capable of producing for the child-centered, nondirective kind of teaching he preached to the receptive ears of Demos. Not that Demos had not an inexhaustible tolerance for inconsistencies, just as Emerson had advised, in the argument that he had been right and good at birth and might expect to develop admirable character if only his spontaneous inclinations were reverently studied and brought to expression. But his still new and insecure class of professional educators felt the need of a persuasive, or at least an esoteric, rationale that would buttress the dogmas of the goodness of human nature and the inevitability of its growth toward perfection. For them, Parker's inspirational hymns to the divine child were a trifle infra dig in tone though not in doctrine.

The more scholarly educational leaders had broken with Christian tradition though they might still profess Christian belief personally and continue the honorific use of Christian terminology. They sought to supply the new education with credentials from philosophy and science. The two most useful sources of materials for the construction of a substitute tradition were Hegelian philosophy and evolutionist biology, both of which not only contained elements that seemed to many continuous with or supplemental to the Christian scheme but also, as J. H. Plumb as observed, provided in "their fundamental dynamic, their belief in development, in change, in an ultimate destiny" prestigious modern backing for the prevalent faith in progress. There were also elements in both that were incompatible with the new education, for example, the notion of the Absolute in Hegel's philosophy of history and the inhumane aspects of "social Darwinism." Nevertheless, Hegel's idea of history as a dialectical process was congenial, while Darwinism seemed to provide the facts that proved progress and "gave a powerful structure to the past, seemingly scientific and not mythical," which was "usable in the totally new contexts of early industrial society."[22]

The Hegelian movement in American education was the more problematical ally of the soft line in education, and the leading Hegelian, William Torrey Harris, was its most formidable critic. In many respects, he stood in contrast to Parker, whose views he often contradicted and implicitly ridiculed. Not for Harris the idea that the teacher must be led by the child. He espoused a classical curriculum and, taking it for granted that "the immature mind of youth" is incapable of making wise choices, did not hesitate to assert that "the wisdom of his instructors," who "know the wants of the pupil and the best mode of supplying them," must be the guide of youth.[23] By the "wants" of the pupil, he meant, not the pupil's desires or interests, but his lacks and deficiencies which must be supplied from without by an authoritative teacher.

Harris made the distinction between nature in general and human nature on idealist and humanistic grounds, thus going against the fundamental emphasis of evolutionism upon continuity. As to the child's spontaneous interest, he bluntly characterized it as "caprice" that "destroys the work of one moment by that of the next. It is only *self-consistent* activity that can be free. . . . What is done through caprice will be controlled by accident." He held that the civilized human being was a product of culture, which could not be learned and assimilated by accident and was not inherent in the individual. Contrary to the concerted prejudices of romanticism, liberal religion, democracy, and optimistic evolutionism, Harris held culture superior to nature. It was the creation and heritage of mind transcendent over nature, requiring intellectual initiation and cultivation of the individual in order that he might live humanely. Harris was thus at odds with the vogue for the primitive and instinctive, his eye more upon the maturation of the individual than upon the evolution of the race.[24]

In spite of the difference in tone between the egregious Parker and the imposing Harris, who had an international reputation as a philosopher, they were not totally opposed in their attitudes. They had Americanism in common, which tended to render inoperative the Hegelian caveats and to excuse the Parkerian absurdities. Americans were attracted to Hegel in part because he "always viewed revolutionary America as the land of the future" and thought "American civilization was a supreme example of what he called 'the concrete universal' expressing itself in the very founding of a civilization in the wilderness."[25] Hegel's system seemed to offer reassurance at the time when the inner contradictions of American society were about to explode in civil war. Harris and Henry C. Brokmeyer started the St. Louis Movement in 1858. They could glory in the Eads bridge, flung across the Mississippi from their frontier city to manifest destiny in the West, as a symbol of their Hegelian faith.

It must, however, have been a comfort in that year to subscribe to a philosophy holding that out of the inevitable clash of antitheses a transcendent synthesis, incorporating the old conflicting elements in a situation inevitably better than the past, must emerge. "Hegelianism was a philosophy of unbounded optimism born out of a virtually infinite series of desperate situations, and it thrived on clashes and confrontations—the fierce contradictions of teeming, ever-changing life."[26] It was a recipe for progressive compromise and consensus and applied to education as well as to other affairs.

Hegel's doctrine of the self and individual freedom, while it implied rejection of the Herbartians' doctrine of interest, offered at least certain slogans which, if left unanalyzed, could be popular with all educational sects. Heavy emphasis was given the self and its development, and of course that was appealing. In the Hegelians' view, "The self as pure being was nothing. . . . the individual could define himself only through past experiences or future expectations . . . and characterize himself only in relation to other individuals or events and hence he took on his identity through a process of identification with the 'other.' " Through interaction between self and other a series of syntheses was thought to occur, always in the direction of improvement, which could be interpreted uncritically as equivalent to "growth" or "unfoldment." The Hegelians described "true freedom" and "true self-definition" as the results of "an ever-widening series of social and institutional relationships." They could subscribe to the view, which Demos could easily mistake as flattering to himself, that "the function of the world was to define the individual." And they postulated "self-activity" as not only possible but necessary in the attainment of freedom, a phrase which does not look very different from kindergarten "creativity" although they probably had in mind something comparable to the later notion of superego formation and the internalization of cultural imperatives.[27]

Nevertheless, Hegelian pedagogics was essentially at odds with every definitive aspect of the emergent child-centered education and Motherteacher. It has been asserted that "the main impulse of Hegelian pedagogics, which came to dominate nineteenth-century America, was controlled creativity—a fostering of the individual's identity exclusively through his relations to the community."[28] However, this seems to overstate the case for the Hegelians' influence. They were a sort of cultural loyal opposition and may have braked but did not redirect the movement toward child-centered methods. Their idealism and determinism led them to demand a much broader curriculum than had been advocated before and to stress school discipline in terms as strong, though within a very different rationale, as any the Boston masters used against Horace Mann. William Torrey Harris was probably the last important American educator who saw the masters as other than bigoted reactionaries. He regarded their criticism of Mann's innovations as penetrating and thought "we are apt to become impatient and blame too severely the conservative party in Massachusetts."[29] Harris was no more prepared than they to accept education on naturalistic principles.

His was a dualistic world in which Reason was supreme and transcended natural law in a way reminiscent of Christian conscience. He saw education in Hegelian terms as the process through which the individual man becomes ethical, the means "to fit him to live in the institutions of civilization—to cooperate with them, and to participate in their fruits."[30] The chief educative institutions with which the individual had to come to terms, reconstituting himself in the process, were the family, civil society, the State, and the Church. Harris conceived of the school only "as supplementary to the family, and propaedeutic to the State, the Church, and civil society," not as itself a cardinal institution. As a civilization became more complex, the school became more important, but only "as a special institution devoted wholly to the work of training the immature individual for taking part in those complex forms of life."[31] It was a cram course in the received culture and inculcated the basis of morality exactly by academic discipline "of the will in correct habit" and "of the intellect in a correct view of the world." The synthesis of practical habit and intellectual view was then definable as character.[32]

A man holding such views could not sympathize with the enthusiasts of child-centered education or with the pretensions of educators who magnified the school as a cardinal institution providing cultural leadership and dictating social reform. It is not surprising to hear that "at one or another interval Harris challenged the tenets, in whole or in part, of Rousseau, Pestalozzi, Spencer, Herbart, Froebel, Darwin, Parker, Stearns, the McMurrys, DeGarmo, James, and Dewey"—a sufficiently complete roll call of the new education.[33] Concerned always for the next and higher stage of development, he was not susceptible to the various calls for a return to nature or to primitivistic glorification of the child.

The Herbartians' notion that will was the product of desire or interest went contrary to Harris's belief that will was transcendental and aroused his fears for the practical consequences: "it will not be a good move," he said, "to make interest a substitute for immediate will training as it exists among us in the form of school discipline." Harris would have had his doubts about those lively Scottish and Prussian schoolrooms which so intrigued Horace Mann in 1843. School discipline, while it did not require that the teacher be a martinet, nevertheless required "a strict adherence to the forms of action that resemble those of a well-drilled company of soldiers." The elements of that discipline were "(1) punctuality, (2) regularity, (3) silence, (4) truth, (5) industry, (6) respect for the rights of others."[34] Pupils must internalize these during their interaction with the curriculum in order to transcend nature and become free but responsible participants in humane society.

Despite his prestige as an intellectual, his reputation as a noble character, and his influence as superintendent of the St. Louis schools from 1857 to 1880 and as U.S. commissioner of education from 1889 to 1906, William Torrey Harris was the advocate of a lost cause and scarcely interfered at all with the emergence of Motherteacher. That was an expression of the culture, and it was part of his institutional theory and understanding of the process of history that education must work from the given conditions. By about 1880, certainly by the time several classes had been graduated from the Cook County Normal School under Parker, Motherteacher had replaced the normalite and was personified in ever larger numbers of classrooms. The Hegelians left their mark, for example in the academically oriented high school curriculum as it was formulated in the 1890s with Harris much to the fore; but the curriculum was steadily subverted by Motherteaching below and increasingly within the high schools. In many cities, at least one high school devoted to preparing students for college continued to function until the time of World War II; but thereafter these schools were merged with the prevalent pupil-centered or "progressive" ones, and colleges altered their admission requirements accordingly.

Harris tried to substitute an idealist and humanistic educational creed for Christian theology and education on what the Boston masters called scriptural principles, but the cultural drift was toward a naturalistic and scientific faith consonant with egalitarian democracy and mass culture. Horace Mann's phrenology of the 1830s and 1840s symbolizes what was desired throughout. As the credentials of phrenology came into question, something better as science and as the source of a rationale for the new education became available in Darwinism. It fell to the chief American adapter of Darwinism to the purposes of psychology and education, G. Stanley Hall, to provide the trappings of science and legitimize Motherteacher. He did so with all the religiosity and chauvinism of Parker, which insured popularity, establishing both what he preached as the "cult of the child" and at the same time what he claimed was scientific "child-study." Although John Dewey has in recent decades been regarded as more influential in education than Hall, I believe Hall anticipated Dewey in all the essential emphases. Taking Dewey's famous sequence of titles, *The Child and the Curriculum, The School and Society,* and *Democracy and Education,* as a series of Hegelian antitheses, the next chapter shows that it was Hall who did most to make certain that the first term in each combination prevailed over the other instead of transcending itself and the other in the kind of synthesis William Torrey Harris and (more ambivalently) John Dewey hoped to see.

Chapter 8

The Prolongation of Infancy and Adolescence

IF THE normalite's credentials derived in part from reaction against Calvinism and in part from out-of-date belief in a species of natural religion with Newtonian connotations, they also reflected the nineteenth-century faith in progress and were compatible in some degree with the genetic world view when this was rapidly popularized after the Civil War. It will be remembered that Horace Mann worked under the direct influence of the phrenologist George Combe, from whose *Constitution of Man* he derived an optimistic developmental, though dubiously scientific, working model of human nature. The normalite's license to teach needed only to be revised in more respectably scientific evolutionary terms that implied development in the teacher leading to Motherteacher, who might be professionally incarnate in male as well as in female teachers.

Humanitarians and, notable among them, the educational reformers were uncomfortably aware that though evolution, as it became known through the formulations of Herbert Spencer before Charles Darwin's were published, might have an immutable millennial tendency, it was unimaginably protracted. The millennium it promised could not be expected within a thousand or a thousand thousand years, to say nothing of anybody's lifetime. It was a predetermined process during which efforts at social reconstruction must be as wrong as they were futile. Furthermore, the evolutionary means of bringing about the millennium was horrible from the point of view of most individuals; for Spencer, taking grim satisfaction from Malthus's theorem of the pressure of population upon subsistence, advanced ruthless competition as the technique necessary to the "survival of the fittest"—a biological elite—and the elimination of the unfit. Spencerianism was, in short, a doctrine of the evolutionary select no more compatible with democratic sentiment and the pedagogy of love than the Calvinist doctrine of God's elect.

Versions of evolutionism more congenial with humanitarian sentiment and reformist vocation had been formulated within a quarter century after the advent of the Spencerian line in the 1850s. While this was elaborated in the social theory of William Graham Sumner, alternative lines were opened up by Lester F. Ward and G. Stanley Hall. Both brought their evolutionist views extensively to bear on educational theory, but it appears that Hall's approach was selected by American attitudes as the viable influence. His recent biographer, Dorothy Ross, has remarked that "Hall first feared that evolutionary theories might require a thoroughly laissez faire theory of education . . . [but] quickly realized . . . that a reliance on the evolutionary gifts of nature did not require such a position; indeed, that they assumed an alert environment to husband and shape them." He undertook empirical study of the child's mind which tended to support "the latest innovations being sought by the educational disciples of Pestalozzi, Herbart, and Froebel" and which "was an affirmation, in the name of science, of the reform efforts of his day which hoped to adjust education to the child's nature."[1]

Although Ward's ideas did not achieve the impact that Hall's did, a brief look at them as an instance of what American culture rejected may illuminate what it preferred. Ward thought that Spencer made a fundamental error in assuming that the human species, like all the others, was still a passive object of the ineluctable laws of genetic evolution. On the contrary, he claimed, "Mind is found only at the end of the series [of evolutionary changes], and not at the beginning. It is the distinctive attribute of the creature, and not of the creator. It resides in man, and not in nature." Man's proper business was, therefore, to be the student, just in order that he might be the master, of nature, including his own by means of education, which Ward thought should be the fundamental function of government.

He did not deny that the basic impulse for change in human affairs was emotion or impulse, the same as in nonhuman nature. Progress could be expected in accordance with the genetic laws of evolution if society continued to rely merely on emotion, but progress in human affairs would continue to be as slow and wasteful as in the rest of nature unless a new element was supplied. "This element," Ward said, "is the guidance of the intellect."[2] The intellect could economize impulse by directing it into adaptive channels. Man could not, by taking thought, increase the quantity of intellect except perhaps over a term so long as to be meaningless to living individuals; but he could increase intelligence, and thereby the impact of actual intellect, by means of education.

This would seem to be doctrine sufficiently heady for any optimist; why was it not preferred to Hall's? The answer will depend largely, of course, on what Hall had to offer instead; but Ward's approach in education was in any case fatally committed to the adjustment of the child's nature to education rather than the other way round. Defining knowledge as "acquaintance with the environment," Ward characterized education as the "universal distribution of extant knowledge."[3] He believed priority should go to the distribution of what was already objectively known—that is, validated by the methods of natural science—about environment, including man and his society. He was not opposed to research and the origination of new knowledge but believed these would be sufficiently stimulated by the diffusion of extant knowledge.

Accordingly, he proposed a hierarchy of specifically prescribed curricula and defined the teacher's function as the inculcation of intelligence or information. Growth was not for Ward the shibboleth of education but rather something to be taken intelligently into account in practical pedagogy, for he understood that evolutionary development occurred at a rate that made it a "wild fancy" to suppose that an individual could be transformed. As to the given pupil in school at a given time, the overriding consideration should be to increase his knowledge as efficiently as possible. This required the full use of books as the chief means of learning intellectually, without having to recapitulate ancestral experience in a wasteful and imperfect manner.[4] In elementary education, he sought to counteract the notion that reading, writing, and arithmetic were in themselves "the rudiments of education" rather than the means of obtaining education which should be mastered expeditiously in order to proceed to education proper.

Holding such views, Ward was squarely opposed to the traditional idea of woman which had conditioned the development of Motherteacher and to the character-oriented pedagogy of love. He thought women made good teachers but no better than men and not because of maternal instinct. "Teachers of the young they must be, whether mothers or not," he said, "and this universal function alone would be sufficient to make their thorough and universal education an imperative duty of society. While the female mind may, and doubtless does, differ from the male in many important and fortunate aspects, it is only [in?] the emotional part of it. Intellect is one and the same everywhere, and the proper nourishment of intellect is truth. Therefore what women require as education is the same that men require, viz., knowledge."[5]

To say that Ward's telic evolutionism led to a curriculum-centered philosophy of education is to arouse the expectation that it must have projected like a boulder against the powerfully running tide of child-centeredness, or perhaps the image should be of submergence. Paradoxically, telic evolutionism provided a sanction for a meliorist attitude and social reform, but the principles of education he derived from his master idea were conservative and even reactionary from the point of view of the dominant educators and the popular attitudes they more or less ambivalently served. In his specificity about curriculum, in his insistence upon the prime importance of teaching given skills and defined subjects to every pupil capable of learning, and in his assumption that emphasis must remain on the learner's accommodating the curriculum rather than the reverse, Ward had more in common, when it came to details of curriculum, with William T. Harris, known as "the Great Conservator," than with Francis W. Parker, G. Stanley Hall, or John Dewey.

With respect to the idea of the teacher, Ward's proposals were inimical to Motherteacher; and Motherteacher represented an irresistible force. He asserted the ability of human society to transcend the laws of genetic evolution that had produced mankind and "undertake the artificial improvement of its condition upon scientific principles strictly analogous to those by which the rude conditions of [nontelic] nature have been improved upon in the process which we call civilization." Therefore, he advocated "an aggressive reform policy guided entirely by scientific foresight" and argued for "man in his social corporate capacity assuming the attitude of a teleological agent and adopting measures in the nature of final causes for the production of remote beneficial effects."[6] These views applied most particularly in education, and his very view of the state was that it should be essentially and positively educative. So true is this that it has been observed, "The state as defined by Ward is chiefly a school."[7] Education according to Ward was nothing if not directive, prescriptive, and common; Motherteacher was nurturant, nondirective, and the uncritical practitioner of ad hominem pedagogy.

It is not surprising, therefore, that evolutionism had its impact on educational theory and practice under the auspices of figures other than Ward and in an eclectic form retaining Spencerian features that happened to support the prevailing prejudices against intellectualism, activist social policy, and authority. It was Spencerian laissez-faire tendencies, above all, that seduced people who wished education to be responsive to human growth and development (conceived on terms different from Ward's) and believed it could be effectual only insofar as the individual pupil spontaneously appropriated it. Educators thus shared, at least nominally, the laissez-faire doctrine of the regnant capitalism, of which they might be critical on other grounds, a circumstance which helps explain why laissez-faire capitalists were not opposed to public education. Laissez-faire in education, manifested in nurturant, child-centered teaching by the sex thought naturally more suited to the work, was newly justified by misapplication of the biological laws of evolution. The understanding of those laws, especially prior to the belated appreciation of Mendelian genetics after 1900, was imperfect, and their social and educational applications were loose; but there was operative belief in the ineluctableness of human growth and its happy and manifest destiny. In pedagogy, this belief guaranteed the emergence and viability of Mother-teacher.

In 1923, toward the end of his life, G. Stanley Hall expressed proprietary satisfaction in what he took to be the settled fact that, in education, "the paidocentric versus the scholiocentric viewpoint has come to stay as surely as its analogue, the Copernican revolution from the geocentric to the heliocentric view of the world, did."[8] He was proud to recall that he had been hailed "as the Darwin of the mind." The result of his application of evolutionism to the study of mental phenomena was "genetic" psychology, which proved more serviceable than phrenology had in the 1840s or than Ward's telic evolutionary theory could in the 1880s as a rationale for "paidocentric" pedagogy. Hall felt he had done more than anybody else, including especially William James and John Dewey, to correct what he considered "a culture calamity without precedent," namely, the fact that toward the end of the nineteenth century "the enthusiasm that every able and trained mind the world over felt for evolution, which was really their confessed or unconfessed religion, was not encouraged to spread its benign infection wherever adolescents are taught."[9] He meant not only that evolution should be taught but that teaching should be evolutionized, according to his understanding of evolution.

Hall was an admirer of Francis W. Parker and visited the Cook County Normal School as a shrine where he might refresh his spirit, circumstances that make one recall that Motherteacher flourished in actuality even as she was justified in theory. The steps he took in deriving his genetic psychology from evolutionary theory and then in elaborating a genetic philosophy of education smack as much of enthusiastic apologetics as they do of scientific reasoning. He believed, as many others including Freud did, in the evolutionary hypothesis, since discredited, represented by the formula "ontogeny recapitulates phylogeny." His belief in evolutionary recapitulation tended to confirm him in his advocacy of paedocentric pedagogy, for in the child (representing ontogeny) he literal-mindedly asserted that all the stages in the evolution of the species were repeated from savagery to civilization. This process, sanctified by nature, was not to be blasphemously interfered with by the imposition of authority and external standards in education.

For underlying the belief in recapitulation was the faith in progress. The child, embodying the latest generation in progressive evolution, not only recapitulated the growth of the species; he grew to a higher stage than his ancestors, even than his parents, ever reached. So it was imperative that the child's growth not be inhibited, that the adult—parent or teacher—respect the child's growth more than tradition in educating him, and that growth be encouraged to continue as long as possible. What adult, fixed by maturity at an inferior stage of evolution, could judge a child growing toward some as yet unexperienced height of humanity?

Hall started the child-study movement, very properly named, that functioned effectually as a propaganda office for paedocentric pedagogy—a theory of education in which emphasis was on the mentor respectfully studying the child rather than on what the child should respectfully study. Child-study was much more popular than the precepts of the competing Hegelian movement, and Hall could afford to patronize William T. Harris despite his eminence. "Few if any teachers in this country understood it [the Hegelian movement]" said Hall, "and I always felt that even Harris himself fell far short of doing so. Although he was not successful as a propagandist, for years nearly all the leaders in public education heard him gladly. They felt that here was something very profound and elemental which emancipated them the tyranny of the old definition-philosophy and gave them *aperçus* in advance even of academic teachers of the subject. It always seemed to me pathetic to see this group gaspingly striving to comprehend these world-bestriding pronouncements."[10] His comment on the meetings of professional educators who heard Harris, if not that on Harris himself, is shrewd. He could not, as he put it, "evolutionize" the Hegelian movement—there was resistant principle there after all; but he could be much more popular than Harris.

The other leading movement in professional education in the 1890s, Herbartianism, was much more compatible with child-study than the Hegelian theory of education. Herbartians might insist on their distinct identity, but Hall thought of them as evolutionized in effect if not entirely in confession. He observed approvingly that Herbartianism "was to a degree paidocentric. Its generalizations were all in the right direction but it fell far short of putting teachers into the sympathetic rapport with the juvenile psyche that child study did, which went far beyond it in appraising the native instincts and capacities of the growing mind."[11] Hall out-Herbarted the Herbartians in asserting that "interest is the very Holy Ghost of education" and stating without qualification the corollary of this, "that so-called formal studies and methods of discipline are only, for the most part, a delusion and a snare."[12] In his messianic mood, he looked to the day when Clark University, of which he was president from its founding in 1888, would "devote all its funds ultimately to the cult of the child."[13] What he called the "benign infection" of evolutionism led to the cult of the child and reinforced the idea of the teacher as devotee of the child. For he believed:

There is really no clue by which we can thread our way through all the mazes of culture and the distractions of modern life save by knowing the true nature and needs of childhood and adolescence. I urge then that civilizations, religions, all human institutions, and the schools, are judged truly, or from the standpoint of the philosophy of history, by this one criterion: namely, whether they have offended against these little ones or have helped bring childhood and adolescence to an even higher and completer maturity as generations pass by. Childhood is thus our pillar of cloud by day and fire by night.[14]

No more extreme formulation of the creed of child-centered education and its implicit pedagogical method, personified in Motherteacher, is conceivable. From such a position—very nearly it would seem that of Moses—Hall resented the claims

being made for the younger sage, John Dewey, at the time Hall
was writing his autobiography in the early 1920s. He then dismissed Dewey as derivative and banal, at most an influence on
"normal school minds," and declared, "To those . . . versed in
paidology Dewey not only has nothing new to offer but seems
obvious if not platitudinous."[15] For Hall had worked out in his
genetic philosophy of education all the implications for curriculum and teaching methods that true belief in the divinity of
the child required and had done so with far less philosophical
sophistication and opaque language than are to be found in
Dewey's work on education. These aspects of Dewey may
reflect a more critical and philosophical mind than Hall's; certainly at the level of "normal school minds" Hall's signals were
easier to read than Dewey's, just as they had been more popular
than those of Harris.

On the basis of his faith in the proposition that ontogeny recapitulates phylogeny, coupled with the assumption that with
each successive generation evolutionary nature recoils upon itself in order to leap beyond the parental mark, Hall magnified
the child as the incarnation of the evolutionary vanguard. The
child was wiser than any member of the parental generation
could be, in the sense that he had the genetic potential to evolve
into a higher form necessarily beyond the comprehension and
criticism of the antecedent generations. His growth through all
the early ancestral stages toward the level of his parents' and
teachers' civilization and beyond was a predetermined biological process, which must be reverenced as progressive. Each
phase of the child's growth and development must be fully
experienced if the highest potential was to be realized at
maturity, but Hall attached more importance to growing than
to maturity, which waited like a presage of death at the end of
growth. What mattered most was the dynamics of growing:
maturity was stability and stability was retrogression in the individual. No matter what height of evolutionary development his
mature state might reach, it would be overtopped by the following generation.

Accordingly, Hall held that the teacher was "to be the chief
agent in the march of progress, and if we are to have a higher

type of citizenship, of manhood, or of womanhood in the world, it is to be done by conscious agencies, and those agencies culminate in the teacher." Taken by itself, this statement might reasonably be attributed to Lester F. Ward, but Hall was thinking in the context of what Ward called "genetic" or animal evolution and so represents a position exactly contrary to the educational principles implicit in Ward's telic or human evolutionary theory. Hall no less than Ward saw the teacher as the conscious agent of evolution, but according to Hall what the teacher must be most conscious of was the sacrosanct rhythm of growth in the child to which education must be subordinated. The implication of Ward's thought was, to the contrary, that education must be synchronized with the growth of the child, but only in order to insure his learning prescribed curricula in common with the rest of his generation. There was no place in Hall's genetic philosophy of education for applying directive intelligence on the part of the teacher. "In the vision of the super-man," said Hall, "if it is ever to be realized, it will be because the school, the college and the university will succeed in bringing childhood to more complete maturity, physically, mentally, and, above all, morally."[16] Again, Ward might be imagined uttering these words, but he would have meant something very nearly opposite to what Hall meant, implying a conflicting notion of education.

What Hall meant may be appreciated in the light of his assertion that the school "stands for the prolongation of human infancy, and the no whit less important prolongation of adolescence."[17] The implicit symbolism is uterine, the school as an environment as nearly womblike or paradisal as possible in the tragic declension from the physical womb to the cradle to the home to the school—where Motherteacher was indispensable. The proof of artful teaching must be continuing growth in pupils to as late a chronological age as genetically possible. Everything must be done to condition and encourage growth and nothing to foreclose it, such as criticism by traditional adult standards or demands that knowledge of some given thing be acquired by any given calendar date.

Hall's concern for growth was paramount at all times but

most intense with respect to adolescence, which he defined generously in chronological terms, suggesting in one place the age of thirty-three as the upper limit by allusion to the Great Adolescent, Jesus Christ. He extended the tradition that began with the common school revival of pushing to ever later stages the period during which pupils might suitably be left in female, or feminized and evolutionized, tutelage. In most passages, he seems to have thought of adolescence as extending into the middle twenties if the right conditions were supplied. The notion that it might last as late as the early thirties may have been an instance of the sentimentality which, since growth was taken paradoxically as an absolute value, could attribute growth honorifically to dotards.

The corollary of the valuation of growth is all important here, namely, that maturity is of comparatively little worth and antecedent experience—history, tradition—epitomized in maturity is of course devalued. That is, the subjective experience of the pupil in growing was accorded precedence over his acquiring knowledge of and intelligent adjustment to objective reality, as Ward had recommended. This being the assumption, the attainment of maturity could be interpreted only as a regrettable conclusion in the individual's participation in the evolution of what Hall termed "man-soul." That grand mystic process allowed "no finalities save formulae of development."[18] The over-thirties, to inject the popular pejorative phrase of the 1960s which may derive from the era of child-study, were in progressive evolutionist terms passé and could serve the rising generation only through sacrificing themselves to it, with at most a pathetic hope of vicarious gratification. Adulthood was, according to Hall's authorized redactor, G. E. Partridge, "a fall and a degeneration. The adult must sacrifice his ideals for himself, but he does not altogether abandon them. He must be content to plan and build so that his offspring can carry on his part, and in them he attains vicariously the wishes of his youth."[19] The apostles of child-study uttered this view cheerfully, and the cheeriness suggests they did not understand the implications. Edgar's dictum that ripeness is all received from child-study an increment of grimness.

Partridge's *Genetic Philosophy of Education,* published in 1912 with Hall's express authority as a systematic presentation of Hall's ideas, opened with an emphatic statement of the case for the young, by now referred to usually as the adolescent rather than as the child, as the first-class members of the species. He followed with unqualified statements of the pedagogic corollaries: the unimportance of intellect and intellectual training as compared with nurture of biological growth, the inferiority of the teacher to the pupil in proportion to her degree of maturity, the teacher's duty to subordinate formal instruction to the natural unfolding of the pupil. Hall had declared that the school was "sacred to health, growth, and heredity, a pound of which is worth a ton of instruction. The guardians of the young should strive first of all to keep out of nature's way, and to prevent harm, and should merit the proud title of defenders of the happiness and rights of children. They should feel profoundly that childhood, as it comes fresh from the hands of God, is not corrupt, but illustrates the survival of the most consummate thing in the world; they should be convinced that there is nothing else so worthy of love, reverence, and service as the body and soul of the growing child."[20]

Partridge stated matter-of-factly, "The most general formulation of all the facts of development that we yet possess is contained in the *law of recapitulation.* This law declares that the individual, in his development, passes through stages similar to those through which the race has passed and in the same order."[21] Thus the genetic philosophy of education referred its fundamental "law of recapitulation" not to the embryo, where it has a certain validity, but to the postpartum individual's growth through adolescence. Partridge took the law of recapitulation for granted and drew the inference that "the welfare of the individual corresponds, in great measure, to that of the race, but that beyond this common good there is a sphere of self-interest, to live in which is to rob the future of its rights."[22] He meant the welfare of the individual corresponds to that of the race so long as the individual is adolescent, i.e., still evolving, as if evolution continued in the individual after the production of the zygote. Apparently, he never said that the important thing was to preserve the individual until he was old enough to reproduce—a proposition itself subject to stipulations—or to manifest his own genetic endowment in society and civilization.

The implication was that it was just during the teachable years that the individual was not to be subjected to the adult impertinence of being taught, except perhaps from the age of eight to twelve, a stage when Hall thought the organism called for drill. To teach was to place intellectual acquisition of specific knowledge by the pupil at the center of the teacher's function, and this meant to impose already dysfunctional adult categories upon the growing pupil. "The intellect is at best a superficial part of the mind," Partridge asserted. "Excessive analysis, introspection, and criticism is [sic] morbid. . . . Reasoned philosophies and theologies pass away, but the deeper philosophy of poetry, folklore, belief—all that comes from the heart—endures. . . . Any philosophy that fails to make youth enthusiastic in the right way . . . is wrong."[23] And we know what that right way, that right direction, was. The profundity of this anti-intellectualism cannot be overstated: knowledge could only be knowledge of the past or the present, and in the Hall-Partridge system inevitably impertinent since the future was what mattered. From this view we derive the demand for "relevance" which has pervaded both popular and professional educational discussion at least since 1960.

"Consciousness," though the latest, is not necessarily "the highest, nor the most central, part of mind," Partridge asserted. "In fact when the mind is most alert in doubt or thought, acting with strained and concentrated attention, it is farthest from that which is most genuinely mental, or the expression of soul life." This phrase "soul life" is obscure but seems to refer to the folk-soul, or "man-soul" as Hall sometimes put it, a metaphysical notion that kept cropping up in this supposedly naturalistic context. Hall and Partridge tended to reverse the usual meanings of *thought, mind, mental,* and similar terms. Thus Partridge continued, "The deepest thought is expressed in movement. . . . The conscious life is unorganized and disjointed, while life is carried on by the deeper instincts and impulses in an even, uninterrupted flow. In thought, personality tends to become confused and superficial: in action we show ourselves as we truly are."[24] This most perdurable of American democratic prejudices in education was thus rerationalized by the genetic philosophy of education, as it would be by succeeding theories.

It should be recalled that Partridge published his book three years after Hall had brought Sigmund Freud to Clark University. Child-study had an affinity with psychoanalysis, which carried Hall's and Partridge's emphasis on the nonrational further and deeper and took the lead in cultural influence. Psychoanalysis had a more direct effect than child-study did on the progressive education movement when it got under way in the 1920s. Although the genetic philosophy of education was warped round to support the American penchant for optimism, it no less than psychoanalysis provided a dark prospect for the individual. Maturity, according to Freud, was dearly bought and must endure the "discontents of civilization" and was practically synonymous with alienation. And according to Partridge, "growth"—the great desideratum of his system—"from this plastic period of adolescence on to maturity, is . . . in a sense a fall from a higher state, for of many promises of the individual but few at best can be fulfilled. . . . If our species ever degenerate it will not be through lack of knowledge and culture, nor from relaxation of industries, but because of the progressive failure of youth to develop normally to maximal maturity."[25] Hall phrased this sad view more flatly: "Childhood is the paradise of the race from which adult life is a fall."[26] On this showing, the teacher must need all the compassion she could muster as she nurtured the growth of pupils into a maturity that could be only comparatively less disappointing than her own.

No doubt Hall meant his paean to childhood to be just that, with the dark implications left as it were patriotically unstated; and teachers took him at his word and not at his implication. Ironically, in view of his tendency to disparage other educational thinkers by stressing the ludicrous aspect of esoteric doctrine in the practice of simple normal school graduates, Hall could depend on teachers and administrators to accentuate the positive in applying his own tenets. As he observed of Sir William Hamilton's work in faculty psychology, his own genetic psychology and its educational implications also "filtered down to the level of the minds of normal pupils and gave them the smuggest primness and complacency, and really did little more than to substitute formulated ignorance for knowledge."[27]

The instructions in method that filtered down to teachers from the genetic philosophy and helped put the finishing touches to Motherteacher were so child-centered as to leave the uncomfortable aspects in peripheral obscurity. Motherteacher needed only to believe, or simulate belief, in Hall's axiom: "To love and feel for and with the young can alone make the teacher love his calling and respect it as supreme."[28] Thus simplified and suffused with the *Gemüt* that Hall had found so pleasant as a student in Germany in contrast with the Calvinistic frostiness of his New England youth, the genetic philosophy professed the grandest goals combined with the smallest of demands for specific results in teaching. Motherteacher was assured, moreover, that the genetic philosophy might "be applied to all grades of school, from the kindergarten to the college. It gives us true ideals for the home, for it makes love of childhood the centre of all its teachings." Teachers were told they had "too readily accepted" as the pedagogical ideal the "perfecting of the art of imparting knowledge" rather than "nourishing and unfolding the child." Seventy-five years after Horace Mann established the pedagogy of love, the genetic philosophy still made the polemical point, "Attention has been too strongly fixed upon subject matter, and too little upon the child."[29]

The denigration of intellect, taken as the definitive characteristic of adulthood understood as the obsolescent stage of individual human life, led to the assumption that the school should not reflect society and fit the young for life and work in the present. For such an ideal "tends to select only such knowledge as the adult mind finds useful for its own purposes, and to neglect the knowledge most suited to the child." So the genetic philosophy held "that the school shall not be made in the image of the past nor of the present, but shall fit man for the next stage of his development." Accordingly, there was no "image" at all that the school should be made to reflect; the teacher must await the pupil's unfolding and fret not at the lack of any known pedagogical goal. "Education must take the biological rather than the logical road to its end."[30] If the biological road did not seem to be going anywhere or appeared to take a sinister turn, the teacher must have faith in the child's genetic program while this superseded the curriculum and dismiss her doubts as the expression of invidious adult intellectualizing or authoritarian compulsiveness.

The extension of mothering from infancy to ever later stages that shaped Motherteacher received a new theoretical justification very specifically from the genetic philosophy. Not only in infancy but in adolescence, generously defined as we have seen, teachers must "be careful not to try to accelerate nature and we must be equally sure that there are no retarding influences. . . . All external forcing is antagonistic to nature. Interest welling up from within shows the way." While much was claimed for child-study as the scientific preparation for knowing just how to exert influences that neither accelerated nor retarded nature, little if anything was said about what to do if interest did not well up in the pupil. It was a question the Boston masters had put in their terms to Horace Mann, and he had no clear answer either. Precocity, in any event, was to be dreaded still. "To linger at leisure in each recapitulatory stage, so that each individual may experience all the life the race has experienced, is the ideal."[31] The teacher was relieved of responsibility: acceleration was worse than retardation, and if a pupil seemed to linger rather too long in one ill-defined recapitulatory stage or another, might not he be a late bloomer?

As Partridge repeatedly confessed, nobody could maintain "that the parallel between the individual and the race is as precise and definite as the law of recapitulation would of itself demand." The science of childhood was not far enough advanced to enable the teacher to know just when a pupil was ready for exposure to the appropriate "culture material." Nevertheless, there was no hesitation in asserting "we have one cardinal principle . . . that interest is the best test of capacity and of pedagogical progress." In yet another theoretical revaluing of what in Horace Mann had been just reaction against repressive Puritan school discipline, the genetic philosophy promoted child's play to the status of "the greatest of all educational forces. . . . For without the interests which play creates the child could not be educated in a true sense at all." No matter how uncertain one might be about the operation of the law of recapitulation and the methods of calibrating the biological stage of the pupil with the culture material, one acted confidently on the principle that the curriculum should be comprised of subject matter "selected according to the stage of development of the child, and not by the logical requirements of the adult's science."[32]

Except for the stage from eight to twelve, the genetic philosophy never allowed "the logical requirements of the adult's science" equality, to say nothing of primacy, with the pupil's "interest." Nature provided for a temporary excursion into a sort of masochism which caused pupils from eight to twelve to desire "drill," the pejorative Partridge used for the process of acquiring grammar and arithmetic, involving as this did the imposition on individual practice of conventional rules. These four years were crucial, for the twelfth was "the last year in which drill can be the predominant method, so that if defects in the rudiments are not now remedied, they never can be."[33] How many pupils passed their twelfth year with defects in the rudiments unremedied? It is an important question that does not seem to have received the attention it warranted; for the genetic philosophy postulated for a long adolescence, spanning all the rest of education, the subordination of curricular logic once more to the pupil's sovereign interest. Neither Hall nor Partridge seems to have thought competence in the rudiments by the age of twelve should be prerequisite to continuing in secondary and higher education, despite their belief that it had to be acquired then or never. That they were correct in this belief seems to have been attested by the increasing prevalence in even reputable colleges and universities since their day of squalid programs of remedial English and mathematics, or of supposedly regular courses which are in fact vitiated by the illiteracy of the students and often enough of their instructors.

Motherteaching was, in fact, more in order for adolescents than for young children according to the genetic philosophy. Hall's position was that "adolescence is a new birth, for the higher and more completely human traits are now born. The qualities of body and soul that now emerge are far newer. The child comes from and harks back to a remoter past; the adolescent is neo-atavistic, and in him the later acquisitions of the race slowly become prepotent. Development is less gradual and more saltatory, suggestive of some ancient period of storm and stress when old moorings were broken and a higher level attained."[34] During adolescence, therefore, it was more important than ever for teachers to understand, as Partridge put it, that "insistence upon logical order before its time, making havoc with the genetic order, is the greatest pedagogic sin against the intellect."[35] Accordingly, "Entrance examinations to college should be abandoned. . . . The high school should be able to dictate to the college rather than the reverse. The college should be obliged to take the product of the high school in the condition which the high school, working according to the principles of genetic education, must leave it; and should then, in its own way, proceed to build the next higher stage."[36]

The college, having respectfully accepted the product of the high school, might be permitted to proceed in its own way—if that was the high school's, and the elementary school's, and the kindergarten's way. Partridge observed:

One of the most prevalent and serious evils of the college work of the present time, one containing many others, is too close specialization in teaching. Professors are too much concerned with the subject-matter of their courses, and too little with the true function of teaching. They are led away from interest in the student by the passion for systematizing, technique, precision, and scholarship within their own departments; and they try to impart to the student the same professional attitude toward their subject that they themselves have. This is wrong, for it is a time when the schoolmaster and his methods and subject-matter are of minor importance. . . . He must, if need be, brave the charge of superficiality and lack of system, if in order to be inspiring he must sacrifice something of precision and form. His aim must be the mental awakening of his students. He should stimulate questions and problems, and answer but few of them. The test of his success is not the amount of knowledge he leaves in the minds of his students, but the state of their interests in things worth being interested in; that is, his effect upon their sense of values in life, and their zeal in adjusting themselves to them.[37]

It is one of the richest ironies in the history of American education that this statement by an archeducationist can be used today without changing a syllable to describe the attitude and procedure of the typical college and university liberal arts instructor.

By gradual accretion, guaranteed by democratic preferences that would have drafted one justifying theory if not another, the empire of Motherteacher extended to all of American education by the time of the first World War, when, surely not without some connection with the evolution of Motherteacher, the country's complacency was prepared to make the world safe for democracy. Partridge concluded that "the chief art of the teacher . . . during most of childhood and youth is to keep the mind of his pupil filled with the proper nourishment." What must Motherteacher's breast provide? It must flow with "a rich knowledge of the subject-matter of his sciences, assimilated to the form best suited to the child, and above all ready to use spontaneously. The teacher must possess a power of free, vivid, and interesting expression—ability which the great majority of teachers, as now trained, lack."[38]

In case the innate interests of students did not extend to English grammar and composition or arithmetic, the properly trained teacher was expected to rely upon "power of free, vivid, and interesting expression" to get results. Hall enjoined teachers not to forget "that of the two aims of education, namely, to give exact and finished results that satisfy and give a sense of finality, on the one hand, and that which, on the other, aims chiefly at the excitement of interest and curiosity, which measures the success of teaching not at all by the volume of acquisition but by the strength and many-sidedness of mental zests and appetites aroused, the latter, although its results can never be weighed and measured by examinations, is by far the higher."[39] So long as the classroom was animated, no matter what the subject, mutual congratulations between teacher and taught were in order, teachers were conveniently interchangeable regardless of subject specialization, and a specious personal warmth could be credited as professional competence.

The lineaments of Motherteacher emerge from the genetic philosophy without great emphasis on Hall's part upon women teachers although he referred casually from time to time to the circumstance that almost all teachers were women. His focus on child-study implied a teacher nondirective by definition whether female or male, and he took for granted the almost absolute majority of women in the teaching corps. His occasional slurs upon "normal school minds" and their tendency to vulgarize educational theory do not seem to have suggested to him that his own doctrine was vulnerable. Partridge stated the case thus: "Less than half of our teachers have had professional training." That meant the necessity of indoctrination in child-study. "Teaching is often taken up, not as a life work, but as a stepping stone to some other occupation. So little is it regarded as a permanent profession, in fact, that the average teaching life is not more than three years." He acknowledged that "professional spirit must be created, and so long as schools are taught predominantly by women, who do not intend to adopt teaching for a life work, and who therefore are unwilling to make serious professional preparation, this will be difficult."[40] But the Chanticleers of American education have never been able to make more than passing references to the issue. They have crowed professionalism and the Pertelotes have clucked their soothing acquiescence.

Hall implicitly associated male gender with "child" or "pupil" and female with "teacher." His attitudes were exactly those of the leaders of the common school revival, and like them he believed in emphasizing the differences between the sexes by education. Pedagogically, the critical, but not very critical, moment was the age of twelve when "boys and girls in the ideal school will be chiefly, tho not exclusively, placed under the care of teachers of their own sex."[41] He calmly noted: "In most public high schools girls preponderate, especially in the upper classes; and in many of them the boys that remain are practically in a girls' school, sometimes taught chiefly, if not solely, by women teachers, at an age when strong men should be in control more than at any other period of life. Boys need a different discipline and moral regimen and atmosphere." Boys should have at their schools the sort of "robust tone and a true boy life" such as he thought Eton, Harrow, and Rugby provided; "feminization of the school spirit, discipline, and personnel is bad for boys."[42] Hall asserted, "The good teacher is a true Pedotrieb, or boy driver."[43]

Like his predecessors, Hall defined woman in terms of maternity, and his readiness to accept a feminized teaching corps reflected the idea of the teacher as uncritically motherly and supportive in the context of his theory of recapitulatory evolution. Woman was the properly unintellectual bearer of the race of men, in his view; and it may be inferred that when he thought of evolution, of those "saltatory" phases of human adolescence above all, it was the human male he had in mind. The only aspect of the idea of woman as teacher that seemed to disturb him related to the intellectual, "scholiocentric" necessities of teaching, however subordinated to the growth of the pupil they might be. "In the progressive feminization of our schools," he observed, "most teachers, perhaps naturally and necessarily, have more or less masculine ideals, and this does not encourage the development of those that constitute the glory of womanhood."[44] He thought that intellectualism in women led to an aversion to maternity, and he equated women who avoided having children with male slackers in war or business competition.[45]

Although Partridge expressed concern about the effect of short-term employment of women in teaching on professionalism, he and Hall were obviously not deeply disturbed by the prevalence of women teachers. The good woman teacher was first and last a good, i.e., maternal, woman whose first duty, the very quality that made her a good teacher, was to marry and bear: it is no accident that, in referring to intellectualism, Hall and Partridge were likely to call it "barren."

Hall never doubted that the influence of women in schools was beneficent, and he could couple this judgment with the observation, "In some states nine tenths of the entire teaching force are women so that this sex now almost monopolizes elementary teaching."[46] The phenomenon elicited a passing reference to its "economic cause." Hall was not nearly so exercised as Horace Mann had been about the low wages of female teachers, for the underlying reasons for approving the feminization of teaching were the same under evolutionist dispensation as they had been under the Unitarian-phrenological rationale at the time of the common school revival.

By the time Hall published his autobiography in 1923, the rationale of the dominant "soft line" in American education and incidentally of the feminized teaching corps had changed again, as he was jealously aware; his genetic philosophy of education has been more or less tacitly assimilated to pragmatism as elaborated by John Dewey. The continuity was at that deeper institutional level of which William T. Harris had been so respectful and of which he thought education could after all be only the reflective servant. Pragmatism no less than (recapitulatory) evolutionism was skewed to serve the purposes of abiding romantic, democratic antinomianism in education. The diluting, distorting process of filtering down to normal school minds was repeated in the progressive education movement, toward which, however, Dewey was more ambivalent than Hall had been toward the child-study movement. Dewey's ideas, too, were mediated by others, preeminently by W. H. Kilpatrick at Teachers College of Columbia University, and brought into the service of that nondirective anti-intellectualism which had characterized American education— "feminized" education, precisely—ever more decisively since Horace Mann.

Chapter 9
Socializing Intelligence and Spirit

To JOHN DEWEY may be attributed the final developments in Motherteacher, not exactly as he would have wished but as a distorted reflection of his thought and its application in the classroom. Before Dewey, Motherteacher was still beholden, if not to the Christian God, at least to some vague absolutist world view and nurtured the child, therefore, in some sense as a responsible individual. Her faith in the innate goodness of the child and the inevitability of its growth as a moral person to a level superior to that of her own generation made her uncritical and tended to subvert the curriculum, but the curriculum was still there for the child to cope with according to his lights if not hers. The effect of Deweyan reforms was to redirect Motherteacher's faith from belief in the goodness of the child to belief in the goodness of society and thus to replace individualism in American education with a type of conformism which went by the honorific title of democracy.

Dewey's philosophy—monist, relativistic, pragmatic: "instrumentalist" was his preference—denied absolutes and so undercut the authority of the traditional curriculum and its constituent subjects of study. He sought, however, to reconstruct a curriculum and even to restore to the teacher a species of authority to teach it "by indirection." In place of any absolute foundation, he proposed society, but society not only recognized but celebrated in evolutionist terms as changing. Whatever was social was moral; and, since society was constantly in flux, change per se must be reverenced, tradition devalued, and in education a premium placed on social adjustment. The school, accordingly, must be an "embryonic" society—a social womb!—and the teacher's role more motherly than ever, with the fundamental qualification that she was to nurture the child not as a responsible individual but as a member of the mystical body of society or the group. As an embryonic society, the school had to be, according to evolutionist optimism, an improvement upon the society operating beyond its walls, which could not, therefore, be more than a provisional model. The teacher must be "creative," motherly in a sense far more demanding than a merely procreative mother is ever asked to be. She was to provide an environment which would in no way inhibit and in every way facilitate the adjustment of the child to what came to be called "interpersonal relations," with an unconsciously ironic emphasis on the personal and subjective in the name of the social.

Dewey was in education, following William James, the representative of the culminating phase of American social thought which Morton White has characterized as "the revolt against formalism." This advocated the dynamic process of experience against logic, contemned as external, static, or dead in all fields. The formal was made pejoratively synonymous with the abstract, the dogmatic, the ideal, the traditional and decorous, which ideas were associated with the authoritarian and the reactionary. The antiformalists arrogated reality and value to human perception, implying a totally anthropocentric world view and a species of subjective idealism queerly at odds with their professed respect for science. Oliver Wendell Holmes in law, Thorstein Veblen in economics, and Charles Beard and James Harvey Robinson in history took lines analogous to Dewey's in education. Morton White places the beginning of the revolt against formalism at 1878, when Charles S. Peirce published the essay that is commonly regarded as the classic formulation of pragmatism. But surely antiformalism only came to impressive philosophical expression and application at this period, subsuming a national attitude traceable to antinomianism in the Bay Colony. It was characterized by what White calls historicism, or the belief that facts are explicable by derivation from earlier facts, and organicism, "the attempt to find explanations and relevant material in social sciences other than the one . . . primarily under investigation." The antiformalists advocated "coming to grips with life, experience, process, growth, context, function."[1]

Motherteacher was finally licensed in this atmosphere of anti-formalism. Despite their professions, their negativism inhibited the antiformalists from coming to grips with life, experience, process, growth, and function because the very idea of a grip on anything was repugnant. Their distaste for anything fixed or prescribed, which they at once stigmatized as dogma taken as necessarily oppressive and prejudicial to all of their "values," was unmistakably expressed in Dewey's educational theory and experimentation. His definition of experimentation, for all his claim that the experimental control known to physics and chemistry could be approximated in sociology and education by studying the genetic history of moral events, was tendentious. He held that experimentation is genetic because it creates. He was not interested in experimentation as a method of determining or discovering pre-existent being or in accepting the results as established truth, knowledge, or information that should be disseminated through education. The paradoxical notion of creative experimentation reflected, in a distorted way, such facts of chemistry as that, if one combines hydrogen with oxygen in certain ways, water is created. To experiment seems to have meant to Dewey very much the same thing as to experience or, more simply, to feel; nothing could be learned or known unless by a "creative" conjunction of learner and object, with learner the determinant element.[2]

When he set up his experimental school at the University of Chicago in 1896, Dewey, like Hall and Partridge, wanted to find out at what stages in the growth of the child various subject matters might be most appropriately presented and the most effectual methods of teaching. In the antiformalists' manner, he knew what he did not expect to discover, namely, traditional forms. His school was emphatically not "for listening"—except on the part of the teachers. He did not think children were little jugs with big ears into which intellectual pabulum should be ladled. Pupils must not be passive "spectators." He rejected in advance "the typical points of the old education," using the epithet "old" pejoratively and as if there had not been a new education every decade since Horace Mann. He said the old education, still only too current, was characterized by "its passivity of attitude [on the part of pupils], its mechanical massing of children, its uniformity of curriculum and method. It may be summed up by stating that the center of gravity is outside the child. It is the teacher, the textbook, anywhere and everywhere you please except in the immediate instincts and activities of the child himself." The cliché of fifty years of school reform followed pat: Dewey observed that a Copernican revolution was proceeding in education and according to its principles "the child becomes the sun about which the appliances of education revolve."[3]

The curriculum, with stress on the definite article, was in Dewey's opinion the epitome of the old education, representing an imposition of adult categories according to adult ways of thinking and adult convenience without due concern about "the construction of a course of study which harmonizes with the natural history of the growth of the child in capacity and experience."[4] The schools of the day relied upon what Dewey dismissed as an outmoded psychology according to which the mind was an individual affair in direct contact with the world rather than a function of social life. It was "a psychology of knowledge, of intellect" that ignored emotion, instinct, and genetic characters, seeing mind as static rather than as "a process of growth" and regarding child mind as the same in kind as adult mind. Modern psychology had, Dewey asserted, shown the error of thinking that "the subject-matter of the adult, logically arranged facts and principles" could be right for the child if only simplified.[5]

Instead of a set of logically organized subjects and grades through which adults manipulated children by the traditional means of emulation and penalties, Dewey meant to contrive a school where "the school life organizes itself on a social basis. Within this organization is found the principle of school discipline or order. . . . If you have the end in view of forty or fifty children learning certain set lessons, to be recited to a teacher, your discipline must be devoted to securing that result." He proposed instead "the development of a spirit of social cooperation and community life . . ."[6] Dewey was here, in *The School and Society*, as frankly engaged in apologetics as Horace Mann had been in his talks to county meetings during the early days of the common school revival in Massachusetts. And, like Mann again, he derogated the practice of having children learn "set" lessons "to be recited to a teacher," as if no change in this practice had occurred and as if it could not conceivably have some purpose other than gratification of the teacher's will, at the expense of the child's. Americans could be expected to prefer rhetoric about "the development of a spirit of social co-operation and community life." Then he could claim for the new education "the only discipline that stands by us, the only training that becomes intuition," which "is that got through life itself."[7]

No doubt; but was not school, no matter how traditionally conducted—even if tradition was merely oppressive as represented—as much life as any other situation? William T. Harris thought of school not as life in toto but as that part of it in which the young might learn from requirements of punctuality, silence, performance, and so on, what they would have to know and practice as civilized adults participating in and deriving the benefits of the cardinal institutions of their culture. Dewey conceived of children not as being more or less passively prepared for life at school but as actually living there on their own terms as adults live on theirs outside of school, beyond tutelage; not as being taught but as having "learning experiences." In order to make sure these occurred, a great deal of stage-managing was obviously necessary on the part of teachers. Dewey apparently never worried about the manipulative aspect of his program, which seems as egregious in its way as the drill it was supposed to replace. His chief idea of a method more truly educative than the old education was to have pupils imitate occupations of "real life"—that is, life outside of school, although by his own argument life should be as real inside as outside—e.g., cloth making. Each child would be persuaded, although I do not think Dewey ever showed convincingly how each and every child could be persuaded and not forced or manipulated, to start with bits of flax, wool, and so on, and follow through to textile engineering, manufacturing, and economics, learning incidentally but internalizing all the related history, geography, mathematics, etc. "The occupation," he said in apparent obliviousness to all of the difficulties of such a program, "supplies the child with a genuine motive; it gives him experience at first hand; it brings him into contact with realities. . . . in addition it is liberalized throughout by translation into its historic and social values and scientific equivalencies."[8]

So far as I know he never recognized the fatuity of this kind of proposal even though, in the palmy days during the 1920s and 1930s of the "project method" which was derived from his ideas, he had misgivings about the capriciousness and intellectual sterility of American education. To William T. Harris's consciousness of the problem of numbers and the necessity of skilled administration in order to make sure of some minimum of learning of specifics by some maximum of pupils, Dewey never provided any equivalent realism. He continued to think that "intelligent and serious attention to what the child *now* needs and is capable of in the way of a rich, valuable, and expanded life" would obviate any subsequent deficiencies in particular subject matter and skill. He merely preached: "If we seek the kingdom of heaven, educationally, all other things shall be added unto us—which, being interpreted, is that if we identify ourselves with the real instincts and needs of childhood and ask only after its fullest assertion and growth, the discipline and information and culture of adult life shall all come in their due season."[9]

It is not surprising, therefore, that he was for "organic" education in full communication with "life" but not, as in the Middle Ages, education as an influence "from the top down"— which, being interpreted, meant he was against education as an influence from adult to child, from head to heart, from university to school. He was concerned, rather, because the " 'lower' parts of our system are not in vital connection with the 'higher.' " It was difficult for him to see how the ends he had in mind could be reached "except as the most advanced part of the educational system is in complete interaction with the most rudimentary,"[10] the power, be it understood, flowing from the rudimentary to the advanced. As Hall out-Herbarted Herbart, Dewey out-Froebeled Froebel. He reported of his University Elementary School (the name seems to have had a meaning not usually appreciated) that "in a certain sense the school endeavors throughout its whole course—now including children between four and thirteen—to carry into effect certain principles which Froebel was perhaps the first consciously to set forth."[11] He actually made the kindergarten proper, for ages four to six, more child-centered than Froebel, omitting particular Froebelian "gifts" and occupations that implied adult direction of the scene.

Dewey was, nevertheless, clearly aware of the child and the curriculum as antitheses and set his "laboratory" school to find experimentally the most effectual methods of promoting the educational synthesis. "The easy thing," he wrote, "is to seize upon something in the nature of the child, or upon something in the developed consciousness of the adult, and insist upon *that* as the key to the whole problem. When this happens a really serious practical problem—that of interaction—is transformed into an unreal, and hence insoluble, theoretic problem."[12] He regretted the wasting hostility of the educational sects that rallied under the sign of "Child," on the one hand, and of "Discipline" or "Curriculum" on the other. The problem was "just to get rid of the prejudicial notion that there is some gap in kind (as distinct from degree) between the child's experience and the various forms of subject-matter that make up the course of study. From the side of the child, it is a question of seeing how his experience already contains within itself elements—facts and truths—of just the same sort as those entering into the formulated study. . . . From the side of the studies, it is a question of interpreting them as outgrowths of forces operating in the child's life." So he urged that "we realize that the child and the curriculum are simply two limits which define a single process."[13] He seems to have been inconsistent in asserting, on the one hand, that the child mind had its integrity and was not the same in kind as adult mind and, on the other, that there was no gap in kind between the child's experience and subject matter, taken as the expression of adult categories.

Nevertheless, more evenly and thoughtfully than anybody else, Dewey formulated the issues of more than sixty years of educational reform. "Just as, upon the whole, it was the weakness of the 'old education' that it made invidious comparisons between the immaturity of the child and the maturity of the adult, regarding the former as something to be got away from as soon as possible and as much as possible; so it is the danger of the 'new education' that it regards the child's present powers and interests as something finally significant in themselves."[14] In Dewey's *The Child and the Curriculum*, published in 1902, Pestalozzi, Froebel, Mann, Harris, James, Hall, and Ward are edited and their valuable elements synthesized in a philosophy of education which, at least as theory, did promise an American "kingdom of heaven, educationally."

The further and crucial problem remained, however, of translating theory into professional teaching practice. Dewey criticized the methods of both the old education and the new and proposed, in his neo-Hegelian fashion, not the rejection of either but a merger in something better than either. He asserted that while "the 'old education' tended to ignore the dynamic quality, the developing force inherent in the child's present experience, and therefore to assume that direction and control were just matters of arbitrarily putting the child in a given path and compelling him to walk there, the 'new education' is in danger of taking the idea of development in altogether too formal and empty a way. The child is expected to 'develop' this or that fact or truth out of his own mind." Instead, Dewey said, "it is development of experience and into experience that is really wanted."[15] This is a simply brilliant proposition, that is, an instance of the simple brilliance of a focused synthesis of diverse elements. The notion of the child's development of and into experience, that is, its development of its own experience as this stands at a given moment into the larger experience of the adult as the heir of history, was the foundation of Dewey's theory of teaching method. It was an advance on the Herbartians' doctrine of interest, allowing for more effectual pedagogical application. It was compatible with the idea of seeing to it by means of education that children's stock of experience included certain common elements by certain ages so that the engrafting of subject matter might be facilitated.

Dewey visualized the child, or indeed the pupil of any age, progressively appropriating subject matter and the teacher tactfully facilitating the process, professionally concerned primarily neither for child nor for curriculum but for the thorough appropriation of the latter by the former. Subject matter, he said, "needs to be *psychologized;* turned over, translated into the immediate and individual experiencing within which it has its origin and significance."[16] This famous statement has been grievously misinterpreted in the process of filtering down to normal school minds and popular perceptions. Dewey did not explicitly phrase what the context of this formulation implies. It is easy to take it in isolation as meaning that there is something wrong about subject matter that needs "psychologizing" and that the teacher is responsible for doing so—that is, that the teacher is authorized to sacrifice the integrity of subject matter and the curriculum to the immediate interest of the child. The context indicates, however, that Dewey meant that society needs its young to psychologize, or internalize and absorb into and thus expand their experience, the subject matter that comprises the curriculum. Nothing in the passage implies that the curriculum, even after such reforms as Dewey recommended, should be forever fixed. Like the Constitution, the curriculum might be amended but stand sacred in its form as given at any particular time.

Accordingly, Dewey defined the teacher equally in terms of responsibility to subject matter and to child. "Every study or subject . . . has two aspects: one for the scientist as a scientist; the other for the teacher as a teacher." His usage of "scientist' reflects the prestige of science at the time he wrote and should be read as referring not just to specialists in natural science but in any field of learning, including of course social sciences, in which investigation subject to empirical validation is carried on.

"These two aspects," he continued, "are in no sense opposed or conflicting. For the scientist, the subject-matter represents simply a given body of truth to be employed in locating new problems. . . . The problem of the teacher is a different one. As a teacher he is not concerned with adding new facts to the science he teaches." Rather, "He is concerned with the subject-matter of the sciences as *representing a given stage and phase of the development of experience.* His problem is that of inducing a vital and personal experiencing [by his pupils]."[17] The pupil's "vital and personal experiencing" is synonymous with the "psychologizing" of subject matter. In order to induce this process, the teacher must know the psychology of the pupil and the "given body of truth" which the pupil must psychologize equally well. This position parallels that of Lester F. Ward in defining the function of education as the diffusion of "extant knowledge" and implies an extremely learned teacher, who, though not engaged in the discovery of new truth as the scientist is, has comparable dignity as a professional diffuser of intelligence.

Despite the association of his name with the permissive education of the twentieth century, John Dewey actually stood squarely against the "soft line" in education, as squarely as William T. Harris and Lester F. Ward. "The radical fallacy . . . ," he said, "is the supposition that we have no choice save either to leave the child to his own unguided spontaneity or to inspire direction upon him from without. Action is response; it is adaptation, adjustment. There is no such thing as sheer self-activity possible." Motherteacher's operative principle was just what Dewey regarded as the radical fallacy of American educational thought. In his view, the teacher must be thoroughly versed in "the formulated wealth of knowledge that makes up the course of study" in order to use it *"to determine the environment of the child,* and thus by indirection to direct." The notion of nondirective teaching, of teaching as uncritical indulgent mothering, shows up as a contradiction in terms in the light of Dewey's words. "The case is of Child," he went on to admit. "But save as the teacher knows, knows wisely and thoroughly, the race-expression which is embodied in that thing we call the Curriculum, the teacher knows neither what the present power, capacity, or attitude is, nor yet how it is to be asserted exercised, and realized."[18]

These formulations by John Dewey did not, however, exorcize Motherteacher, who flourished partly on distortions of his doctrine and partly because, in his general antiformalist posture, Dewey was himself a product of the same social forces that produced Motherteacher. On the key issue of a specifically defined and logically organized curriculum, implying an intellectual and authoritative (not authoritarian!) teacher professionally responsible as much for certifying according to objective standards the degree to which pupils learn prescribed subject matter as for facilitating their learning through applied psychology, Dewey was a negative force. His instrumentalist development of the pragmatist theory of knowledge militated against prescription of subject matter, against respect for the logic of subject matter, and against all fixed principles except that of growth. For all his emphasis on social values in education, his influence told against the common schooling because the "psychologizing" of subject matter meant in practice that there was no guarantee, though there was a naive expectation, that a maximal number of pupils would learn any given things in any given order. The radical empiricism of William James as elaborated by Dewey and reflected in pedagogy led to peculiarly irresponsible and potentially antisocial individualism based in an unavowed subjective idealism. Pupils were the arbiters of their own education and Motherteacher was confirmed as the ideal American teacher, operating on a meretriciously personal basis without real professional authority or responsibility.

Dewey further undermined the curriculum by his conception of democracy and of education as pragmatically devoted to its advancement. A Marxist critic has accused Dewey of wickedly concealing "the essence of bourgeois education through making it appear as the unfolding of the innate instincts and impulses of the child."[19] There is insight in this, but it is astigmatic. The charge of cynical intention to indoctrinate with capitalist ideology is surely wrong, but Dewey's philosophy of education did rationalize, in the sense of a largely unconscious tendency, as others had done before the antinomian element in American democracy. From Mann to Dewey, American theorists of education were themselves implicated, albeit on higher intellectual levels, in the popular ideology, not playing cynically upon a weakness of the masses. As Dewey said, "the case is of Child," and at bottom I think he identified with "Child" and, under all the philosophizing, resented "Discipline." Like G. Stanley Hall, though for other reasons, he was for prolonging infancy and, therefore, for the infantilizing pedagogy, honorifically billed democratic, which Mother-teacher purveyed.

In the most frequently quoted paragraph from *Democracy and Education* (1916), Dewey said, "Since a democratic society repudiates the principle of external authority, it must find a substitute in voluntary disposition and interest; these can be created only by education." He offered this as an explanation of the "devotion of democracy to education," but it is hard to see how education can "create" specifically "voluntary" disposition and interest. The interpretation may be that he was using "voluntary" with connotations of pragmatist voluntarism, according to which we can "will to believe," what we will to believe habitually we actually believe, and—for all practical purposes—what we actually believe is. Dewey, however, made interpretation of his statement more difficult by defining democracy as "more than a form of government," since his antiformalist bias made any form of government, i.e., any actual source of external authority, uncongenial. Rather than a form of government, democracy was "primarily a mode of associated living, of conjoint communicated experience." So, of course, must be any social organization, whether tyranny, monarchy, feudalism, or democracy. Presumably, Dewey must be taken as meaning democracy as a particular mode of associated living with rules that particularize it. But the antiformalist must resist rules, and Dewey injected necessary vagueness by giving as a synonym for a mode of "associated living" the phrase a mode of "conjoint communicated experience."[20] Dewey had said seventeen years earlier that a school should not be "for listening." If one takes him at his word, thinks of democracy as a mode of conjoint communicated experience, with stress on "conjoint," and of the school as an embryonic democracy implicating teachers as well as pupils, then the school would not be for listening because nobody could hear himself think.

For the progressive-pragmatist-democratic case was indeed "of Child" in the grandest cosmological sense, implying a totally anthropocentric view of the universe and parceling out creativity to every man. Emerson at his most prophetic, Whitman at his most rhapsodic had gone no further. Ironically, the hard-won naturalism and vaunted scientific experimentalism of American thought had come back to idealism, only of a crudely subjective rather than an objective type. The world was just what it was perceived to be, not by God, but by every child, and truth coterminous with every child's experience. William James had declared, "The true . . . is only the expedient in the way of our thinking."[21] And he had made it clear that the expedient was what every man found useful in serving whatever interest he, individually, and society only incidentally felt at the moment. "Any idea upon which we can ride, so to speak; any idea that will carry us prosperously from any one part of our experience to any other part, linking things satisfactorily, working securely, simplifying, saving labor; is true for just so much, true in so far forth, true *instrumentally.*"[22]

So science, according to Dewey, cannot disclose the properties of reality apart from human experience: there is no Being that was, is, and ever shall be world without end that stands in objective integrity beyond human nature and imposes upon men external constraints justifying external authority in our affairs and "Discipline" in education. Within a world that was only a womb of human experience, we needed to learn only to satisfy ourselves by intelligent arrangements replacing the automatic arrangement whereby as fetuses we were satisfied in our mothers' wombs. "Now," Dewey assured his readers in 1920, "old experience is used to suggest aims and methods for developing new and improved experience."[23] Current experience, the breathing moment, mattered chiefly insofar as it was expediently directed toward greater satisfaction in the future. Old experience—the cultural heritage—mattered not for its own sake, either, or as a model but just for whatever "cash value" (James's phrase) it might have. If its cash value were not immediately apparent, who could be expected to value it sufficiently even to find out whether it might after all have cash value? Far from being concerned about the disavowal of intrinsic value and the possibility of objectivity, Dewey went on to assert in 1929: "It is because of injection of an irrelevant philosophy (materialism) into interpretation of the conclusions of science that the latter are thought to eliminate qualities and values from nature. Thus is created the standing problem of modern philosophy: the relation of science to the things we prize and love and which have authority in the direction of conduct. . . . Drop the conception that knowledge is knowledge only when it is disclosure and definition of the properties of fixed and antecedent reality; interpret the aim and test of knowing by what happens in the actual procedures of scientific inquiry and the supposed need and problem vanish."[24]

The distance from epistemological theory to the schoolroom where a normal school mind might be expected to apply it in teaching was long and tortuous, and it was only what a normal school mind could apprehend as tone and slogan that survived the journey. "The case is of Child"—that arrived. Dewey might allow the importance of subject matter as relics of "past collective experience" that should be studied, but he added caveats that came through more clearly than the concession. "But," he said, "this process tends to set up subject matter as something of value just by itself, apart from its function in promoting the realization of the meanings implied in the present experience of the immature. Especially is the educator exposed to the temptation to conceive his task in terms of the pupil's ability to appropriate and reproduce the subject matter in set statements, irrespective of its organization into his activities as a developing social member."[25] What, practically, had he to suggest as a replacement for the curriculum regarded, as he said it generally was, "as a kind of composite made by the aggregation of segregated values"?[26] He usually substituted "living" for "schooling," and the educative living he visualized was a form of roleplaying in which pupils imitated vocations of the urban-industrial setting. He thought it possible in this way for the young to get the equivalent of what he supposed had been the "organic" education of the agrarian past. "The positive principle is maintained," he said, "when the young begin with active occupations having a social origin and use, and proceed to a scientific insight in the materials and laws involved, through assimilating into their more direct experience the ideas and facts communicated by others who have had a larger experience."[27] He did not address himself to the staggering practical questions that immediately arise. To mention only two: what could guarantee pupils' advancing to "scientific insight in the materials and laws involved"? What conceivable training could guarantee teachers' competence to found teaching in the variety of "active occupations having a social origin and use"?

He wanted the school to be "a miniature community and one in close interaction with other modes of associated experience beyond the school walls" although schooling was necessary just because under urban-industrial conditions children no longer had the opportunities for informal education that farm and village life supposedly had provided so richly.[28] He believed that education, as distinguished from memorized lumber, was for the most part an incidental effect of social activities, customs, occupations, and so on, that is, an unplanned effect of environment. It did not strike him as paradoxical to propose that the school should be a planned environment that would have unplanned but consistently desirable, though not prescribed and predictable, educational effects. "What conscious, deliberate teaching can do is at most to free the capacities thus formed for fuller exercise, to purge them of some of their grossness, and to furnish objects which make their activity more productive of meaning."[29] The test of the unplanned effect of the planned environment upon a pupil was thus a subjective one on the part of the pupil, who had only to assure the teacher he had had a "meaningful experience" in order to get credit for having advanced to scientific insight. It was only too easy for Motherteacher to obtain such assurances through personal relationships with pupils without exacting objective proofs of particular learning.

Dewey's contradictory notions of formal education proceeding informally, of school as "life," of pupils as persons not in tutelage and teachers as personal manipulators without impersonal authority appear all the more puzzling in the light of his reformist inclination. Be he ever so subtly manipulative, an antiformalist reformer is hard to imagine. He may destroy the existent form that he dislikes, but can he replace it with another, however superior in conception, if it is form per se that he cannot tolerate? The pragmatic and instrumentalist answer was that if forms there must be, let them be in continuous transformation as temporary expedients, for the world is dynamic. In American educational theory, the scientific conclusion that matter is in motion was readily translated into the cliché that children must be educated for "our changing world of today" by dissolving the curriculum.

Implicit here was faith in the propositions that change is constant, for the better, and so rapid that nothing taught definitively to a pupil will be relevant to his situation a few years later when he is an adult. Education must be above all things relevant—that is, freed from the past; but since nothing that happens to be relevant today will be so tomorrow, nothing in particular need be taught now except the desirability of an open, though empty, mind and mutual acceptance of openness and emptiness. According to Dewey's instrumental view of truth, one is led to a logical absurdity that might be punningly characterized as infinite progress instead of infinite regress. As Bertrand Russell pointed out, to hold that things may be called true or good only in terms of their consequences involves validating the consequences in terms of their consequences ad infinitum, so that judgment is never possible. One result would be that nothing in the curriculum could ever be settled on, even provisionally, either to anathematize, except stability, or to propose as a substitute, except change.

In fact, however, John Dewey was a dogmatist; and he, no less than his enthusiastic followers in progressive and democratic educational propaganda, vended truth. The basic article of faith was his belief in "the principle of continunity."[30] This was his variety of evolutionism, which did not, as Lester Ward's had done, postulate a distinction between genetic and telic evolution but held the universe to be a seamless unity and man, therefore, as one with all. His idea of democracy was rooted here; the universe was "democratic" in that it disallowed distinctions or "discontinuities," and the same held for democratic society. Man was in no sense a special creation or a species that had evolved to a distinctive status under a new evolutionary dispensation. He was not, therefore, a responsible individual prior to social relationships. Instead, in the gospel according to Dewey, man was primarily a social product, not responsible but responsive to others. The good society must of course be democratic in the sense that it encouraged the most inclusive possible "communication," which meant that it must discourage all kinds of distinction, whether economic, racial, or intellectual. Communication implied integration; segregation implied "barriers" and nature abhorred a barrier, a division, or a discrimination.

From the dogma of naturalistic continuity, Dewey derived that of growth. The term had, of course, been a commonplace of liberal educational theory long before Dewey or even Darwin; but Dewey gave the idea a social connotation. "Growth, or growing as developing, not only physically but intellectually and morally, is one exemplification of the principle of continuity." The idea of growth still dressed the old faith in the inevitability of progress in evolutionist terms, but as "an exemplification of the principle of continuity" it pointed to the central desideratum of Dewey's political and social theory, "the experiential continuum."[31] The creation and preservation of some such social glue had always been among the aims of common prayer and common schooling, but Dewey held that the experiential continuum, reflecting the continuum of nature, was democracy. Growth was not so much a vertical experience of the individual as a lateral multiplication of contact among the members of the body politic. He had said subject matter must be psychologized; now he said experience must be democratized; and this meant indoctrination with emphasis upon the most widely accessible experience and discouragement of the less accessible.

"The necessity for democratic experience in the fulfillment of the concept of continuity," Rushdoony has observed, "makes mandatory an essential aspect of Dewey's faith, namely, *integration downward.* Democracy requires identification with the continuum, and such identification necessitates a surrender of all exclusive and aristocratic concepts."[32] Although in theory he advocated a synthesis of impulse or emotion with intellect in education, or as education, Dewey's democratic faith required in fact a preference for feeling since that was more widely distributed than intellect. "How do you feel?" instead of "What do you know?" or "What can you do?" was the democratic question, and Motherteacher asked it of pupils. Intellectuality was damned as undemocratic—elitist being still today the more biting synonym—and increasingly regarded as an inconvenience, an abnormality, by the democratic school lumping the bright with the retarded under the euphemism "exceptional." Dewey went so far as to advise the National Education Association to moderate its efforts to professionalize teachers, thus setting them undemocratically apart; they ought to seek "identification of sympathy and thought" not with limited groups such as the professions but with the masses.[33]

Dewey's idea of "the Great Community" was echoed and sentimentalized in educationist doctrine, emerging, for example, in Harold Rugg's idea of the "Great Society." Community was thought of as the result of socialization so complete that divisive factors, including criticism and dissent, would be obviated. Like the maladapted in the evolutionary theory of biology, critics and dissenters, presumably, would be eliminated in Dewey's sociology. The socially adjusted survivors would be living proof of "growth" into what Dewey called "socialism of the intelligence and the spirit," and their reward would come as a result "of the growing recognition that the community owes to each one of its members the fullest opportunity for development."[34]

But he was defining development in terms of the paradoxical notion of the individual already socialized in intelligence and spirit by paradoxically informal formal education. The individual being taken as no longer responsible prior to society for the degree of cooperation necessary to preserve social order and profit from civil liberty, stress fell on what society and the "democratic" state owed the individual. And the state, no less than the school under Motherteacher, was thought of in imagery connoting the womb, that is, as a controlled environment in which the members of society would be in symbiotic relationship. Dewey's ostensibly pragmatic but covertly idealist emphasis on experience as the arbiter of reality was the inclusive, cosmic sanction for indulgence of "Child" and subversion of "Discipline" not only at school but in life then and thereafter.

With the institution of the welfare state after 1932, the American school became very nearly the embryonic society Dewey thought it should be, in which pupils were not so much prepared for autonomously individual responsibility in a representative democracy as conditioned to continue as adults a pattern of infantile dependency and gratification in a socialist state. "The teacher is engaged," he said, "not simply in the training of individuals, but in the formation of the proper social life." If the proper social life was that of the Great Community, it followed that the teacher must be Motherteacher with a social-democratic allegiance. The "dignity" of the teacher's calling lay in the fact "that he is a social servant set apart for the maintenance of proper social order and the securing of the right social growth." Like Froebel's kindergartners who, for all their reverence toward children's sacred impulses, never doubted they were privy to God's intentions for children, Dewey's ideal teacher, serving not God but society, knew which was the "proper" social order and the "right" social growth. Furthermore, Dewey's teacher understood that growth was social growth, which is not necessarily individual growth, pace his notion of the individual socialized in intelligence and spirit. He added that "in this way the teacher always is the prophet of the true God and the usherer in of the true kingdom of God," an egregious formulation which has often been taken approvingly as a pious echo of faith in education but which on analysis reveals his bias.[35]

The true kingdom of God to which Dewey alluded was presumably his version of democracy; and if the teacher's function was "the maintenance of proper social order and the securing of right social growth," it could not be the teaching of a curriculum keyed to literacy and through that to the fostering of autonomous responsibility and critical intelligence. Dewey asserted allegiance to subject matter and intellectual development, and there is no reason to suppose he was insincere in doing so. Nevertheless, his social emphasis in education, which made it an instrument of planners of a particular kind of society, implied and has indeed led to the devaluation of literacy as the elementary educational goal. This has meant the abandonment of the idea of education as a curriculum, for literacy—verbal and mathematical—is prerequisite to the study of the several subject matters. "Democratic education," as Dewey and his followers used the phrase, is another contradiction in terms rather than a synthesis. If the purpose of the school is to foster social "continuity," the curriculum must be inimical to schools; for by definition the curriculum is a course to be run, at every stage and branching of which capacities are discriminated and specialized. The fruitlessness of decades of debate between educators in the tradition of progressive education and the defenders of the curriculum has been the inevitable result of talking at different levels of discourse. The parties have used the same words but with opposite meanings, to the point at which for a quarter century (racial) integration of teachers and student bodies has been equated with (academic) "quality education."

Continuing the strange abuse, amounting to reversal of meanings, of terminology which has characterized American educational thought since Horace Mann, Dewey declared in 1929 that "the American people is conscious that its schools serve best the cause of religion in serving the cause of social unification; and that under certain conditions schools are more religious in substance and in promise without any of the conventional badges and machinery of religious instruction than they could be in cultivating these forms at the expense of state-consciousness."[36] Like Mann, with differences more apparent than real, he regarded education as a propaganda, designed to indoctrinate people with a species of statism substituting for religious faith. "Apart from the thought of participation in social life the school has no end nor aim," he asserted.[37] It celebrated the secular communion, in which the part of God was taken by society. Since the society was democratic, it could not countenance a division of its members into categories paralleling the saints and sinners of Christian theology. Social unification and participation being all in school as well as in society at large, the curriculum, with its inevitably discriminating categories of failure and achievement, was antidemocratic and heretical. The point may be made as well in terms without religious connotation: the curriculum was irrelevant to education as Dewey conceived it, and the strident demand for "relevance" in education which characterized the 1960s and continues more matter-of-factly in the 1970s is a mass rejection of external "structure" embodied in the curriculum.

Yet the curriculum could not be frankly scrapped. Instead it has been taught for half a century in increasingly bad faith while all of its detested divisions, definitions, and discriminations have been steadily blurred by a train of "integrative" and "interdisciplinary" schemes that have subverted the logic of subject matter in the cause of social unification at the most inclusive and therefore a low level: "integration downward." Dewey's apostle, William H. Kilpatrick, developed the model of such schemes and popularized it through the immense classes of teachers from all over the country that he taught at Teachers College of Columbia University between 1913 and 1938. Known as the "project method," after an article Kilpatrick published in 1918,[38] it was a translation into operative classroom terms of Dewey's educational theory and of his practice as well, since it derived from the vocation-centered play Dewey experimented with in his laboratory school at the University of Chicago. The project was to be, in the school of the urban era, the equivalent of the idyllic agrarian past when life at large was supposed to have been informally educative. Kilpatrick did nothing to explain away the difficulty in the notion of informal formal education and either countered critics with the mere animus of antiformalism or assured his followers that "somehow" soundly educated people would emerge from school projects.

Whatever else the project method was designed to accomplish, it was a guarantee that "the capable one" would develop only in step with the mass, a flat rejection of the Christian dependence upon the salt of the earth, the saving remnant. The old curriculum encouraged individually responsible study along the logical lines of subject matter without imposing limits on how far "the capable one" might go, regardless of how far behind he might leave the mass. The project method, however, was group effort and brought social pressures to bear on individual pupils who went autonomous ways, appealing to objective standards against the feelings of the group. To repress "the capable one" was not, however, recognized as cruelty. Did not Kilpatrick teach that "man's nature is social" and that the greatest privation in life is therefore "exclusion by others, the sense of not being accepted by the group"?[39] He did not make clear in what sense the development of "the capable one" might be "at the mere expense of others," as he suggested; but frustration of that development was apparently richly compensated, in his view, by group acceptance. The stultification of the capable was matched, in the cause of social unification and integration, by the redefinition of the incapable, who became known as "the disadvantaged" and were hospitably drawn into the group as well.

By 1928 John Dewey was avowedly anxious about the formlessness of the schools to which his own antiformalist views had led. Writing in *Progressive Education,* he credited the new education with "the elements of a distinctive contribution to the body of educational theory: respect for individual capacities, interests, and experience; enough external freedom and informality at least to enable teachers to become acquainted with children as they really are; respect for self-initiated and self-conducted learning; and perhaps above all belief in social contact, communication, and cooperation upon a normal human plane as all-enveloping medium." But he asked the crucial question: what had the new education produced in the way of "a body of verified facts and tested principles which may give intellectual guidance to the practical operating of schools?"[40]

The question for him was at this time of "Curriculum," for the new education was too exclusively committed to "Child." "An experimental school," Dewey observed, "is under the temptation to improvise its subject-matter," but a school ought to arrive at least at "some significant subject-matters undergoing growth and formulation" even if these differed from school to school. He feared that the progressive schools would improvise forever, so opposed were they to "orderly organization of subject-matter" on the grounds that this was "hostile to the needs of students in their individual character." Accordingly, he issued a clear warning:

But individuality is something developing and to be continuously attained, not something given once and ready-made. . . . It is quite possible for teachers to make such a fuss over individual children, worrying about their peculiarities, their likes and dislikes, their weaknesses and failures, so that they miss perception of real individuality, and indeed tend to adopt methods which show no faith in the power of individuality. A child's individuality cannot be found in what he does or in what he consciously likes at a given moment; it can be found only in the connected course of his actions. Consciousness of desire and purpose can be genuinely attained only toward the close of some fairly prolonged sequence of activities. Consequently some organization of subject-matter reached through a serial or consecutive course of doings, held together within the unity of progressively growing occupation or project, is the only means which corresponds to real individuality. So far is organization from being hostile to the principle of individuality.

He then flatly asserted that the progressive schools were "under the necessity of finding projects which involve an orderly development and interconnection of subject-matter, since otherwise there can be no sufficiently complex and long-span undertaking" in the classroom.[41]

Dewey's own antiformalist ambivalence licensed the progressive educators to ignore this warning against the complete subversion of the curriculum. His temperamental and philosophical commitment to growth and democracy prevented him from defining a common curriculum, so he weakened his assertions with vagueness. A school should arrive at least at "some significant subject-matters." It was only "some" organization of subject matter that was necessary to encourage "real" individuality in students. The blandly plural "subject-matters," the "somes" and "somehows," the "reals" and "trues," the mock-modest acknowledgments of educational "challenges" that could never be definitively met in "our changing world of today" which still characterize educationist jargon are not without their sanctions in the usage of John Dewey. Out of multifarious unspecifiable and unpredictable projects, differing not only from one school to another but within a given school and from one year to the next, all supposedly founded in the atomistic initiatives of pupils, he expected teachers so to manipulate the situation that pupils should learn particular, though ever unparticularized, subject matter. I am not aware that he ever got down to cases and specified subject matter and the proper sequence of it in relation to the maturation of pupils. Nor, so far as I know, did he ever discuss teaching method in relation to the logic of subject matter rather than in relation to "finding the conditions which call out self-educative activity"—as if initiation into the logic of subject matter might not do this!—and "cooperating with the activities of the pupils so that they have learning as their consequence."[42]

The more democratically socialized intelligence and spirit of W. H. Kilpatrick brooked none of Dewey's reservations and made it plain, at last, that the new education was at war with "Curriculum" and that "Curriculum" meant education keyed to literacy. It is idle to search so child-centered a writer for specifics as to what should comprise any curriculum, to say nothing of a curriculum supposed common. Kilpatrick relied on the master's comfortable words to the effect that if one seeks the kingdom of heaven educationally, all the needful specifics will be added unto one; but he was bound to tell teachers how to teach the unspecified.

He averred that "teaching exists to encourage and develop a good quality of living, living of a quality fit to be built into abiding character." Whether "abiding" is the same as "all-round" character, which he had adduced earlier as the aim of education, it is hard to say; nor is it any easier to infer what a "good" quality of living may be than it was to understand what he meant by the "proper" behavior to which all-round character was said to lead. He assured teachers that they, like anyone else, possessed a "map" or "aggregate" of values, which, though "for the most part not consciously organized," must be relied on "as aims in guiding those under [their] care." Kilpatrick did not suggest that teachers try to organize their values more consciously but said they "should aim continually at keeping this aggregate of values alive and growing."[43] Undefined to start with, it should not even remain the same. Perhaps all he meant was that teachers should be ever receptive to the professional educationist line as paid out to them by professors like Kilpatrick in summer schools where teachers had to acquire credits for certification and advancement.

Whatever aggregate of values the teacher might have, Kilpatrick was strong to assert the verity, "We must start where the learner is; for the new can be learned only as the learner already has in mind and heart enough relationship between new and old to make him see, understand, value, and wish (accept) the new." Thus sixty years after the heyday of Herbartianism the doctrine of interest remained central. "Let it be noted, emphatically, that in teaching at its best we do not first choose subject matter, then ask how to make it interesting." That was the error of the old education: "the new . . . starts where the child is so as to capitalize on the child's personally directed activity springing from his real interest." Just as he said the teacher possessed a "map of values," though not "consciously organized," so he asserted, "Each learner has a stock of interests, most of which are lying dormant."[44] One is asked to imagine, as teaching at its best, a situation in which the teacher uses conscientiously changing "values," most of them never consciously organized, as a guide in assessing the "interests," mostly dormant, of each pupil and then in encouraging each pupil to develop his interests apart from any prescribed subjects of study.

From such mutual unconsciousness and dormancy, the teacher—none other than Motherteacher—as only first among peers in the classroom, must reach through group discussion techniques a choice of class activity. Kilpatrick assumed that from the infinitely diverse interests of pupils selection of one as the index for a class activity was possible on the basis of their age. "The teacher, having in mind the whole class and the promising lines of activity for this age of pupil, may on the first school day have lying around the room specimens of art or craft work or books used or made in previous years, or may start discussion of what the summer vacation yielded, or ask openly for suggestions as to the line of work the class should take up first."[45] Kilpatrick thought it would be helpful to list all the pupils' suggestions on the blackboard and then set about choosing among them. It was then up to the teacher to manipulate the situation so that the group would choose a feasible activity, make a "commitment" to it, and educate themselves with it.

From the hour of commitment, the teacher's function was "to help the learners to help themselves."[46] They would learn what they lived, and "the school should be *a place of living,* living of a kind to help build the desirable all-round character to serve the all-round good life." His reiterations, with increments of evangelical tone only, took the place of development. Accordingly, *"the new curriculum becomes the total living of the child so far as the school can influence it or should take responsibility for developing it."*[47] Kilpatrick sought to exorcize vacuity by italicizing it.

Under the chapter heading "Curriculum Making," Kilpatrick resorted to mere exhortation. For example: "Since the pupils will learn what *they* live as *they* accept it and *in the degree* they accept and live it, it is *their* living which is to be sought, the finest quality of living that teachers and pupils together can effect— create or contrive or develop." Or: "But if the pupils are to learn the fine qualities of this living—and build these into character—they have to *live* precisely these fine qualities and *accept them in their hearts* to live by."[48] He could use the demonstrative adjective—"this living"; he could exhort teachers to contrive fine qualities of living and get pupils to "live precisely" these qualities; but he supplied no substantive for the adjective and never defined the qualities.

It remains to observe that Kilpatrick, like his predecessors in the tradition of child-centeredness, advocated the extension of the methods he advocated for elementary school to the higher levels of education. He described the work of the elementary school as "general" education, characterized with his usual vagueness as the education "that all should have to fit them as well as possible for full living, full living now of a kind to add continually to growing and richness of living as the years advance," and said "this must go on all through high school and even into college." Kilpatrick said "specialized" or "departmentalized" work must, regrettably, have a place in high school and college, but he meant to restrict the place it had and, furthermore, to have the teaching of it "as far as possible remade on the general principles of teaching hitherto discussed." "It would be better," he wrote, "if those preparing to teach specialized subjects did not as now major under subject matter professors, but rather in teaching of their subject or area. As a rule subject-matter professors fail to appreciate the fuller and truer aim of modern education and often indoctrinate their students against the modern point of view." Even in college, he recommended that "general," i.e., child- or student-centered, work should continue through all four years, accounting for one and three-quarters of the total. "The chief and most urgent need is to release the American college from the Alexandrian grip," said he, having absurdly fastened upon the scholars of Hellenistic Alexandria responsibility for the academic tradition he detested. Only when this had been accomplished, he added with snide hostility, would we cease "to hear of college teachers saying that college work would be fine if it were not for the students."[49]

Chapter 10
Humbly and Lovingly Muddling Along with Children

KILPATRICK represents the full development of hostility to "Curriculum" which was immediately grounded in Dewey, whether or not Dewey was happy with the improvisations of progressive education; but another figure, Harold Rugg, exemplifies better than Kilpatrick the ultimate fatuities of "democracy" in education. The whole line of child-centered educators and "schoolmen" since Horace Mann can be interpreted as pandering the services of Motherteacher to Demos, but Kilpatrick and Rugg together stand for certain further qualitative aspects, above all for the false and oleaginous tone of American education that has been unmistakable since the 1930s. It is a factitiously personal tone, "warm" and "compassionate," which turns stridently defensive when questioned. It is of course more emotive than intellectual, democratically pious and progressive but with a weak obbligato of cynicism arising from "professional" conformity. It turns realistic only in lobbying for legislative appropriations, asserting bureaucratic power, or coping with breakdowns in student discipline.

Harold Rugg was for education as "challenge," "adventure," "drama," "meaningful experience." Under a typically phrased chapter heading, "The School Curriculum and the Drama of American Life," he bewailed the "gap" between the traditional "essentially academic" American school and the "dynamic content of American life," on the one hand, and between the curriculum and "the growing child" on the other. What he thought was needed to close the gap was a corps of "750,000 teachers (or even, say, 300,000) who, like William Rainey

Harper, 'could teach Hebrew as though it were a series of hair-breadth escapes' "; with such teachers "the *curriculum* itself would stand merely as a subordinate element in the educational scheme. The teacher would occupy the important place of guidance we have given to the materials of instruction." The teacher ought to see to it that the school matched the "American tempo," which he characterized as "*prestissimo*" and "*fortissimo*." Alas, the school had "lagged far behind" the "tor-rential" current of American life, which he said was "personified by the pervading hum of motors and the dynamic syncopation of our new national music"—though how a cur-rent could be personified by motors and music he did not pause to explain.[1]

For want of enough sufficiently "dynamic" teachers who could dispense with the curriculum, Rugg proposed at least to jazz up the curriculum for so long as curriculum there must regrettably be. His idea of a curriculum (as of 1926) was pre-sumably in itself enough to have spurred John Dewey to protest the tendency of progressive schools to improvise subject matter (in 1928). If the curriculum as Rugg imagined it was manage-able by the less than dynamic teachers then in service, one would be helpless to think what and how the superior teachers he confidently expected in the future could teach—if one had not witnessed what has in fact occurred in American schools and colleges in the meantime. Rugg asked:

> Lacking half-a-million dynamic teachers, are we not forced to put into our schools a dynamic curriculum? A curriculum which deals in a rich vivid manner with modes of living of people all over the earth; which is full of throbbing anecdotes of human life? A curriculum which will set forth the crucial facts about the community in which the pupils live; one which will interpret for them the chief features of the basic resources and industries upon which their lives depend in a fragile, interdependent civilization; one which will introduce them to the modes of living of other people? A curriculum which will enable pupils to visualize the problems set up by human migration; one which will provide them with an opportunity to study and think critically about the form of democratic government under which they are living and to compare it with the forms of government of other

peoples? A curriculum which is built around a core of pupils' activities—studies of their home community, special reading and original investigation, a constantly growing stream of opportunities for participation in open-forum discussion, debate, and exchange of ideas? A curriculum which deals courageously and intelligently with the issues of modern life and which utilizes in their study the cultural and industrial as well as the political history of their development? A curriculum which is constructed on a problem-solving organization, providing continuous practice in choosing between alternatives, in making decisions, in drawing generalizations? A curriculum which recognizes the need for providing definite and systematic practice upon socially valuable skills? Finally, a curriculum which so makes use of dramatic episodic materials illustrating great humanitarian themes that by constant contact with it children grow in wise insights and attitudes and, constructively but critically, will be influenced to put their ideas sanely into action?[2]

Many details of this Whitmanesque rhapsody on educationist themes commend themselves to analysis, but perhaps it is enough to point out that in it what Kilpatrick called "concomitant learnings" are cited as comprising the "dynamic" curriculum. As Rugg used the terms, they make one more of the characteristic contradictions, the one canceling the other, of the ever new education. The inanity of personifying the curriculum and proposing it in the absence of competent teachers is very striking, but he reached further extremes of inanity with every grandiose function that he proposed for it.

The curriculum must be seen "whole," as Dewey had said— so, of course, must the child; but Rugg opined that the "creative artist" is the type most able to see wholes. "The poet who sings of America (be his rhythm set in verse or prose), the dramatist, the novelist, the lay critic of American life, prose essayist, the student of society—all must be brought into this task of setting the great objectives of the school. Deep-seeing analysts must cooperate with the man of science and his fact-founded laws. For in the last analysis it is the creative artist and the student of society who will set the far-off, deep-guiding, *ultimate* objectives."[3] No surprise was in store when, in later effusions, Rugg, unconsciously echoing Francis W. Parker, extolled the "artist teacher" as the particular manifestation of the dynamic teacher of which he held so many hundreds of thousands were needed.

In *The Child-Centered School*, published in 1928, Harold Rugg and Ann Shumaker purported to take a critical view, as suggested by their subtitle, "An Appraisal of the New Education"—it was still new, be it noted. They advanced as the main goals of education the "drawing out of the child's inner capacities for self expression," in which they were only repeating the old "soft line," and second, the development of "tolerant understanding of self and society," in which something new did come to expression. The emphasis on tolerant understanding, as if understanding might not lead as reasonably to intolerance as to tolerance, was prophetic. They subscribed to the fundamental illusion of all optimistic philosophy that to understand is necessarily to forgive. They did, it is true, say that the goal should be "tolerant understanding and . . . critical questioning," but it appeared that the critical questioning was to be of society by mutually tolerant egoisms prior to any prescribed training. It was a recipe for impertinence. Rugg and Shumaker gave a nod to social adjustment in passing, but their presumption was that the individual pupil should develop "his potential for improving the world through the release of his powers of creative self-expression."[4]

This advocacy of indulgence of the child's "creative self-expression" was based less on consciousness of the evolutionist rationale than on childishness in the authors manifested in cultural parochialism as extreme as that of the "now generation" of the 1960s, in relation to which Rugg and Shumaker stand as godparents. "We are living today in a totally new civilization," they asserted. "In this erection of a new civilization the American people have assumed a position of strategic leadership."[5] And they meant global leadership, to which the new education was in their minds essential. The ancient bias of the new education against the past was now increased, for was not the old curriculum the product of college professors bound to the past? They had written the school textbooks with an eye to the history and integrity of their different disciplines.

"Now," wrote Rugg and Shumaker, "being primarily interested in the logic of their generalizations, knowing little of child interests, needs, and capacities, they organized the textbooks, hence the materials of instruction, on the lines prescribed by the limits of the academic research in which they were engaged. . . . The curriculum thus came to consist of a program of narrow and non-useful school subjects, for each of which a specific textbook determined the content of instruction."[6] This was no way to release the creative self-expression of American children that would unify American society and then Americanize the world!

Although they asserted their devotion to seeing the curriculum whole and blamed college professors for having made it an unphilosophical patchwork imbued with wicked elitism, the progressive educationists conceived it no tyranny on their part when they reversed matters and imposed the methods of the lower on the higher levels of education. With them, "curriculum-making" was a never-ending process—for was the world not in flux?—to be carried on by committees drawn from among themselves. If the result was studiedly too vague for definition, it was accompanied by an explicit characterization of the teacher that epitomized the development of Motherteacher. A report by the Committee on Curriculum-Making of the National Society for the Study of Education, published as the *Twenty-sixth Yearbook* of the society in 1926, is the classic statement.

Chaired by Harold Rugg, this committee comprised a brief who's who of the new education. It included figures who, compared with Rugg and Kilpatrick, counted as conservatives, notably William C. Bagley of Teachers College, Columbia University, and Charles H. Judd of the School of Education, University of Chicago. But the differences were not radical; and the summary of the committee's approach to curriculum making by one of its members, Stuart A. Courtis, professor of education at the University of Michigan, is an index to the views prevalent at the time among the educationist leadership of the country. Courtis's summary may not represent the views of the leading educators of the 1970s, but these are not discontinuous

with the 1920s and in any case the advanced position of that period is the cliché of ours.

Courtis drew up a table from scattered parts of the committee's report to illustrate the direction in which the committee
believed education in 1926 was moving.

Education To-Day Is Moving

Paragraph
Number

(4) *From* "imposition on children of adult forms of thought, feeling, and behavior"* — *To* "goals dictated by children's interests, needs, capacities for learning and experiences, as well as by the larger demands of society."

(5) *From* disregard of the individual — *To* "work adjusted to contribute most fully to the development of the individual."

(6) *From* formal, academic, non-social standards — *To* the "test of the effectiveness with which subsequent situations are met by the individual." "It is of paramount importance that the individual participate effectively in social life."

(14) *From* subjective, unchecked bases of selection and organization of curriculum-materials — *To* bases of selection and organization established by scientific studies of both children and society.

(16) *From* disregard of life values — *To* "definite consideration of the problems of economic, political, social, and individual life."

(21) *From* a narrow academic content of conventional skills and knowledges — *To* a content that "includes important attitudes, generalizations, and appreciations, and an understanding of the important institutions and problems of life as well as the conventional skills and knowledges."

Paragraph
Number

(22)	*From* mass education	*To* "provision for individual differences."
(24)	*From* education as "subject matter set out to be learned, repeated, accepted ready made, given back without adequate understanding"	*To* education as "change in control of conduct," as "ways of responding *to be built by the learner* into his own character."
(28)	*From* a teacher-controlled process	*To* a process in which the learner, with a "maximum of self-direction, assumes responsibility for the exercise of choice in terms of life-values."
(40)	*From* a curriculum organized by subjects	*To* "materials of instruction assembled from the starting point of the needs of the learner, irrespective of the content and boundaries of existing subjects."
(44)	*From* a criterion of value based upon adult opinion	*To* a "criterion of value based upon measured contributions to facilitation of 'true learning.' "
(47)	*From* "curriculum-revision by individuals and by subjects"	*To* curriculum-revision by adequate groups of specialists, and as a whole.
(49)	*From* "measurement by mere subject-matter tests and examinations"	*To* measurement by tests "corresponding in type to the advances made in the curriculum."

_____

*Quotation marks are used whenever a phrase or sentence is practically a quotation, even though a few words may be changed in order or form to fit the tabular form.[7]

Courtis believed that curriculum making should begin with the formulation of "a basic philosophy," which he said in the loose grandiose style of his kind "should be derived from a study of cosmic evolution and should formulate the purpose of

life, and the destiny of man, as far as these ultimate goals may
be discerned." The selection and organization of "curriculum-
materials" should then be governed by the basic philosophy.
Courtis reported that there was, however, "no need" to go
through the preliminary philosophizing. "The record of past
changes in education is *in itself* an expression," he asserted, "of
the evolutionary process." There is no clearer instance of the
evolutionist pieties in pragmatic use than Courtis's conclusion
that the "evidence of change in education," as shown in his table, was equivalent to an organic philosophy in terms of which
the curriculum might be reconstructed.[8]

Evidently, the new educationists could not speak of any given
curriculum but only of curriculum making; details of the
contents and organization of the curriculum could be only
ephemeral and one was freed to dwell magniloquently on goals.
There might be reactionary pockets of resistance here and
there, but American education had rejected knowledge as its
goal. "The success of educational effort," as Courtis put it, "is to
be judged by the *types of individuals* produced, not merely by
what these individuals know." This was only the common
school revival emphasis on character as against "mere"
knowledge rephrased once more. The educationist of 1926,
however, defined character, or the type of the individual, in
evolutionist rather than moralistic terms. "In cosmic evolution
the sequence of emergence has been energy, matter, life, intelligence, personality," Courtis opined confidently. "Personality is the latest, most complex, most influential product of
the creative process." He argued, "In curriculum-revision,
therefore, decisions as to selection, organization, and administration of both materials and methods are to be made more and
more in terms of their contributions to integration of personality."[9]

But what was an integrated personality? Courtis said the
committee, though it did not address itself to this question any
more than it did to formulating a basic philosophy, implied an
answer. An integrated personality was fully "developed"; could
"participate effectively in social life because he has built into his

own character, by the assumption of responsibility and the exercise of choice in terms of life values, desirable controls of conduct"; had "definitely considered the problems of economic, political, social, and individual life"; and had acquired "a sense of responsibility for social as well as for individual progress." If that was the committee's idea of an integrated personality, it would seem that the curriculum designed to produce it must be formidable indeed. But to Courtis and his colleagues the function of the teacher and the school seemed clear enough. *"Throughout* their school careers—that is, from kindergarten through college, and to an ever increasing degree—pupils must be given opportunities to develop 'attitudes of understanding and tolerance,' and 'to perfect habits of right conduct and creative self-expression.' "[10]

Nevertheless, the question will not down; what, exactly, was the teacher to do in the classroom day after day? The sample curricula in Rugg and Shumaker's *The Child-Centered School* propose, as might be expected, everything in general and nothing in particular. Theirs would be, of course, an "activity" school, and the book illustrated this fundamental point with a frontispiece contrasting photographs of a classroom symbolizing the hateful old education (orderly rows of pupils' desks oriented to the teacher's) and a classroom symbolizing the blessed new (jumble of tables and chairs and small groups of pupils buzzing about different activities). It hardly needed saying that the authors took "child interest as the orienting center of the school."[11] It did need saying how, given all the different child interests, there could be any "orienting center." Rugg and Shumaker seemed to recognize as a problem "the extent to which the pupils must themselves initiate the units of work which constitute the curriculum": there was "the problem of expert guidance by the teacher. Can the stage be set so that pupils will recognize those problems which are suggested by the teacher as of enough importance to stimulate whole-hearted effort and thus to bring about intense and broadly integrated learning?"[12]

So they declared, in an ingenuous tone, that the teacher had only to present and the pupils had only to accept as "a center of interest . . . any one of the host of problems of international affairs, industrial life, government, immigration, population, or those that contribute to effective individual living." The authors professed surprise that even in the new schools "it is impossible to find . . ., for example, a curriculum program designed to give an understanding of the current impact of the great agricultural nations of the earth upon the industrial nations which are their masters. We find little reference to the thrilling story of the unique industrial civilization which has been produced from Germany westward to Japan since 1800."[13] How could "child-interest" have failed to demand such thrilling "curriculum material"?

Rugg and Shumaker felt that the new schools, whatever little shortcomings they might have, rightly scorned to teach "isolated facts" and left "mostly to chance and to the succession of spontaneous events the evolution of ideas and generalizations." In this context "generalization" seems to have meant something other than a proposition derived from any given particulars ("isolated facts"). Naturally, Rugg and Shumaker would not "propose to determine in avance the details of the specific units of work"—which units could not, therefore, have been very specific—in any given school, much less for schools in general. They only recommended that the teacher "have a large array of units, analyzed in advance for their ideational possibilities, their concept-developing power; to determine what relationships of cause and effect may be reasonably expected to appear from participation in them." And the teacher would need, as a basis for curriculum planning (Dewey called it improvisation), "adequate lists of the fundamental meanings, concepts, generalizations, and problems of contemporary society, and the controlling themes and movements which modern civilizations are rapidly evolving."[14]

Sadly, but of course tolerantly, Rugg and Shumaker admitted that the new schools were imperfect although their heart was in the right place and they must at all events be preferred to the old. "Emphatically," they confessed, "intellectual development is avoided by many of these schools. They stand for informality and they secure the outcomes of informality. Their centers of interest (they are well named) lack intellectual rigor in plan and development."[15] In another place, Rugg and Shumaker confessed further that the "extreme individualism of the teachers" was a defect. "No school has visualized the whole educational program," they said; and they remarked the "conspicuous absence of clear thinking about the psychology of the creative act"—in schools dedicated to the subtitution of creativity for program! "It is to be intensely regretted that in thirty years we have not succeeded in producing adequate measures of the outcomes of the new education." Nevertheless, they rose from the confessional to say that such defects were as nothing "compared to the revolutionary contribution of the new schools," especially their "untrammeled attitude toward the philosophy of child growth." The new education had correctly rejected "the philosophy of subject-matter-set-out-to-be-learned, discarded the concept of knowledge for knowledge's sake, and explored the concept of freedom."[16] In their late epitome of the paedocentric tradition, Rugg and Shumaker were finally content with schools whose educational activities lacked all unity except that of the hero, the child. It was a unity still more illusory than Aristotle had indicated, for the case was really not of child but of every individual child and every individual teacher at last herself credited with childish rights to self-expression.

More than ten years after *The Child-Centered School,* Harold Rugg, nothing daunted, was the leading contributor to another volume ominously titled *Democracy and the Curriculum.* The subtitle translated these incompatible terms as *The Life and Program of the School,* and Rugg's foreword was significantly titled "Studying the American Problem." The American problem was not, as the uninitiated might think, the life and program of the school as decreed by the child-centered educators. The problem was, rather, their country, of which pupils were still being encouraged to seek "tolerant understanding," for "if the democratic process is to be anything more than the will-o'-the-wisplike political fluctuation of a blind and credulous people, the process must take on the very nature of *education.*"[17]

The school was presented now as the tolerant critic of society, whose fumbling efforts at developing the democratic process since the founding of the Republic had amounted to very little. Following Rugg, the teacher must take an alarmed view of the "immaturity of our society" rather than that of the child.[18] It was the "task" of the school "to bring forth on this continent—in the form of a cooperative commonwealth—the civilization of abundance, democratic behavior, and integrity of expression and of beauty which is now potentially available."[19]

It was a Motherteacher of uncommon fecundity who was required for such a magnificent bringing-forth, and Rugg and Shumaker had already drawn her portrait as the final touch in *The Child-Centered School.* "With respect to the heart of the school, the teacher," the chief qualification sought by the new school was a negative one, namely, "liberation from academic concepts of the nature of learning." The new school had started from "scratch" with teachers as with everything else, so it was necessary to define the liberated teacher largely in terms of what she had been liberated from. "In order to free the child it was necessary first to free the teacher," Rugg and Shumaker declared. Freeing her (they used the feminine pronoun) meant nothing less, they said, than "re-creating the teacher!" There could be "no place at all" for "the traditional discipline-teacher in this atmosphere of activity and creative expression." In contrast to the discipline-teacher, whom Rugg and Shumaker further derogated as *"mécanicienne,"* the new teacher was *"artiste."*[20]

In order to bring out the parallel with the views on curriculum as tabulated by Courtis, the following table contrasts the traditional or mere "artisan" teacher and the creative new "artist" teacher, as described in the conclusion of *The Child-Centered School.*[21] It will be as instructive to see how the traditional academically oriented teacher, ninety years after the graduation of the first normalites, was conceived as to study the portrait, done in bald bold strokes, of Rugg and Shumaker's ideal.

The Traditional Discipline- or Artisan-Teacher	The New Artist-Teacher
Rarely listens, talks constantly. An exhibitionist. Impresses her individuality and her ideas on pupils. Domineering, authoritative, demanding her place in the schoolroom sun; every desk must converge toward her place at the front.	A listening teacher. Self-effacing, quietly observant, an unassuming influence in the background.
Assertive. Knows the conventional rules of what seems to her a set game. Has preconceived scheme of inflexible standards to which all pupils must measure—so many arithmetic examples to be worked per minute.	Humble, searching, ever doubtful concerning the success of her concrete achievements. Respect for the unique personalities of pupils forbids assumption of too much authority. Standards not rigid and absolute, principles flexible, adaptable to the unique capacities of her children.
Knows subject matter of her trade. Has memorized the content of the history book she teaches, underlined paragraphs of the geography, has eyes on the answers to the arithmetic problems. Lacking interest in growth, has missed the significance of the psychology of mental and emotional life.	Understands the psychology of growth and has a rich mastery of interrelationships, movements, fundamental ideas, in that broad sector of life in which she may be dealing.
Lives by slogans such as knowledge of set facts, skills, orderly quiet, at-	Lives by slogans such as growth, freedom, individuality, initiative. A guide.

tainment of norms and standards. A taskmaster, a kind of section boss for the huge railroading system known as school.	A student of the child, a student of society.
A blind, helpless cog in the great machine of enforced mass education.	True master of the techniques of teaching, both scientist and artist. Her art has a scientific foundation, and her very science is an art. She constantly submits the subjective inspirations of art to objective evaluations of science, supplements the nearsightedness and incompleteness of pigeonhole science with the full vision of artistic intuition.
Has no chance to be a person in her own right; duty, discipline, the requirements of authorities higher up bar her from human contact with the children.	Knows when to abandon technique and fall back on the more human method of "humbly and lovingly muddling along" with children.

At the end, Rugg and Shumaker held out to the wretched geese of the old dispensation a hope of flocking with the swans of the new. All that was really required was a change of heart. "Thousands of teachers in public schools could, within limits, reproduce the atmosphere of the new schools. The change requires not so much in the way of additional financial aid or years of training, as a fundamental modification in point of view." The main thing had been accomplished: "The new education has reoriented educational thinking about its true center—the child."[22] No matter if it was planless and failed to evaluate its results objectively, they said; for "none who have been touched by the stirring promise of the new education can deny that here is possibly something too great to be measured by the limited standards we now employ. As profitably measure the horizon with foot rules."[23]

One of the most important points to be observed in these contrastive treatments by child-centered educationists of the old and the new curricula and the old and the new types of teacher is the misrepresentation, amounting to evidence of honest ignorance, of academic principles. Courtis began with the view of the Committee on Curriculum-Making that the traditional education gratuitously and undemocratically, even sadistically, imposed on children "adult forms of thought, feeling, and behavior," as if it might not have been a matter of initiating them with charitable concern for their interests as well as society's and as if it had never been done with tactful regard for childish capacities. The modern American educationists could not credit any received, external forms valuable enough to warrant the deliberate subjection of the child's immediate interests (always supposing he had strong ones) to forms. This was interpreted by the committee as "disregard for the individual." So far was the committee from understanding commitment to academic objectivity that it accused the old education of relying upon "subjective, unchecked bases of selection and organization of curriculum-materials." Commitment to the logic of subject matter was only a blind, in the opinion of the committee, behind which subject-centered teachers hid personal authoritarianism.

If that were the case, the committee could not be blamed for believing that the old education consisted of "subject matter set out to be learned, repeated, accepted ready made, given back without adequate understanding." The committee presumably took this as a cynical "teacher-controlled process." It was at any rate wrongheaded because it employed "a criterion of value based upon adult opinion." Adults though the committee members were, they apparently stood firm in the faith that child opinion was superior at least so far as the education of the young was concerned.

But if adult opinion was unacceptable as a criterion of value in education, what else was available? The committee provided two answers, neither of which referred to the underlying evolutionist rationale, so that one cannot be sure the committee was aware of it. Possibly not, for in its indifference to the past the committee may have overlooked even the recent history of American education. First, the committee thought adult opinion should be replaced by "a criterion of value based upon measured contributions to facilitation of 'true learning,' " which seems mere obscurantism. Second, the committee asserted that the old education went in for "curriculum revision by individuals and by subjects," whereas the new did it "by adequate groups of specialists, and as a whole." The committee nursed regard for the individual, but the individual socialized in spirit and intelligence. Group opinion, even though the group were comprised of adults, was preferable to an individual's opinion no matter how specialized his academic qualifications; and if the group also happened to be professors of education ("specialists" in education per se), its opinion must be acceptable as a criterion of value. This second criterion had at least operative or pragmatic meaning. The opinion even of an adequate group of educationists was held to be subject to scientific evaluation of the results of its curriculum making. But whereas the old education used "measurement by mere subject-matter tests and examinations," the new used tests "corresponding in type to the advance made in the curriculum." So if the curriculum no longer consisted of prescribed subject matter, teachers and students were reduced to personal "adjustment."

Courtis said the committee believed that the old education employed "formal, academic, non-social standards." As antiformalists, the committee members could say nothing harsher; but the context shows that they meant by these terms something other than they usually mean, at least outside the circles of professional education. To the committee, the formal was the empty, the fossilized, the repressive, the authoritarian. The academic was to them the useless and irrelevant; the nonsocial was the discriminating and judgmental. By a social standard for measuring the results of schooling, the committee meant "the effectiveness with which subsequent situations are met by the individual," a standard which could not be applied while the individual was still in school or convincingly referred back to his school activities once he was graduated. The only standard that could be applied to him while a pupil was a species of conformism, a sufficiently ironical result for antiformalists to claim. The individual pupil could only be referred to the opinion of the others in his group—his class, his school; what Kilpatrick called "the competent others"—for approval or disapproval. In such a situation, the competence of the others must be accepted as given. In practice, this means indulgence of every opinion, criticism of none, and consequently the emergence of none as authoritative or conclusive.

In this atmosphere, Motherteacher herself was rendered a child among her children in the sense that she no less than they was allowed to be "creative" and entitled to have her opinion respected as much, but no more than, any other in the group. For her, the children were "the competent others." What she had to say on any subject was regarded as merely her opinion, to which she was personally entitled. Let her insist upon it, however, to the point of correcting a sum in arithmetic or a solecism in English usage and she could expect from pupils the classic sullen response: "I just didn't understand what *you* wanted." The question of correctness according to commonly held standards was defensively mistaken by pupils as a question of whim, backed by power, on the part of the teacher. In this attitude, pupils were reinforced by a greater power than the teacher's, namely, that of the system of activity education triumphantly expressing the soft idea of democracy cherished by American society.

Rugg and Shumaker characterized Motherteacher in her full development by setting up the straw figure of the "discipline-teacher" as a horrible example of everything Motherteacher was not and then by describing Motherteacher—their "artist-teacher"—in terms that purported to be positive but which on analysis vanish in self-contradiction. They could not conceive of a teacher who was impersonally, disinterestedly, responsibly, and humanely devoted to academic standards because they could not conceive of academic standards as objectively there. They could not endure the idea of an ineluctable reality of which the human species was an element and to which it must adapt itself. They could not conceive, therefore, of maturation as adaptation to external powers and dominions. It was not even, for them, adjustment to other individuals or the group, for all their pretensions to democracy. They proposed staving off adjustment by their formulas of "acceptance," by blinking differences, by ignoring standards in cultivating an inevitably mindless "tolerant understanding."

Therefore, to Rugg and Shumaker, who I think spoke for modern American education in general, the subject-centered teacher was the discipline-teacher, by which they connoted punitiveness more than devotion to a field of study. They presented the subject-centered teacher just as Horace Mann had libeled the Boston masters as neurotic, compulsive, authoritarian, domineering, totally egocentric. They were obsessed with the traditionally quiet and orderly schoolroom with the pupils' desks oriented to the teacher as a symbol of the teacher's "exhibitionism," as if no teacher had ever had anything to exhibit other than ego, as if the focus might not be through the teacher to the subject under study, an arrangement for facilitating concentration on impersonal matters about which pupils need to know. It was a corollary of the dogma that school must be "life," that it must not be just part of life designed to rule out, for limited periods, the distractions of the random and the personal in order to promote the learning of information and skills that might otherwise never be acquired.

For them, everything went in polemical black and white; over against the subject-centered martinet they posed a teacher whose "respect for the unique personalities" and the also "unique capacities" of pupils caused her—and it has very much the she-teacher that was under discussion—to breach academic standards and subcribe to "flexible" principles. The term *principle* retained honorific connotations and could not be dispensed with, but it could be used so as to evade the thing while advancing the word. The stress on the uniqueness of personalities and capacities destroyed the integrity of subjects and the logic of curriculum and predicated a teacher whose tendency was to assume as a transcendent value the pupil as he was. It destroyed pupil status: a unique personality—and uniqueness was made to connote superiority—which is to be preserved in its uniqueness must not be taught anything on the grounds that it ought to learn common knowledge. All the terms dissolved in this way, "teacher" prominently among them; Motherteacher is no-teacher.

From the beginning of the soft education in the common school revival, special contempt and moral outrage were reserved for memorizing since this was taken as the instance par excellence of the subordination of personality to externals, symbolized by the textbook. It is doubtful that there ever was a time when many teachers forced pupils to memorize textbooks and were content with verbatim reproduction without under- standing as the exclusive goal of education. But Rugg and Shu- maker faithfully repeated, and so added another of the finish- ing touches to the portrait of Motherteacher, that she was no grind. They ridiculed the subject-centered teacher for knowing the "subject matter of her trade," apparently assuming that the pejorative connotations of "trade" would clinch the sneer, al- though in other places they were fulsomely democratic about the workers of the world. They belittled her understanding of subjects as something dully memorized. They thus presented her knowledge as proof of her pathetically uncreative passivity and a fatal impediment to her grasping "mental and emotional life." Their "artist-teacher" would never do anything so absurd as to underline, as the discipline-teacher slavishly did, "para- graphs of the geography" or to keep her "eyes on the answers to the arithmetic problems."

They said scathingly that the subject-centered teacher lived and, presumably, taught in what at first glance might seem a reasonable belief that pupils should learn facts and skills and at- tain to norms and standards in an atmosphere of orderly quiet. But at second glance, the telltale epithet stands out: according to Rugg and Shumaker, the facts and skills to be learned were "set," and that was enough to warrant dismissing them as "mere." The teacher who set what was to be learned might be passive but she was also, in their view, a "taskmaster," "a kind of section boss for the huge railroading system known as school." Although railroading anybody seems to imply a certain degree of initiative, albeit vicious, the outmoded type of teacher must be further denigrated as "a blind, helpless cog in the great machine of enforced mass education."

In contrast, Rugg and Shumaker's ideal teacher had, in place of knowledge of subject matter and concern with students' learning the specifics of it, "a rich mastery of interrelationships, movements, fundamental ideas." These interrelationships do not seem to have referred, as usual in educationist writers, to personal interrelationships but vaguely to those among fields of study that might impinge upon "that broad sector of life in which she may be dealing." One is left to imagine as well as he can the impinging of interrelated fields of study upon some broad sector of life. If one asks for instances of such broad sectors, the answers provided by the educationists came in very broad terms, such as international relations or industrial development.

It came down to personality and personhood and personal relations. The discipline-teacher was regarded as having "no chance of being a person in her own right" and therefore as incapable of "human contact with the children." The ancient idea that academic learning could be liberalizing, that is, humanizing—that it was such by definition—had been forgotten; and the "human" contact now desiderated was really of animal character, a prostituted form of mothering in the biological sense. The discipline-teacher was all the while travestied as meanly subservient to "the requirements of authorities higher up," as if Rugg and Shumaker could not conceive of a teacher professionally certified as an authority in his or her own right.

The new-created and creative teacher, however, fell back on "technique" or "method" in which, according to Rugg and Shumaker, she was not merely an artist but a scientist, too—"her very science is an art." Teaching was a matter of "subjective inspirations," which Rugg and Shumaker said would be scientifically evaluated. Since, however, the subjective cannot, by definition, be objectively measured, science was here accorded only lip service. The teacher was said to have a technique for evading the difficulty; she knew how to supplement "the nearsightedness and incompleteness of pigeonhole science with the full vision of artistic tuition." Science was, after all, only a filing system, a pedantic insistence on classification of mere knowledge quite incompatible with life. And so, when even technique failed, the teacher need not be dismayed—she had "a more human method" in reserve, that is, an altogether unmethodical method of "humbly and lovingly muddling along with children."

This is what the feminization of American education had come to by the middle decades of the twentieth century, an attitude of almost unfathomable sentimentality and complacency which by the 1970s had permeated colleges and universities almost as thoroughly as the kindergartens, elementary schools, and high schools. The terms of the formula should be understood. There is no humility in that "humbly," no love in the "lovingly," and only a monstrously prolonged youthfulness in these "children." Motherteacher, flattered to be further described as the creative artist-teacher, is only humble as an excuse for irresponsibility and incompetence. She—or he—is loving only as very bad mothers are who never develop a realistic relationship with their children but fob them off with a squalid kind of symbiosis between mutually idealized images of one another. The schizoid muddle to which this leads is only too real and much too dangerous for humor or toleration today.

Like her ancestress, the goddess Dulness in Alexander Pope's *Dunciad* whose insidious progress through London from the rough and raffish quarter of Smithfield to the center of civilization and government at Westminster represented the vulgarization of taste and learning, Motherteacher has extended her reign from low to high, from kindergarten to university. Pope ended his account of the triumph of Dulness on an apocalyptic note that was prematurely struck. We may have lived to see in Motherteacher an even more formidable deity than Dulness. Motherteacher's children all, now supplied with nuclear toys and beset with frustrations, we are capable of the ultimate acts in honor of Motherteacher that would guarantee the realization of Pope's prophecy:

> Lo! thy dread Empire, CHAOS! is restor'd;
> Light dies before thy uncreating word:
> Thy hand, great Anarch! lets the curtain fall;
> And Universal Darkness buries all.

Epilogue
Beyond Motherteacher:
The Need for Intellectual Vertebrae

WHO is Motherteacher?

>. . . What is she?
>That all our swains commend her?
>Holy, fair, and wise is she;
>   The heaven such grace did lend her,
>That she might admiréd be.

>Is she kind as she is fair?

Indeed Motherteacher has long been kind, in the Shake-spearean sense, and regarded as fair for this equivocal reason. In return for pay so modest as to mask corruption, she lays to our souls that flattering unction that we come to the world not only unspotted but already of positive worth and graced, divinely or biologically, to grow and develop as uniquely valu-able individuals if not inhibited by external criticism and constraint. Taking us at whatever sacrosanct stage of growth she finds us, Motherteacher professes to teach us nothing about the world beyond ourselves we do not profess ourselves ready to learn. She compassionately connives at keeping each student in his own genial environment, a womb of subjectivity. While assuring each of the perspicacity and charm of his solipsistic murmurings, she labors in the name of democracy to prevent the various communications of the class from working out to any conclusion since that would imply invidious distinctions.

The smile of compassion and caring becomes a little fixed upon Motherteacher's visage as her pupils reach puberty. Dis-cipline, in fact, is the chief characteristic of democratic educa-tion under the regime of Motherteacher, even though she had her origins in the pedagogy of love as against discipline. Hers is not, of course, the discipline of the rod, nor is it particularly academic discipline, but that of personal manipulation intended to keep the class bottled up more or less quietly in the classroom. The situation would drive her more often to brawling, despite her heart of gold, if it were not for an aspect of her pedagogy according to which history and tradition are of no account, the present is all that matters, and the future will be an improvement over both if only she and her charges live. Although admittedly a poor substitute for the womb, the parochialism of the hour and the person has proved a workable simulation of the infantile present tense, so that as students reach high school and proceed to college she manages them by infantilizing them.

In order to provide this ultimate kindness, Motherteacher subverts the curriculum and discredits the idea that there should be one or even several curricula designed for different talents and capacities. For to maintain the integrity of any curriculum whatever is to impose requirements on the child or the infantilized youth, and requirements are antilife! Motherteacher sees curriculum as the dead hand of the past stifling the now-generation. She cannot imagine any established curriculum that would be other than an engine of oppression operated by the establishment that established it. That she herself might be the creature of an establishment that has had its reasons for winking at the perversion of teaching never occurs to her. The curriculum stands, in her feelings, for that most un-American of ideas, authority, which has for her the connotation always of personal or class repression.

But where, today, do we see this character of Motherteacher most nearly approximated in the flesh? She is to be observed not only in the elementary and high school classrooms but in those of colleges and universities, and the purveyors of her services inhabit the administrative offices and, beyond educational institutions proper, the offices of state and federal education and culture bureaucracies, professional education and accrediting associations, foundations, and testing agencies. Her ubiquity is best appreciated by considering her incidence among college and university faculties. She is at her most effulgent not in the college of education but in that of arts and sciences, despite the continuing snobbery of the latter with respect to the former, and more tellingly manifested in the male than in the female liberal arts instructors. The growing minority of women who have achieved college faculty rank, mostly in liberal arts departments, have been selected for strength but their male colleagues for fecklessness by the feminized educational system.

Motherteacher's services are sanctioned today by all propagandists, most of them male administrators, bureaucrats, lobbyists, and members of education association or foundation staffs, for "quality" education defined only in grandiloquent terms of goals and never in concrete academic terms. To this group have been recruited over the past twenty years agitators for minority rights in education. Their demands are only the latest and most extravagant expression of the American antinomianism that has skewed our educational institutions since the Jackson era. Instead of honest testing of specific knowledge and skill, as grounds both for admission to a prescribed curriculum and for certification of achievement after admission, Motherteacher's propagandists and superiors prefer to test aptitude and intelligence. They manipulate the results so as to affirm the educability in general terms of virtually the whole population at every academic level. Where the results resist such manipulation, the case is made for quotas regardless of qualification but never for a more rigorous curriculum that might in time produce qualified students among the group in question.

The legitimation of Motherteacher proceeds today from the most exalted purlieus of the university and the federal bureaucracy. In September 1974, for instance, the president of Yale University welcomed the freshman class to "this largely permissive university" by assuring them, "Yours is the burden of having to find out for yourself what matters most, what you care most about, what you believe, what you most want to do with your life." Yale, he said, refused to tell students "what to think, what to believe" because it had a "deep conviction that purposes, values, and convictions will be more durable if they have taken into account a great variety of human thought and experience, and have withstood the buffeting of doubt." He did not explain how purposes, values, and convictions take human thought and experience into account but promised them, "Yale College tries to make it hard for you to use specialism or professionalism as a substitution for purpose." Did he imagine specialism or professionalism could be at odds with purpose, or was he after all sneaking in advice on what to think, what to believe, namely, that specialized or professional purposes should be suspect? He urged commitment to "the search for compelling purpose," one of those grandiloquent goals that Motherteacher's propagandists commonly extol. It is a formula for the academic antinomianism that Motherteacher exists to indulge.[1]

The way in which cultural leaders generate the atmosphere in which Motherteacher flourishes may be further illustrated by a speech which a member of the Federal Communications Commission delivered early in 1975 to a group of Spanish-speaking people who were protesting the programming of one of the leading stations in the Public Broadcasting System, WNET in New York City. The commissioner attacked WNET and the Public Broadcasting System in general for conceiving of themselves "as an electronic Harvard liberal-arts course" and for having "forsaken those less privileged and influential whose culture and educational needs are far more on a 'street academy' or community college scale." The programming, he declared, derived far too much from the civilization of Western Europe and amounted to the "Caucasian intellectual's home entertainment game" while it "overlooked the intellectual needs and sensitivities of that core of the population which, after years of third-rate education and cultural repression, is just emerging from the 18th and 19th centuries." The polemic fetched up in a cant phrase which, like that of which the president of Yale was guilty, is a cliché of the sentimentality which sanctions Motherteacher. He recommended that WNET turn over its facilities to blacks and Puerto Ricans and allow them "to do their own thing."[2]

Since so much of current discussion of education is focused on the rights of blacks, it is worth stressing further the Americanism of the blacks' attitude, including as it does devotion to

Motherteacher. Even in what purports to be a root-and-branch attack on the American public school as inimical to the interests of the children of the poor in every generation since Horace Mann and especially today to those of urban black children, Colin Greer's *The Great School Legend* (1972), it is after all only Motherteacher's services that are pandered. Historically, Motherteacher has been white and the servant of the white middle class, and Greer thinks the public school has been little more than the engine whereby that class has oppressed the poor, especially poor blacks, in the name of social order and stability but actually just in its own interest. He does not seem to think of social order apart from white middle-class privilege but makes them synonymous and so asserts indifference to the survival of social order. Motherteacher, suitably adjusted to black slum children, so now a black Motherteacher or a sort of revival of Norman Mailer's idea of the white Negro, is the latest expression of the idea of democracy as anarchy with a schoolmistress. Nothing in the current scene is more troubling than the spectacle of apologists for blacks demanding racially integrated schools, getting them preferably at the cost of "court-ordered busing" to formerly all white schools, but taking it for granted that "quality" education waits at the end of the bus line. In fact, Motherteacher presides there, her license renewed with their connivance; and the children arrive only to be indulged in "their own thing"—which is to shortchange them cruelly.

In the foregoing discussion, Motherteacher has not been summoned as a reproach just to women. No matter how far we have taken dissolutive permissivism in education, there can be no temptation to revert to a paralyzing authoritarianism founded in a doctrine of depravity and expressed in a masculinized teaching corps. For all her excesses in the meantime, Motherteacher represented amendment at her beginnings. The question now is how to retain the true qualities of the female while retrieving those of the male teacher, an ambition which implies a disabused but fundamentally optimistic view of human nature and democratic institutions.

Motherteacher can be no more a reproach to women than to men, for she embodies nineteenth-century sex-typing which involves one sex as much as the other. As we increasingly free our behavior from sex-typing, the idea of the teacher as definitively either masculine or feminine should weaken. With respect to the sex-typing of women, the fundamental differentiae have been maternal instinct and motherhood; these have been also the fundamental elements in the stereotype of Motherteacher. If the controlling idea of woman-as-mother loses influence, Motherteacher must fade away. But then so must the reciprocal idea of man-as-child, and of education as a man-child-centered affair.

Although Motherteacher appears in this perspective as a travesty of female nature, her critics still generally regard her as a debilitating influence on male students but not on female students. Until people understand that Motherteacher is no better for girls than for boys she will not be retired. She was originally thought to be a wholesome moral (and only incidentally an intellectual) influence on young boys but a questionable one on adolescent boys and young men. From the beginning, however, she was taken for granted as a proper influence on female students of all ages. This judgment remains an unexamined cliché masking the circumstance that the formal education of girls is not yet of particular concern.

People have all along acknowledged, even if unwilling to correct the situation, that male students tend to rebel against women and, therefore, against the women who happen to be their teachers. This aspect of the development of boys is related to the unfortunate consequence in education that boys rejected what women taught along with the women who taught. The effect has been reinforced by the secondary social status of women. Since women taught everything that is honored only to be subverted as culture in America, the feminization of education has produced male American muckerism, which dominates the scene.

But girls, no less than boys, have understood in their bones the unequal status of the sexes and known, to their own stultification, that culture was associated with the second sex. Of those "concomitant learnings" that W. H. Kilpatrick was wont to exalt above the curriculum, none has been more thoroughly absorbed than this, by girls as well as boys. Being members of the second or teacher sex, girls have suffered subtle ambivalence in their comparatively amenable behavior as students. The boys flout and reject, the girls profess to honor but trivialize culture under the influence of Motherteacher. The boys' stronger feeling, if ever redirected, is more likely to lead to critical-mindedness and creativity than the girls' ambivalence is. Their attitude typically produces the bland, the mechanically correct, the genteel performance in school and leads to more or less conscious obeisance to male moneymaking and continued subversion of culture by adult women in their roles as "docents" of our art galleries, patronesses of our symphony orchestras, advocates of "beautification," and so on.[3]

The continuing lack of concern about the effect of feminized education on girls and women is exemplified in the writer who has most explicitly treated the feminization of education. Patricia Cayo Sexton's position in the 1960s differed little from that of the Male High School Teachers' Association of New York City in 1904. She deplores, rightly, "a rapidly growing breed—the 'feminized male'—whose normal male impulses are suppressed or misshapen by overexposure to feminine norms" in school.[4] She does not, however, give an account of the "feminized female," that is, of the female warped as much as the male by exposure to the anachronistic typing of woman embodied in Motherteacher. Quoting Otto Fenichel to the effect that feminized education discouraged aggressiveness, the loss of which he held to be a handicap to a boy as great as the loss of "his sexual abilities" would be, Sexton has proposed as the first means of mitigating this atrocity "decreasing the school bias that favors girls."[5] But feminized education does not really favor girls. Sexton means that girls make better grades and stay in high school longer than boys do, but a second glance reveals an undesirable kind of conformism in the girls' performance.

Sexton's discussion, although ahead of its time in its emphatic recognition of feminization as an important issue in American education, was confused as a result of an unresolved approach to sex-typing. She was still comfortable, for example, with the usage of "feminized" as a pejorative when applied to men and to "strong" as a pejorative when applied to women. She could casually equate "to feminize" with "to humanize," evidently unconscious of the irony of arrogating the inclusive generic term to one sex to the exclusion of the other; for she used it in the secondary, sex-typing sense of softening, personalizing. She felt that (masculine) engineering needed "a woman's touch" and, conversely, that the arts and humanities needed to be "masculinized."[6] One knows in general what she meant, but in the meantime our attitude toward sex-typing has changed to a degree at which many are uncomfortable with the practice of identifying any of an ever wider range of occupations and behavior with either sex. Such identifications import into our affairs a species of pathetic fallacy increasingly perceived as irrational and unrealistic.

It may, therefore, conceivably be practical now to suggest the exorcism of Motherteacher by balancing the sexes numerically at all levels and in all functions of the educational system. That the balancing of the sexes in the teaching corps, though not in educational administration, has been a panacea prescribed in bad faith since the 1880s should be no deterrent. Of the three great obstacles to carrying out such a reform, two seem less formidable than they did as recently as ten years ago and the third, though still looking like Gibraltar, would fall according to a sort of domino theory if the others did.

The first obstacle to balancing the sexes in education has been the sex-typing of which Motherteacher is an incarnation, and it appears that some decisive changes have occurred in this respect. How many Americans still think, as Patricia Cayo Sexton did in the 1960s, that men, but not women, should be courageous, inner-directed, masterful, technologically skilled, and so on, or that women, but not men, should be polite, clean, neat, and nice?[7] Such culturally determined sex-characters have reflected in part the physical disparities of the sexes and, above all, their different roles as the bearers of and providers for the young. Technology has reduced the need for and the incidence of male strength and aggressiveness, at the same time compensating for female weakness. We are increasingly ready to credit arguments for the organismic equality or superiority of women. In the meantime, growing worry about overpopulation has worked to undercut parenthood as the chief justification of human existence, with greater effect on the idea of woman than on that of man since woman has traditionally been defined as mother, dependent on man for such human fulfillment as she might be capable of. If we are entering an era when most women will bear no more than one or two children and many none at all, and will be regarded as serving society as well by forbearing as by bearing, women will be redefined as independently of the maternal role as men are of the paternal.

The second obstacle is the one Horace Mann took to be permanently fixed, namely the unwillingness of the American taxpayer to provide equal wages at rates as attractive to men as to women for equal work in education. Mann's argument from "expediency" for the use of women as teachers has been pretty well invalidated within education, feminized in Mann's sense though it still is. One no longer expects a woman teacher to make a fourth to a third what a man teacher makes, and the woman teacher now has legal recourse against such discrimination. The unionizing of teachers, expressing a demand for a wage scale comparable to that enjoyed by skilled labor and other professions, has reached a point at which it seems reasonable to think teachers' pay will continue to rise. If it reaches a level competitive with other occupations that men have preferred, the men who enter teaching will be more prepared than earlier generations to find themselves paid on a parity with female colleagues.

The third and most durable obstacle in the way of balancing the sexes in education is the American distaste for hierarchical education dating from the founding of the Republic and reflecting the attitudes that transformed the Republic into a Democracy. Whether Americans will become any more respectful of the need for thorough common education or of the integrity of academic disciplines erected upon it remains to be seen. Only the most chastening experiences could be expected to affect Demos' complacency or reduce the arrogance of his ignorance, but he has now had several that may have begun the work. The humiliation of losing (not the willfulness and stupidity of waging) the long war in Vietnam, the political bankruptcy of the Johnson administration to which the war led, the moral bankruptcy of the Nixon administration that followed, and the economic depression which in due course appeared have been at least temporarily sobering.

In the meantime, the ecological crisis brought on by overpopulation and overconsumption of resources is bound to call into question the old American faith in growth and progress and place a new premium upon conservation, planning, and stability. At the heart of the matter is the blind anthropocentricity that we inherit—along with its nursemaid, Motherteacher—from the expansive nineteenth century, which is faithfully confessed in the egocentricity of individual Americans. If we are now forced to take an objective view of ourselves in relation to the rest of humanity and of humanity in relation to nature, and to adjust our behavior accordingly, certainly our philosophy of education will be revolutionized.

Whether a shifting of the value system is in fact occurring, one in the midst of events can only speculate; but the dislocations of the last ten years have been unmistakable. They seem to confirm Morton White's analysis of American social thought, first published in 1947, referred to above in connection with John Dewey. White felt, in the aftermath of the Depression and the Second World War, that the general attitude that he called antiformalism was no longer tenable. Ten years later, however, the liberal tradition of which he had been critical was under "a very different kind of attack" with which he felt "no sympathy." He was anxious, in preparing a new edition published in 1957, to make it clear that his volume was "in no sense to be identified with the more recent revivals of religious, conservative, and obscurantist thinking which have attempted to discredit and seriously lower the reputation of liberalism and secularism in social, political, and moral affairs."[8] Nevertheless, he remained persuaded of the correctness of his analysis, which he had concluded with a chapter titled "Yes and No," in which he indicated elements of the liberal or antiformalist tradition that continued to deserve respect while naming others that seemed questionable. Motherteacher, as a phenomenon associated with American liberalism (as that has been reflected in the "soft line" in education), should be viewed in the same judicious way. American democratic liberalism has tended, while defending the rights of the individual and of groups regarded as underdogs, to skimp the specification of the responsibilities of the individual and such groups. Motherteacher has reflected this bias in the schools, where its effects have been dangerously magnified. Education for democracy is one thing, education as democracy quite another and ruinous to democracy itself; so yes and no to Motherteacher.

White traced the weaknesses of American antiformalism to "a distaste for intellectual and moral rigidity, a distaste which was temperamentally associated with the spirit of progressive education and of social liberalism in politics." He raised a question whether the antiformalists had not confused rigidity in some pejorative sense with commitment to principle and method and the values, perhaps deliberately adopted, of common culture. Thinkers such as Dewey proclaimed allegiance to science but were after all something other than scientific in their approach. As White observed, "Attitudes were involved which went beyond scientific method"—or perhaps, one may add, never were submitted to scientific method. The antiformalists of Dewey's generation were in revolt, not just against formalism, but against the "constraints of previous morality and ideology" which had been rigidly dogmatic; they were advocates of a more liberal ideology and could, ironically, be dogmatically undogmatic. This kind of reaction was foreshadowed in their precursors of Horace Mann's generation, who identified the bête noire as Calvinist orthodoxy.[9]

It appears that Morton White's strictures against the antiformalist attitude in 1947 were more correct than he later came to feel under the impact of the Eisenhower administration and the McCarthy episode. Now, after even darker episodes have occurred, some in the name of dogmatic liberalism, White's judgment of the antiformalists not only stands but is applicable to popular attitudes. Speaking of Holmes, Veblen, Robinson, Beard, and Dewey, White concluded:

> Unfortunately they were unable to set limits to this revolt against rigidity and sometimes they allowed it to run wild. It is not exaggerat-

ing to say that the revolt was speedily followed by a reign of terror in which precision and logic and analytic methods became suspect. This is typified not only in the animus which institutional economists felt against deductive theory but also in Dewey's persistent failure to see the virtues of logical analysis in philosophy. Nor is it an exaggeration to say that this same fear of rigidity has caused liberalism's anxiety about having principles turn into dogma. It is easy to show how the whole reaction against these anti-formalist liberals in philosophy, politics, economics, and education was part of a search for intellectual vertebrae and not the result of a neurotic quest for certainty. The espousal of deduction and abstract theory need not lead to totalitarianism as some of the wilder anti-formalists have thought. An interest in the precise formulation of philosophical premises and conclusions with the help of formal logic is no sign of reaction. Nor is it necessarily a regression to search for political principles that go beyond simple methodological exhortations to be intelligent in social matters.[10]

In education, as in other departments of social thought, White's essay should be remembered for its advice to the effect that, in the event a "cohesive successor" to antiformalist thought should appear, "that successor will do well to preserve the virtues of the older group. It will do well to combine humanitarianism with principles; it must be anti-formalist without being anti-intellectual or opportunist."[11] It had not appeared in 1947, or in 1957, according to White; it seems not yet to have appeared. Presumably, if it is going to appear at all, we are closer to its advent and may reasonably anticipate it as the general condition for the exorcism of Motherteacher. In this particular, one could hardly do better than adopt White's motto "combine humanitarianism with principles" as the effectual spell.

Problematical as the matter stands, it may be to the purpose to seek in the history of American educational thought and practice elements which, though rejected or forgotten, might prove available in a new fusion. That history is replete with roads not taken, or taken a short distance and abandoned, down which it may be inspiring to take a new look if the road we are still on seems to have led up to disappointment. Colin Greer recently made the amusing suggestion that "in place of the line that established educational historiography draws from Jefferson to Mann to Dewey, why not a line which runs from Tom Paine to Thoreau to Paul Goodman?"[12] He seems to take the established educational historiography rather too much at its own word, for Jefferson certainly does not belong in any line it might honestly draw; and the line he wishes to substitute is by no means irrelevant to the public schools as we know them. But, to adapt his idea, let us first rehearse the line that leads to Motherteacher and then make certain deletions, additions, and changes of emphasis that may lead beyond Motherteacher to schools with "intellectual vetebrae" taught and administered by men and women more or less in numerical balance throughout the classrooms and administrative offices of the system of public education.

That this could be more than idle speculation about history is suggested by two related circumstances. American society is under the necessity of making deliberate choices in fundamental values since these can no longer be left to chance, to unanalyzed trends taken optimistically on faith, or to God, natural law, evolution, or some other more or less articulated cosmology. The two grand issues of the day, the control of human population and the control of nuclear power, are such rude imperatives they cannot be ignored. In both the operative word is *control*. It seems obvious that they cannot be resolved by a new retreat into "religious, conservative, and obscurantist thinking" and, therefore, if they are to be resolved, that they must be approached through critically amended "liberalism and secularism in social, political, and moral affairs," to apply Morton White's phrases quoted earlier. American society is already having to act responsibly on unvarnished existentialist terms, sobering as these are for the most sophisticated, to say nothing of their effect on people in general. This circumstance will become more obvious to everyone as efforts to control population and nuclear power continue, and nowhere more so than in education.

But it happens that in political theory and practice we have had a viable and in education an aborted tradition of deliberate choice with provisos for amendment in cases of error, obsolescence, and unforeseen need. The curriculum is or ought to be to the school what the Constitution is to the state. While abiding more or less faithfully by the Constitution, we have subverted the curriculum and, therefore, the Constitution to the degree that it was predicated upon common education. The second circumstance that may make it useful to edit anew the history of American education and as it were realign our legitimacy is just that we have long experience, comparatively successful in politics, comparatively unsuccessful in education, of constitutional behavior and responsibility. What Colin Greer derogates as the established line in the historiography of American education is that which led to Motherteacher, her very name being a contradiction in terms and an incitement to anarchy. This line, the "soft line" in American education, was consciously inaugurated in the Jacksonian era, not without opposition from a "harder" line then and thereafter. Perhaps we still have the power of choice and revision enabling us to modify tradition, the elements to be retrieved being no less American than those now to be questioned.

The soft line runs from Mann to Sheldon to Parker to Hall to Dewey to Kilpatrick and Rugg. But what if we extend it back into the eighteenth century to include Edwards, Washington, Jefferson, and Rush; expand it to include James G. Carter, Catharine Beecher, and Joseph Hale as well as Mann; then trace it through Harris and Ward to Dewey; and ask what points of departure Dewey offered that were not taken? The names symbolize values, attitudes, emphases. Detailed analyses of the thought and influence of each figure would no doubt reveal countercurrents, no matter which line we set it in, that would attest to the Americanism of every one.

What is most interesting in the eighteenth-century group, despite differences in their religious and philosophical commitments, is a common affinity for empiricism combined with stress on individual responsibility as well as rights. They all required of the individual educated decision and commitment to common values, more or less rationally and deliberately adopted and maintained. Commitment to common values had to be, in their opinion, the result of education, meaning, at the minimum, common literacy as the means of access to the terms of covenants—a religious covenant in the case of Jonathan Edwards, a political one in the cases of Washington, Jefferson, and Rush. Education was conceived as instrumentally by the eighteenth-century figures as it was by John Dewey, but they were far more specific than he in regard to the goal. The movement from Edwards to the founding fathers of the Federal Republic was from a less to a more specific covenant, from the Bible in all its complexity and ambiguity to the simplicity and explicitness of the Constitution and its provisions for amendment in the light of further experience.

A high level of literacy was no less the sine qua non of Federalism and Republicanism than of Puritan biblicism, implying, apart from the particular religious or political motives of the time, the focusing of education on language, the most distinctively human and social of attributes. We should recall the derivation of the term *academic*, which has come in our day to such equivocal usage, from the seventeenth- and eighteenth-century concern for the scrupulous observance of linguisitic convention and technique, regarded as indispensable to civilized conduct. Decay of language was regarded as both cause and symptom of moral and social decay and political dissolution, and this view is as valid today as it ever was. It has been legitimized anew for us by the key importance of language in human development as understood by modern biology and anthropology.

We thus inherit, if we choose to claim the inheritance, a cleanly defined conception of the content and purpose of common education from the founding fathers, redirected from religious to secular goals. The curriculum consisted primarily of reading, writing, and arithmetic, together with instruction in the basic documents that may be thought of as comprising the social covenant. Responsibility for abiding by it or for amending it in the covenanted way rested with the individual. If one inquires what level of competence individuals were expected to attain, the answer is that they were expected to reach a level that would today be considered oppressively high. It is regrettable that demonstration of ability to read and interpret the Constitution has been discredited through long abuse as a qualification for voting, for this was originally the level which citizens were supposed to reach through common education. Only a small fraction of American college graduates reach this level today, a circumstance which should not, however, be interpreted to mean that the goal was unrealistic. The founding fathers adjusted their expectations in the direction of realism, for it was certainly easier to read the Constitution than to read the Bible and the penalties for not doing so were much less horrendous. We have evidence of their realism in the quality of journalism and political argumentation during the latter half of the eighteenth century.

To the notion of common education taken to a level that would fit the citizen to vote intelligently for representatives to govern him constitutionally, the founding fathers added that of selective higher education to guarantee common culture among the leadership of the country at a level commensurate with the responsibilities of government. Inseparable from this idea was frank recognition of differences in capacities of individuals and preference for leadership and government by individuals of superior capacity and education. So it followed that education was hierarchically conceived, with common elementary education designed as basic to, not independent of, secondary and higher education, and the whole system controlled from the top down in the interests of homogeneity: integration upward. Not that there was any idea of preventing individuals from going beyond the common culture at any level, but the main concern was to make sure they possessed in common a base large enough to insure communication throughout society. There was here an element of rational choice and commitment to a particular form of government, a commitment too large, as things turned out, to ask; a small population with a huge territory to exploit was able to avoid the issue. We now can no longer avoid it and may, therefore, be inclined to review the case for hierarchical education directed to the development of a common culture from which a modern democratic state might grow.

By exercising the historical imagination to the extent of taking an antecedent perspective on the common school revival, it is possible not only to keep the idea of hierarchical education in

the picture but to appreciate afresh the merits of proposals that
were lost in the event. James G. Carter, Catharine Beecher, and
Joseph Hale represent a range of alternatives to public education as Horace Mann actually developed it by feminizing the
teaching corps in the interest of social control through primarily moral education. Carter is of particular relevance because he was the disappointed aspirant to the secretaryship of
the Massachusetts Board of Education that went to Mann in
1837. He seems to have been much less in reaction to Calvinism
than Mann and so to have taken a more secular view of the purposes of education, emphasizing, for example, the need for
physical training and the diffusion of knowledge in a scientific
spirit. He, too, had a plan for the professional education of
teachers, but it did not envisage the substitution of women for
men teachers.[13] Together with Hale and the other Boston
masters, Carter reminds us, as Hale reminded Mann, of the
agitation for school reform which had gone on in Massachusetts for ten or fifteen years before Horace Mann suddenly
preempted the field. And though identified with a rejected orthodoxy, Hale and his colleagues in their controversy with
Mann in 1844–45 must attract the attention of anyone
interested in reviewing the role of authority in education and in
strengthening the curriculum. As for Catharine Beecher, she
stood for the feminization of teaching in a sense less sentimental than Mann's and one which seems as compatible with Carter's secularism and Hale's defense of authority as
with Mann's moralism.

Miss Beecher had something in common with William T.
Harris which enables us to parley with her Calvinism and sexism and with his Hegelianism while finding useful recruits to
tradition in their specific educational ideas. These owed as
much to their experience of the West's inspiriting vision of the
nation's manifest destiny—which was not necessarily the same
as the East's—as to the religious and philosophical systems they
professed. Miss Beecher's experience of Cincinnati in the 1830s
and Harris's of St. Louis in the 1850s, when each town, one
after the other as the frontier advanced, imagined itself replacing Washington as the capital, lent to their views a largeness

and confidence not available in Mann's more limited New England experience. They each expected more of the intellectual part of human nature than he did and, although, like him, they thought of education as social control, had a freer conception of society and the pleasures of participation in its institutions.

Harris is interesting in that he provides a route alternative to the normal school line from Mann to Dewey. We may get to Dewey as handily via Harris's Hegelianism and institution-centered philosophy of education as via the child-centered philosophy represented by Sheldon, Parker, and Hall. American Hegelianism, for all its unpopular esoteric subtleties, provided in some ways a more satisfactory rationalization for the cult of progress than evolutionism did, especially so long as the latter had the Spencerian brutality about it. The dialectic of history, speciously rationalistic though it may have been, was thoroughly congenial in the American scene. The program of antitheses transcending themselves in syntheses expressible in a series of "concrete universals" encouraged the native optimism and at the same time allowed for a considerable degree of realism that was reflected in Harris's espousal of a rigorous curriculum.

Taking the individual and society as interacting antitheses, Hegelian educators could think in terms both of progressively social individuals and society sensitive to individual rights. This constant development toward ever more civil liberty could be seen as mediated by the curriculum, according to Harris's position that the school was not itself a cardinal institution but a secondary one whose function was to instruct the young in the given culture and prepare them to participate effectually and with personal benefit in its institutions. The authority of culture and tradition, and thus of the teacher, was defended. It did not follow that individual creativity should be undervalued or repressed, for creativity was regarded as a function of culture that the individual could acquire only through formal education. The assumptions that the dialectic of history would continue, the culture would keep changing for the better, and the school would reflect this improvement made for prudent conservatism in education with guarantees, however, against mere reactionary rigidity. Dewey, and more particularly the popularizers of his doctrine, tended to reverse the terms, assume that the school should reform the society, and yet supply no program, depending rather on the creativity of the young to produce desirable social change. If, as it appears, this tendency in education has contributed to debasement of American culture, a comparison of Harris's and Dewey's approach to what Dewey called the socialization of spirit and intelligence might be instructive. It might turn out that the culture has continued to control education, as Harris expected, but having been debased—in part by permissive education— continually debases education.

To recall Harris is at least to review an alternative process philosophy and so to gain a chastened perspective on evolutionism as another in the series of rationalizations of the American belief in the absoluteness of individual rights deriving from innate creativity and in the necessity of social change to accommodate such rights. In this perspective, Lester Frank Ward may prove a useful corrective to G. Stanley Hall. Ward's telic evolutionism may not be any more respected today by biologists and geneticists than Hall's recapitulatory evolutionism, but the immediate question is only the value of the two emphases as rationalizations of the given cultural bias and thus as influences on educational philosophy and method. Whereas Hall promoted a species of optimistic determinism that supported child-centered education, Ward's notion of man's ability and responsibility for controlling evolution implied the possibility of failure and an education focused on the environment rather than on the child. It led to emphasis on the authoritativeness of the curriculum as a means of insuring an adequate diffusion of specified knowledge or what Ward called intelligence, which no doubt includes that respectful attention to the cardinal institutions of the culture that Harris believed necessary. Evolutionism according to Hall implied individualistic atomism in education for students and uncritical irresponsibility (which is here seen as perverted mothering) for teachers. Evolutionism according to Ward implied common education for students and scientific authority for teachers. If evolutionism may be imagined as having entered Dewey's thought colored more distinctly by Ward than by Hall, it is not fanciful to consider what would have happened and look for points of departure in Dewey other than those which were in fact employed.

For Dewey remains indispensable to any imaginable line one could trace in modern American educational theory and practice and so to any imaginable reforms. The antitheses between school and society, child and curriculm, and democracy and education enshrined in the titles of his works on education remain the central issues; but the exigencies of our time require a different weighting of the elements from that of the 1890s when he made his experiments. The liberal and progressive motives of Dewey's youth did not yet look, as they do now, negative—antiformalist—and had not led to such destruction of forms and such ineffectualness in reconstruction as we have experienced. Perhaps the elements of educational thought and experience must remain analyzable entities, unresolvable into any transcendent synthesis. School cannot literally become society, child cannot become curriculum, education cannot become democracy: those would not in any case by syntheses but only the triumph of one element in each pair over the other. The integrity of each must be taken as given, but forms must be allowed precedence as they stand at any given moment although subject to controlled amendment.

The exorcism of Motherteacher requires a return to the type of experimentation Dewey conducted in the Laboratory School at the University of Chicago but without the antiformalist bias. The work of Jerome S. Bruner and his associates seems most to the purpose in recent years. Bruner's publications of the 1950s and 1960s seem to have overestimated the effects of the flurry of concern about the curriculum which followed the launching of the first Sputnik by the Soviet Union, yet general reform if it comes may prove traceable to that period. It may be that what Bruner, writing in 1964, prematurely thought had become generally appreciated has become more obvious, namely, "that the idea of 'readiness' is a mischievous half-truth . . . because it turns out that one *teaches* readiness or provides opportunities for its nurture, one does not simply wait for it."[14] "Waiting for Readiness" might serve as a theme for a Beckett satire on Motherteacher. To question the doctrine of readiness is to question child-centeredness in education, and to question that is to question at last the dominance of elementary education and to open discussion of the need for hierarchy in education.

Although he did not explicitly apply it to the history of the United States, presumably Bruner would not deny the applicability of the following observation:

> In recent years I have wondered, particularly in connection with work in West Africa, why societies are not more mindful of the role of education in shaping their futures. Why in Africa, for example, is the short-term political allure of universal primary education given priority over training a corps of administrators, teachers, and technicians? In many cases, the second is financially precluded by the first, and the long-run result may prove a terrible time bomb as semi-literate youths flock into the new urban Africa with no marketable skills, their familial and tribal boats burned, and no properly trained corps of teachers and civil servants to maintain stability or to teach the untrained.[15]

The equivalent timing for asking this question in the United States was the period of the common school revival, and indeed it was asked by proponents of hierarchical education directed from above in the service of republican institutions. To ask it now is not to revise history but to criticize historical choices and elicit from the criticism sanctions for the reform of traditional attitudes in education.

With regard to motivation, which in his terms may be understood as the teaching of readiness, Bruner has argued for the rehabilitation of the curriculum as the means to that end. One is not dependent either on the combination of punishment and emulation that Horace Mann detested, not without reason, or on the maternalistic love that he advocated as the substitute. Either line leads to an undesirable extreme. Nobody can wish a return to the "hard line," represented at its mid-nineteenth-century extreme by Dickens's "old Grinder of savage disposition, who had been appointed schoolmaster because he didn't know anything, and wasn't fit for anything, and for whose cruel cane all chubby little boys had a perfect fascination." It is harder and harder to defend the "soft line," represented at its twentieth-century extreme by Motherteacher. Bruner suggests, rather, that the curriculum should be conceived as a calculated means of facilitating "the mastery of skills that in turn lead to the mastery of still more powerful ones, the establishment of self-reward sequences." The "spiral" curriculum, as he has described it, reflects the proposition "that there is an appropriate version of any skill or knowledge that may be imparted at whatever age one wishes to begin teaching—however preparatory that version may be. The choice of the earlier version is based upon what it is one is hoping to cumulate. The deepening and enrichment of this earlier understanding is again a source of reward for intellectual labors."[16]

To think this way is to return with new insight to Dewey's problem of how "to psychologize" subject matter. The thing cannot be done without a defined, prescribed, and authoritative curriculum, representing, however, not social or class repressiveness or privilege, but the structure of the skills and knowledge one has determined should be taught, edited to suit the capacities of learners at different ages. The problem Dewey failed to solve in his Laboratory School, just as G. Stanley Hall's "genetic philosophy of education " failed to solve it, was how to calibrate the growth and development of the child to what Hall and Partridge called the "culture material" to be taught. They failed to solve it because of their antiformalist and, therefore, child-centered bias, which prevented the development of what Bruner terms "a theory of instruction." Such a theory, he holds, must be *"prescriptive* in the sense that it sets forth rules concerning the most effective way of achieving knowledge or skill . . . [and] provides a yardstick for criticizing or evaluating any particular way of teaching or learning." It must also be *"normative"* in that it "sets up criteria and states the conditions for meeting them." A theory of instruction is needed because the attempt to construct curricula on the basis of theories of learning and development has proved disappointing in application. The latter are "descriptive rather than prescriptive," whereas a theory of instruction is "concerned with how what one wishes to teach can best be learned, with improving rather than describing learning."[17]

It needs stressing more than Bruner had occasion to do how idle it is to talk about a theory of instruction unless one is willing to prescribe in detail and, therefore, to limit "what one wishes to teach." Few American teachers are yet prepared to do this, and few taxpayers push them to do this. Their common allegiance remains with "Child," usually referred to protectively as "the whole child" wherever Motherteacher and her constituency remain in place. Given the probability that they will have no choice but to change or collapse into frank anarchy, one may consider a theory of instruction such as Bruner's as more than speculation.

While it is no doubt true that the intrinsic rewards of intellectual labor, which result from the student's faithful application to the structure of different fields of knowledge and skill, are the most truly motivating, it remains to be seen how much of the population is capable of the necessary application. The spiral curriculum would be as selective in operation as any other and so excite the ingrained American distaste for external constraints. Any theory of instruction, however, can be so applied as to maximize students' success and the variety of curricula in which different talents may succeed. There is, furthermore, such a thing as a democracy of excellencies in kind, that is, mutual respect among people who are unquestionably good and productive at whatever they know or do; invidious comparisons need not be made, for example, between manual and intellectual work.

Bruner has specified four major features of a theory of instruction. First, it "should specify the experiences which most effectively implant in the individual a predisposition toward learning," e.g., the "sorts of relationships with people and things in the preschool environment [that] will tend to make the child willing and able to learn when he enters school." The plain implication here is that institutions and agencies other than the school must be responsible for predisposing children toward learning and that the school program must not be sacrificed if those other agencies fail. Second, Bruner thinks a theory of instruction "must specify the ways in which a body of knowledge should be structured so that it can be most readily grasped by the learner." Third, it "should specify the most effective sequences in which to present the material to be learned." And fourth, it "should specify the nature and pacing of rewards and punishments in the process of learning and teaching." Bruner has suggested "that as learning progresses there is a point at which it is better to shift away from extrinsic rewards, such as a teacher's praise, toward the intrinsic rewards inherent in solving a complex problem for oneself."[18]

Whether or not the theory of instruction Bruner has outlined is correct, certainly a theory of instruction, predicated upon a prescriptive curriculum, is the fundamental reform needed in American education. The development of a theory of instruction would break Motherteacher's hold upon the schools. It seems doubtful that a theory of instruction could be developed, much less successfully applied, in the schools without the achievement of a balance of the sexes among teachers and administrators throughout the educational system. Whether one must come before the other is impossible to say. The two eventualities would be reciprocal influences reflecting changes in social values of the most pervasive sort, chiefly in our antinomian liberalism and in our sexism. Either change might, and assuredly both together would, prove inimical to Motherteacher.

Notes
Index

Notes

Chapter 1

1. Alexander Hamilton, James Madison, and John Jay, *The Federalist,* ed. Benjamin Fletcher Wright (Cambridge: Harvard Univ. Press, 1961), p. 22.

2. Ibid., pp. 112–13.

3. Paul L. Ford, ed., *The Writings of Thomas Jefferson* (New York: G. P. Putnam's Sons, 1892–99), III, 24.

4. Dagobert G. Runes, ed., *The Selected Writings of Benjamin Rush* (New York: Philosophical Library, 1947), p. 101.

5. Ibid., p. 104.

6. Victor Hugo Palstits, ed., *Washington's Farewell Address* (New York: The New York Public Library and Arno Press, 1935), p. 254.

7. Rudolph Frederick, ed., *Essays on Education in the Early Republic* (Cambridge: Harvard Univ. Press, 1965), p. 290.

8. Linda K. Kerber, *Federalists in Dissent: Imagery and Ideology in Jeffersonian America* (Ithaca: Cornell Univ. Press, 1970), p. 178.

9. Fred L. Israel, ed., *The State of the Union Messages of the Presidents, 1790–1966* (New York: Chelsea House–Robert Hector, 1966), I, 244.

10. Ibid.

11. Ibid., p. 248.

12. John Quincy Adams, *Memoirs,* ed. Charles Francis Adams (Philadelphia: J. B. Lippincott & Co., 1874–77), VIII, 546.

13. Ibid., IX, 416.

14. Sidney L. Jackson, *America's Struggle for Free Schools: Social Tension and Education in New England and New York, 1827–42* (Washington, D.C.: Council on Public Affairs, 1941), pp. 165–69.

15. Lyman Beecher, *A Plea for the West* (Cincinnati: Truman & Smith; New York: Leavitt, Lord & Co., 1835), p. 39.

16. Ibid., p. 75.

17. Rush Welter, *Popular Education and Democratic Thought in America* (New York: Columbia Univ. Press, 1962), pp. 57, 50.

18. Ibid., p. 57.

19. Ibid., p. 4.

Chapter 2

1. Anne L. Kuhn, *The Mother's Role in Childhood Education: New England Concepts, 1830–1860* (New Haven: Yale Univ. Press, 1947), p. 186.

2. Ibid., p. 31.

3. William Ellery Channing, "Unitarian Christianity," *Works* (Boston: American Unitarian Assn., 1886), p. 377.

4. Quoted in Sandford Fleming, *Children and Puritanism* (1933; rpt. New York: Arno Press, 1969), p. 119.

5. Kuhn, p. 53.

6. Ibid., p. 186.

7. Quoted ibid., p. 31.

8. Quoted in H. Shelton Smith, ed., *Horace Bushnell* (New York: Oxford Univ. Press, 1965), p. 33.

9. Horace Bushnell, *Christian Nurture,* with an introduction by Luther A. Weigle (New Haven: Yale Univ. Press, 1947), p. 4.

10. Ibid., p. 48.

11. Ibid., pp. xxxiv, xxxvi.

12. Ibid., pp. 12–13, 14.

13. Ibid., pp. 15, 17.

14. Ibid., p. 21.

15. Ibid., p. 39.

16. Ibid., p. 140.

17. Ibid., p. 199.

18. Ibid., p. 44.

19. Ibid., p. 229.

20. Ibid., p. 202.

21. Ibid., p. 219.

22. Quoted by Fleming, p. 193.

23. Kuhn, p. 72.

24. Quoted ibid., p. 73.

25. Quoted ibid., p. 55.

26. Ibid., p. 102.

27. Quoted ibid., p. 104.

Chapter 3

1. Since the following account was written, Paul H. Mattingly has published a detailed study of the status problems of early nineteenth-century male teachers, *The Classless Profession: American Schoolmen in the Nineteenth Century* (New York: New York Univ. Press, 1975). See especially his discussion of William A. Alcott's career as a teacher in chap. 1, pp. 1–43 passim.

2. Kathryn Kish Sklar, *Catharine Beecher: A Study in American Domesticity* (New Haven: Yale Univ. Press, 1973), p. 182.

3. Catharine E. Beecher, *The True Remedy for the Wrongs of Women; with a History of the Enterprise Having That for Its Object* (Boston: Phillips, Sampson, 1851), p. 101.

4. Sklar, p. 173.

5. Note the usage here of "feminized" in the nineteeth-century ideological sense comprising the sex-typing of the time as well as in the sense of a majority or monopoly of women; in the first sense the term may be applied to men as well as women.

6. Quoted by Sklar, p. 42.

7. Quoted ibid., p. 272.

8. Quoted ibid., p. 48.

9. Ibid., pp. 48–49.

10. Ibid., pp. 38, 39.

11. Ibid., pp. 85–86.

12. Ibid., p. 153.

13. Ibid., p. 59.

14. Quoted ibid., p. 91.

15. Quoted ibid., p. 93.

16. Ibid.

17. Quoted ibid., p. 91.

18. Ibid.

19. The Dedication, Catharine E. Beecher, *Woman Suffrage and Woman's Profession* (Hartford: Brown and Gross, 1871).

20. "An Address on Female Suffrage," ibid., pp. 19, 28, 60.

21. Ibid., p. 61.

22. See ibid., p. 5.

23. "An Address to the Christian Women of America," ibid., p. 171.

24. "An Address on Female Suffrage," ibid., p. 58.

25. Beecher, *The True Remedy,* p. 47.

26. Catharine E. Beecher, *The Evils Suffered by American Women and American Children: The Causes and the Remedy* (New York: Harper & Bros., 1847), pp. 3, 5.

27. Ibid., p. 11.

28. Ibid., pp. 12, 15.

29. Catharine E. Beecher, *Educational Reminiscences and Suggestions* (New York: J. B. Ford and Co., 1874), p. 109.

30. Ibid.

Chapter 4

1. Horace Mann, *Tenth Annual Report,* p. 112. This and subsequent citations of Mann's annual reports are from the facsimile series entitled Massachusetts Board of Education, *Report, together with the Report of the Secretary of the Board—1st–12th* (Washington, D.C.: National Education Assn., 1947).

2. Rousas J. Rushdoony, *The Messianic Character of American Education* (1963; rpt. Nutley, N.J.: Craig Press, 1972), p. 18.

3. Ibid., pp. 19, 20, 23.

4. Quoted in Mary Peabody Mann, *Life of Horace Mann* (Boston: Walker, Fuller & Co., 1865), pp. 13–14.

5. Ibid., p. vii.

6. Quoted ibid., p. 73.

7. Quoted ibid., p. 80.

8. Horace Mann, *First Annual Report*, p. 25.

9. Ibid., p. 46.

10. Horace Mann, *Third Annual Report*, pp. 39–40.

11. Horace Mann, *First Annual Report*, p. 60.

12. Ibid., p. 51.

13. Ibid., p. 63.

14. Ibid., p. 11.

15. Ibid., p. 62.

16. Ibid., pp. 58, 66.

17. Horace Mann, *Second Annual Report*, pp. 27–28.

18. Ibid., p. 8.

19. Ibid., p. 45.

20. Ibid., p. 69.

21. Horace Mann, *Third Annual Report*, p. 9.

22. Horace Mann, *Fourth Annual Report*, pp. 43, 44.

23. Ibid., pp. 44–45.

24. Ibid., pp. 45–46.

25. Horace Mann, *Sixth Annual Report*, pp. 28–29.

26. Ibid., p. 29.

27. Horace Mann, *Eighth Annual Report*, pp. 60–61.

28. Horace Mann, *Eleventh Annual Report*, p. 24.

29. Horace Mann, *Twelfth Annual Report*, p. 21.

30. Horace Mann, *Fourth Annual Report*, p. 46.

31. Michael B. Katz, *The Irony of Early School Reform: Educational Innovation in Mid-Nineteenth-Century Massachusetts* (Cambridge: Harvard Univ. Press, 1968), pp. 59–60.

32. Horace Mann, *Ninth Annual Report,* pp. 35–36.

33. Horace Mann, *Eleventh Annual Report,* p. 25.

34. Ibid., p. 26.

35. Ibid.

36. Horace Mann, *Sixth Annual Report,* pp. 30, 31.

37. Horace Mann, *Eighth Annual Report,* p. 62.

38. Horace Mann, *Eleventh Annual Report,* p. 30.

39. Ibid., pp. 30–31.

40. Quoted in Sklar, *Catharine Beecher,* p. 235.

41. Ibid.

42. Edward Wagenknecht, *Harriet Beecher Stowe, The Known and Unknown* (New York: Oxford Univ. Press, 1965), p. 35.

Chapter 5

1. Dismissive treatment of the Boston masters has been echoed recently in Frederick M. Binder, *The Age of the Common School, 1830 – 1865* (New York: John Wiley and Sons, 1974), pp. 74–76.

2. See the discussion of Mann and his supporters as "soft-line" and the Boston masters as "hard-line" educators in Katz, *Irony of Early School Reform,* pp. 139–43.

3. *Remarks on the Seventh Annual Report of the Hon. Horace Mann, Secretary of the Massachusetts Board of Education* (Boston: Charles C. Little and James Brown, 1844), pp. 3, 5.

4. Mattingly, *The Classless Profession,* pp. 2–3.

5. *Remarks,* pp. 6, 7.

6. Ibid., pp. 7–9.

7. Ibid., p. 13.

8. Ibid., pp. 16, 17.

9. Ibid., p. 28.

10. Ibid., pp. 37–38.

11. Ibid., pp. 45–46.

12. Ibid., pp. 51, 53.

13. George Combe, *Notes on the United States of North America during a Phrenological Visit in 1838–40* (Philadelphia: Carey & Hart, 1841), II, 169.

14. *Remarks,* p. 103.

15. Ibid., p. 104.

16. Ibid., p. 105.

17. Ibid., p. 108.

18. Ibid., p. 121.

19. Ibid., p. 112.

20. Ibid., pp. 125, 126.

21. Ibid., pp. 127–28.

22. Ibid., p. 137.

23. Quoted in Mary Peabody Mann, *Life of Horace Mann,* p. 224.

24. Quoted ibid., p. 230.

25. Horace Mann, *Reply to the* Remarks *of Thirty-one Boston Schoolmasters on the Seventh Annual Report of the Secretary of the Massachusetts Board of Education* (Boston: W. B. Fowle and N. Capen, 1844), pp. 128–30.

26. Ibid., p. 130.

27. Ibid.

28. Ibid., p. 131.

29. *Rejoinder to the* Reply *of the Hon. Horace Mann, Secretary of the Massachusetts Board of Education, to the* Remarks *of the Association of Boston Masters* . . . (Boston: Charles C. Little and James Brown, 1845), p. 40.

30. Ibid., p. 11.

31. Horace Mann, *Answer to the* Rejoinder *of Twenty-Nine Boston Schoolmasters, Part of the "Thirty-one" Who Published* Remarks *on the Seventh Annual Report* . . . (Boston: Wm. B. Fowle and Nahum Capen, 1845), p. 92.

32. Ibid., p. 109.

33. *Remarks,* p. 110.

34. Horace Mann, *Answer,* p. 117.

35. Ibid., p. 121.

36. Quoted in Mary Peabody Mann, *Life of Horace Mann,* p. 241.

37. Quoted ibid., p. 246.

38. Horace Mann, *Answer,* pp. 105–6.

39. *Remarks,* pp. 128–29.

40. *Rejoinder,* p. 26.

41. Horace Mann, *Answer,* p. 105.

42. Mary Peabody Mann, *Life of Horace Mann,* p. 424.

43. *Common School Journal,* VII, nos. 19–23 (Oct. 1, 1845–Dec. 1, 1845), 317–19.

44. Ibid., pp. 322, 323.

Chapter 6

1. Charles W. Eliot, "Wise and Unwise Economy in Schools," *New England Journal of Education,* I (May 29, 1875), 254.

2. Ibid.

3. Ibid., p. 256.

4. Ibid.

5. Ibid.

6. Ibid.

7. Mattingly, *The Classless Profession,* p. xi.

8. *Report of the U.S. Commissioner of Education,* 1873, pp. cxxxiii–cxxxiv.

9. Ibid., 1878, p. 258.

10. Ibid., 1880, p. lxxxii.

11. Ibid., 1886–87, pp. 213–14.

12. Ibid., p. 141.

13. Ibid., 1891–92, pp. 668, 669.

14. Ibid.

15. Ibid.

16. Ibid.

17. Ibid., 1892–93, pp. 544–45.

18. Ibid., p. 544.

19. *Reports of the Mosely Educational Commission to the United States of America, October–December, 1903* (1904; rpt. New York: Arno Press, 1969), p. 166.

20. Ibid., pp. 13, 14.

21. "Are There Too Many Women Teachers," *Educational Review,* XXVIII (June 1904), 98–99.

22. Ibid., p. 100.

23. Ibid., pp. 100–101.

24. Ibid., p. 103.

25. Ibid., p. 102.

26. Ibid., p. 103.

27. Ibid., p. 102.

28. "Teachers' Salaries in New York," ibid., XXXV (Feb. 1908), 211.

29. Ibid.

30. Ibid.

31. "The Equalization of Teachers' Salaries," ibid., XXXIX (March 1910), 292–93.

32. Ibid., p. 293.

33. C. W. Bardeen, "Why Teaching Repels Men," ibid., XXXV (April 1908), 352, 355, 357.

34. C. W. Bardeen, "The Monopolizing Woman Teacher," ibid., XLIII (Jan. 1912), 20, 23.

35. Ibid., p. 31.

36. Ibid., pp. 31, 32.

37. Ibid., p. 37.

38. Ibid., p. 202.

39. F. E. Chadwick, "The Woman Peril in American Education," ibid., XLVII (Feb. 1914), 113–114.

40. Florence H. Hewitt, "The Woman Peril," ibid., XLVII (April 1914), 411, 413.

Chapter 7

1. Rushdoony, *Messianic Character,* pp. 44–45.

2. Ned Harland Dearborn, *The Oswego Movement in American Education* (1925; rpt. New York: Arno Press and The New York Times, 1969), figs. XI, XII.

3. Rushdoony, p. 46.

4. Quoted ibid., p. 268.

5. Quoted ibid., p. 274.

6. Ibid., p. 269.

7. Friedrich Froebel, *The Education of Mankind* (New York: Appleton, 1891), p. 114.

8. H. Courthope Bowen, *Froebel and Education through Self-Activity* (New York: Scribner, 1897), pp. 180–81.

9. Quoted by Rushdoony, p. 276.

10. Ibid., p. 91.

11. Quoted ibid., p. 94.

12. Quoted ibid.

13. Francis W. Parker, *Talks on Pedagogics* (1894; rpt. New York: Arno Press, 1969), p. 1.

14. Ibid., p. 18.

15. Ibid., p. 7.

16. Ibid., p. 21.

17. Ibid., p. 138.

18. Ibid., pp. 10–24.

19. Ibid., p. 24.

20. Ibid., pp. 434–36.

21. Ibid., pp. 450–51.

22. J. H. Plumb, *The Death of the Past* (Boston: Houghton Mifflin Co., 1970), p. 97.

23. Quoted by Rushdoony, p. 68.

24. Ibid., p. 66.

25. William H. Goetzmann, ed., *The American Hegelians: An Intellectual Episode in the History of Western America* (New York: Alfred A. Knopf, 1973), p. 11.

26. Ibid., p. 15.

27. See ibid., p. 14.

28. Ibid., p. 268.

29. Quoted in Neil G. McCluskey, *Public Schools and Moral Education* (New York: Columbia Univ. Press, 1958), p. 83.

30. Ibid., p. 120.

31. Quoted ibid., p. 122.

32. Ibid., p. 127.

33. Ibid., p. 128.

34. Quoted ibid., pp. 135, 149, 151.

Chapter 8

1. Dorothy Ross, *G. Stanley Hall: The Psychologist as Prophet* (Chicago: Univ. of Chicago Press, 1972), pp. 123, 127.

2. Lester Frank Ward, *Dynamic Sociology,* introduction by David W. Noble (1883; rpt. New York: Johnson Reprint Corp., 1968), II, 11; I, 19.

3. Ibid., II, 108.

4. Ibid., II, 186.

5. Ibid., II, 619.

6. Ibid., II, 2.

7. Ibid., I, xii.

8. G. Stanley Hall, *Life and Confessions of a Psychologist* (New York: D. Appleton and Co., 1923), p. 519.

9. Ibid., pp. 360, 362.

10. Ibid., p. 497.

11. Ibid., p. 499.

12. Ransom A. Mackie, *Education and Adolescence*, introduction by G. Stanley Hall (New York: Dutton, 1920), p. xiv.

13. Hall, *Life and Confessions*, p. 405.

14. Quoted in Rushdoony, *Messianic Character*, p. 128.

15. Hall, *Life and Confessions*, p. 500.

16. G. Stanley Hall, "Remarks on Rhythm in Education," *NEA Journal*, 1894, pp. 84–85.

17. G. Stanley Hall, "The Ideal School as Based on Child Study," in *Health, Growth, and Heredity*, ed. Charles E. Strickland and Charles Burgess (New York: Teachers College Press, 1965), p. 116.

18. G. Stanley Hall, *Adolescence* (1905; rpt. New York: Arno Press and The New York Times, 1969), I, viii.

19. G. E. Partridge, *Genetic Philosophy of Education: An Epitome of the Published Educational Writings of President G. Stanley Hall of Clark University* (New York: Sturgis and Walton Co., 1912), p. 86.

20. Hall, "The Ideal School," p. 116.

21. Partridge, p. 28.

22. Ibid., p. 4.

23. Ibid., pp. 8–9.

24. Ibid., p. 60.

25. Ibid., p. 31.

26. Quoted by Rushdoony, p. 128.

27. Hall, *Life and Confessions*, p. 496.

28. Hall, *Adolescence*, I, xix.

29. Partridge, pp. 98, 99.

30. Ibid., pp. 102, 108.

31. Ibid., pp. 109, 116.

32. Ibid., pp. 30, 117, 128, 198.

33. Ibid., p. 317.

34. Hall, *Adolescence*, I, xiii.

35. Partridge, p. 194.

36. Ibid., p. 316.

37. Ibid., p. 327.

38. Ibid., p. 193.

39. Hall, *Life and Confessions,* p. 367.

40. Partridge, pp. 224, 225.

41. Hall, "The Ideal School," p. 126.

42. G. Stanley Hall, "Coeducation in the High School," in Strickland and Burgess, p. 183.

43. Hall, "The Ideal School," p. 126.

44. Hall, "Coeducation," p. 183.

45. Hall, *Adolescence,* I, 609.

46. Hall, *Life and Confessions,* p. 509.

Chapter 9

1. Morton White, *Social Thought in America: The Revolt Against Formalism,* with a new preface and an epilogue (Boston: Beacon Press, 1957), pp. 12–13.

2. Ibid., pp. 18–21.

3. John Dewey, *The Child and the Curriculum* and *The School and Society,* introduction by Leonard Carmichael (Chicago: Univ. of Chicago Press, 1956), p. 34.

4. Ibid., p. 97.

5. Ibid., pp. 101–3.

6. Ibid., p. 16.

7. Ibid., p. 17.

8. Ibid., p. 22.

9. Ibid., p. 60.

10. Ibid., pp. 78–79.

11. Ibid., p. 117.

12. Ibid., p. 4.

13. Ibid., p. 11.

14. Ibid., p. 15.

15. Ibid., pp. 17–18.

16. Ibid., p. 22.

17. Ibid., p. 23.

18. Ibid., pp. 30, 31.

19. Harry K. Wells, *Pragmatism, Philosophy of Imperialism* (1954; rpt. Freeport, N.Y.: Books for Libraries Press, 1971), p. 77.

20. John Dewey, *Democracy and Education: An Introduction to the Philosophy of Education* (1916; rpt. New York: The Free Press, 1966), p. 87.

21. William James, *Pragmatism* (Cleveland and New York: World, 1955), p. 222.

22. Ibid., p. 58.

23. John Dewey, *Reconstruction in Philosophy,* enlarged edition, with a new introduction by the author (Boston: Beacon Press, 1957), p. 94.

24. John Dewey, *The Quest for Certainty* (1929; rpt. New York: Putnam, 1960), p. 100.

25. Dewey, *Democracy and Education,* p. 193.

26. Ibid., p. 249.

27. Ibid., p. 193.

28. Ibid., p. 360.

29. Ibid., p. 17.

30. John Dewey, *Experience and Education* (New York: Macmillan, 1948), p. 26.

31. Ibid., p. 28.

32. Rushdoony, *Messianic Character,* p. 149.

33. Ibid.

34. Quoted ibid., p. 150.

35. John Dewey, *My Pedagogic Creed* (1902; rpt. Washington: The Progressive Education Assn., 1929), p. 13.

36. John Dewey, *Characters and Events,* ed. Joseph Ratner (London: George Allen & Unwin, 1929), II, 515.

37. Quoted by Rushdoony, p. 156.

38. William H. Kilpatrick, "The Project Method: The Use of the Purposeful Act in the Educative Process," *Teachers College Record,* XIX (Sept 1918), 319–35.

39. Rushdoony, p. 205.

40. John Dewey, "Progressive Education and the Science of Education," in *John Dewey on Education* (New York: The Modern Library, 1964), p. 171.

41. Ibid., pp. 176–77, 179

42. Ibid., pp. 180–81.

43. William H. Kilpatrick, *Philosophy of Education* (New York: Macmillan, 1951), pp. 303, 304.

44. Ibid., pp. 304, 305.

45. Ibid.

46. Ibid., pp. 306–7.

47. Ibid., p. 314.

48. Ibid., p. 315.

49. Ibid., pp. 325, 327, 329.

Chapter 10

1. Guy Montrose Whipple, ed., *The Twenty-sixth Yearbook of the National Society for the Study of Education: The Foundations and Technique of Curriculum-Construction* (Bloomington, Ill.: Public School Publishing Co., 1926), I, 3, 4.

2. Ibid., pp. 7–8.

3. Ibid., p. 52.

4. Harold Rugg and Ann Shumaker, *The Child-Centered School: An Appraisal of the New Education* (Yonkers-on-Hudson, N.Y.: World Book Co., 1928), p. 13.

5. Ibid.

6. Ibid., p. 18.

7. Stuart A. Courtis, "Reading between the Lines," in Whipple, II, 93.

8. Ibid., p. 92.

9. Ibid., p. 94.

10. Ibid., pp. 94–95.

11. Rugg and Shumaker, p. 60

12. Ibid., pp. 107, 109.

13. Ibid., pp. 121, 123.

14. Ibid., pp. 125, 126, 127.

15. Ibid., p. 129.

16. Ibid., pp. 315, 317, 318, 319.

17. Harold Rugg et al., *Democracy and the Curriculum: The Life and Program of the School*, Third Yearbook of the John Dewey Society (New York: D. Appleton-Century Co., 1939), p. xi.

18. Ibid., p. 28.

19. Ibid., p. 27.

20. Rugg and Shumaker, pp. 320–21.

21. Ibid., pp. 321–24.

22. Ibid., pp. 324, 325.

23. Ibid., p. 324.

Epilogue

1. Kingman Brewster, Jr., "Collegiate Words of Wisdom," *Commercial Appeal* (Memphis), Sept. 18, 1974, p. 7.

2. "TV Distorts Blacks' Images, FCC Official Believes," ibid., March 10, 1975, p. 3.

3. As this goes to press, a study charging the sentimentalization and debasement of American culture in general to the influence of nineteenth-century women and clergymen has been published by Ann Douglas; see her *The Feminization of American Culture* (New York: Alfred A. Knopf, 1977).

4. Patricia Cayo Sexton, *The Feminized Male: Classrooms, White Collars, and the Decline of Manliness* (New York: Random House, 1969), p. 4.

5. Patricia Cayo Sexton, *The American School: A Sociological Analysis* (Englewood Cliffs, N.J.: Prentiss-Hall, 1967), p. 81.

6. Sexton, *The Feminized Male*, p. 21.

7. Ibid., p. 17.

8. Morton White, *Social Thought in America,* p. x.

9. Ibid., pp. 240–241.

10. Ibid., p. 241.

11. Ibid., pp. 241–42.

12. Colin Greer, *The Great School Legend: A Revisionist Interpretation of American Public Education* (New York: Basic Books, 1972), pp. 16–17.

13. See James G. Carter, *Essays upon Popular Education* (1826; rpt. New York: Arno Press and The New York Times, 1969).

14. Jerome S. Bruner, *Toward a Theory of Instruction* (New York: W. W. Norton and Co., 1968), p. 29.

15. Ibid., p. 31.

16. Ibid., p. 35.

17. Ibid., p. 40.

18. Ibid., pp. 40–42.

Index